Elizabeth Bishop
in Brazil and Aft

Elizabeth Bishop
in Brazil and After

A Poetic Career Transformed

GEORGE MONTEIRO

McFarland & Company, Inc., Publishers
Jefferson, North Carolina, and London

LIBRARY OF CONGRESS CATALOGUING-IN-PUBLICATION DATA

Bishop, Elizabeth, 1911–1979.
    Elizabeth Bishop in Brazil and after : a poetic career
transformed / George Monteiro.
        p.   cm.
    Includes bibliographical references and index.

    ISBN 978-0-7864-6693-1
    softcover : acid free paper ∞

    1. Bishop, Elizabeth, 1911–1979 — Criticism and
interpretation.   2. Bishop, Elizabeth, 1911–1979 —
Influence.   3. Poets, American — 20th century —
Influence.   4. Brazil — In literature.   I. Monteiro, George.
II. Title.
PS3503.1785Z79 2012
811'.54 — dc23   2012018234

BRITISH LIBRARY CATALOGUING DATA ARE AVAILABLE

Front cover: Guanabara Bay, Rio de Janeiro, Brazil; cover design
by David K. Landis (Shake It Loose Graphics)

Manufactured in the United States of America

McFarland & Company, Inc., Publishers
  Box 611, Jefferson, North Carolina 28640
  www.mcfarlandpub.com

To
Brenda, Kate, Stephen, and Emily

Table of Contents

Acknowledgments. ix
Preface 1
Introduction. 4
Prologue: The Map 9

———————————— BRAZIL ————————————

1. The Unwritten Elegy. 11
2. Unravished Brides 23
3. Driving to the Interior 33
4. Rainbow, Rainbow, Rainbow 46
5. Fire and Light 52
6. Eye of the Sparrow 58
7. Good Times at Cabo Frio 64
8. An Ordinary Evening 70
9. Promenade 74
10. In the Middle of the Road. 81
11. Crusoe in the Land of Vera Cruz 88
12. A Tale of Jam and Jelly 91
13. "A Miracle for Breakfast" 96
14. The Brazil Book 98
15. Scenery, Storms 123

———————————— ELSEWHERE ————————————

16. Different Hats, Different Folks. 127
17. Village Matters 130

18. The Art of the Scapegoat 140
19. Burning Bridges 150
20. The Misprint and the Mouse 155
21. Building a Rhyme for Ezra 161
22. Send in a Toy 167
23. Down to the Sea 170
24. Free to Be Free 173

Epilogue: The Last Book 179
Chapter Notes 183
Bibliography 201
Index 207

Acknowledgments

I owe a debt to my first teachers of American literature. My awakening to the riches and complexities of that literature came in college, in a survey course taught by A. D. Van Nostrand, with discussion sections led by Charles H. Watts II and Carlin T. Kindilien. Some years later, A. D. Van Nostrand suggested that I apply for a Fulbright grant to teach American literature in Brazil. There is no doubt, of course, that if not for my subsequent Brazilian experience, this book would not have been undertaken.

I want to thank those students at Brown University, the University of Massachusetts at Dartmouth, and the Universidade Federal de Minas Gerais who read Elizabeth Bishop's poems and stories along with me. I am grateful, too, for the consideration accorded me by the University Press of Kentucky for consenting to the use of material I first published in *The Presence of Camões*, and to Vassar College and Farrar, Straus and Giroux for permission to quote from Bishop materials.

For reading the manuscript, posing good questions, and suggesting helpful changes, I am grateful to my daughter Katherine A. Monteiro, who as a child shared some of my first Brazilian experiences. Finally, I wish to thank my wife, Brenda Murphy, for her ever-considerate critical reading of my work, her informed counsel, and keen advice.

Should we have stayed at home, wherever that may be?
—*Questions of Travel* (1965)

Preface

"I was in a trance with poetry that made it as distasteful to listen to" the famous Shakespearean, George Lyman Kittredge, talk about poetry, "as it would have been to read Freud or Havelock Ellis or Kraft Ebbing [*sic*] when I was in love."[1] Never mind that when the complainant was in the mood for it, he could do a pretty good imitation of Harvard's good professor — Robert Frost's point is well taken. Well, this is not a book for poets. It is a book intended for those who like to talk about poetry and poets — the Kittredges among us, if you will. I am mindful, too, that poems invite multiple readings and various interpretations. What Elizabeth Bishop said about translation — "it is impossible to translate poetry, or perhaps only one aspect can be translated at a time, and each poem needs several translations" — holds true for commentary on poems, as well as their interpretation.[2]

The year 2011 marked the 100th anniversary of the poet Elizabeth Bishop's birth. She shares this centenary with William Golding, Terence Rattigan, and Tennessee Williams. "Each of these names has had its heyday," reports the *TLS*, "but all now appear as hares lagging behind the tortoise Elizabeth Bishop ... who published a modest book of verse once a decade from the mid–1940s onwards," but "is now more fashionable than any of those mentioned above."[3] In the literary history of the United States perhaps only Emily Dickinson's case offers a rough parallel to Bishop's. In each instance, an enormous critical reputation and great overall popularity have come after death. There have been dozens of editions of Bishop's poetry and prose, a selected edition of her letters, a beautifully illustrated edition of her amateur's drawings and paintings, a collection of her unpublished (largely unfinished) poetry, and collections of the correspondence she exchanged with Robert Lowell. In the works is a collection of her correspondence with her fellow poet May Swenson. And of course there have been biographies, introductions, and monographs, special editions of journals, several symposia and colloquia with proceedings publications, and, last but not least, at least thirty critical works — I count that many on my shelves and I do not have them all. She is represented by a volume in the Library of America series (2008). New, enlarged volumes of her prose and her poems have marked her publisher's celebration of her centenary year.

There is little risk in saying that she has emerged as the poet of her generation, outstripping erstwhile rivals such as Theodore Roethke, Randall Jarrell, John Berryman, Anne Sexton, Adrienne Rich, and — what was unthinkable in 1980 to most readers of American poetry — Robert Lowell. And, in the ways that matter, she has caught up with (some would say surpassed) the redoubtable Sylvia Plath.

Bishop once said in an interview conducted by the poet George Starbuck that "it takes probably hundreds of things coming together at the right moment to make a poem and no one can ever really separate them out and say this did this, that did that."[4] If one is doomed to failure when one tries to separate out some of the things that come to make a given poem, the scholar interested in sources and analogues makes the effort nevertheless to find such nascent things. His only justification for doing so is that often such knowledge enhances a reader's understanding of a word, an image or a line in a poem, if not the poem's overall purpose or intention. Anything, in my opinion, that tells us something about the way the writer's imaginary works in the making of his poem is ipso facto of value. Identifying sources (sometimes broadly fundamental, sometimes indirectly allusive) has its further justification in the way it contributes to a deeper understanding of the biographical poet herself. Wallace Stevens had just been talking about two poets of his acquaintance — William Carlos Williams and Bishop — when he generalized: "The fact remains that we are always fundamentally interested in what a writer has to say. When we are sure of that, we pay attention to the way in which he says it, not often before."[5] Sometimes, however, we do not know what the poet is saying exactly until we attend to the way in which she says it. In Bishop's case this is often at the essence of her poems, especially those that start out "obliquely," with "the fire balloons, the Nova Scotia Picture, the hen in New York," as Robert Lowell observed, "something beside the point and unimportant (seemingly) but is not."[6]

"[T]he drinking and the working both seem to have improved miraculously," wrote Bishop to Anny Baumann, her doctor and friend, on September 16, 1952. "Well no, it isn't miraculous really — it is almost entirely due to Lota's good sense and kindness. I still feel I must have died and gone to heaven without deserving to, but I am getting a little more used to it."[7] *Elizabeth Bishop in Brazil and After* is intended to be, not a comprehensive or exhaustive overview of the sentiments that Bishop suggests in her message to Dr. Baumann, but an account of the instances and ways in which Bishop's direct and literary experience in Brazil influenced her work both while she was in Brazil and in the decade following her return to the United States (permanently, it turned out). As a result, I have not felt required to deal comprehensively with Bishop's work prior to 1951, except in poems such as "The Prodigal," "Faustina, or Rock Roses," or "The Bight," to select only three examples, which can be seen now to have anticipated specific attitudes, images, and major themes in Bishop's work after 1951. And I have not commented on Bishop's translation, *The Diary of "Helena Morley,"* which deserves to be studied on its own as a translator's odyssey through the intricacies of the Portuguese language as it expresses Brazilian culture, or a poem such as "The Riverman," which reworks closely material from *Amazon Town: A Study of Man in the Tropics* (1953), the anthropologist Charles Wagley's book. (To Robert Lowell, Bishop confided that Lota did not like the poem and she herself didn't "approve of it."[8]) Rather I have limited myself to considering those poems and stories about which I think I have something useful to say.

I should also add that I am largely in agreement with the view expressed by C. K. Doreski in one of the early works of criticism devoted to Bishop: "She was not very successful in empathizing with people of distinctly different ethnic or racial backgrounds, and the voices and personae derived from her observations of the inhabitants of Brazil, for example, are not always convincing or effective." But I am less inclined to agree with Doreski when she continues on to say: "However, this is a particular aesthetic failing, and does not negate the principle involved, which is Shakespearian, Keatsian, and at the very heart of the metaphor of creativity as Bishop understood it."[9] It seems to me that in these aesthetic failures what is most apparent is that behind them are the poet's personal failures of sympathy or empathy with those "others," sometimes seen as exotic, at other times as social or cultural inferiors.

"The entire corpus of her [Bishop's] work has to be understood as the record of one hypersensitive person's cautious, watchful, self-conscious inching towards the truth," writes Anne Stevenson. "It asks to be read as autobiography, but as an autobiography told from the 'inside looking out.' Instead of a year-by-year chronicle of a life, we are given a series of impressions or 'looks' — a slide-show of places, people, creatures and small events, all of which have been seen, enacted and carefully noted down to be carried ever afterwards in the clear mirror of the writer's memory."[10] To this thoughtful characterization of Bishop's aesthetic life, I would add only that one must be willing to accept the idea, especially so in Bishop's biography, that the experience of encountering a literary text (or, for that matter, any text) also contributes to one's overall life experience — even, or, especially, perhaps, when one is also interested in the biography of a writer.

Introduction

Elizabeth Bishop's stint as Consultant in Poetry to the Library of Congress (1949–50) came towards the end of a five-year period when she had been much honored and well rewarded. In 1945, she received the Houghton Mifflin Poetry Prize which brought with it publication of her first book, *North & South*, in 1946. The following year she was awarded a Guggenheim Fellowship. Following her appointment as Consultant in Poetry to the Library of Congress in 1949, she received an award from the American Academy of Arts and Letters in 1951 and the first Lucy Martin Donnelly Fellowship from Bryn Mawr College, also in 1951, and she was privileged to spend time as an invited guest at Yaddo, the writers' colony in Saratoga Springs, New York. But by fall 1951, she was undecided about where to live, and, worse, indecisive about what to do next. After much vacillation, she came to a decision, one that effectively put off the need to make the other important decisions. On November 10, 1951, she left New York on the SS *Bowplate*, a freighter headed for Tierra del Fuego, with the intention of eventually circling the globe. She would take advantage of the ship's stop in Brazil to visit with Mary Stearns Morse in Rio de Janeiro. It was there that Bishop's life took a sharp turn, one that would turn Brazil into her permanent home for most of the next 20 years. An allergic reaction to the fruit of the cashew tree, one so severe that she had to prolong her stay until her recovery, caused her to miss the date of her ship's departure. In the meantime she had come under the care of Maria Carlota Costallat de Macedo Soares, a Brazilian, known to all, simply, as Lota.[1] Lota invited Bishop to stay in Brazil, offering to share her Rio apartment as well as the new house she was building in Petrópolis. Bishop stayed. And for the next decade and more, Bishop experienced the longest stretch of happiness of her entire life. Moreover, despite its attractions and distractions, Brazil proved to be a congenial place for work. She continued to write and publish her poetry, mostly in the *New Yorker* (which did its best to sell her as travel-poet, adding place names after the titles of her Brazilian poems), and in collections such as *Poems:*

North & South—*A Cold Spring* (1955), *Questions of Travel* (1965), *The Burglar of Babylon* (1968), and *The Complete Poems* (1969). And she continued to win prizes and awards—for the rest of her life: Shelley Memorial Award (1953), membership in the National Institute of Arts and Letters (1954), Pulitzer Prize for Poetry 1956, Amy Lowell Traveling Fellowship (1957), Chapelbrook Foundation Award (1960), Academy of American Poets Fellowship (1964), Ingram-Merrill Foundation Grant (1968), National Book Award (1969), (Brazilian) Order of Rio Branco (1971), Harriet Monroe Poetry Award (1974), *Books Abroad*/Neustadt International Prize for Literature (1976), National Book Critics Circle Award (1977), Guggenheim Fellowship (1978), and honorary doctorates from several universities—Princeton (1969), Rutgers (1972), Brown (1972), Brandeis (1977), and Dalhousie (1979).

A Brazilian poet imagines the figure of Bishop in situ, at Samambaia: "From a Petrópolis hilltop / watering can in hand and wearing a pointed hat, / Elizabeth reconfirms, 'Losing is easier than you think.'"[2] A less Olympian Bishop is revealed in an interview conducted in Boston toward the end of the poet's life. The interviewer for the *Jornal do Brasil* tells of an exchange with Bishop on what might still have been a delicate matter for the poet: "'As a child I often went to Samambaia,' I tell her. 'I remember entering your house, on tiptoe, and overhearing my neighborhood friends saying: "Two strange women live here; they never leave the house."'" To which Bishop responds: "That's not true. It's a child's exaggeration. We didn't go to parties every night, but neither were we hermits. We had plenty of friends. Some of them, like Carlos Lacerda, were neighbors in the same part of town."[3]

The compelling and extraordinary story of those "two strange women," living their lives privately in Petrópolis and somewhat more publicly in a Rio apartment above the beach in Leme, is told sympathetically and responsibly by Carmen L. Oliveira in her dual biography, *Flores Raras e Banalíssimas*, published in 1995, and in 2002, in a translation by Neil K. Besner, as *Rare and Commonplace Flowers*. It offers a sympathetic account of Bishop's midlife Brazilian years (the better part of two decades) and of Lota's vexed professional career and, finally, tragic life.

Late in life, more than a decade after Lota's death, Bishop acknowledged that Lota was the great passion of her life. She planned to write a long memorial poem but did not live to compose it. According to Brett C. Millier, who quotes from Bishop's notes, her "Elegy" would celebrate Lota's "'reticence and pride'; her 'heroism, brave & young'; her 'beautiful colored skin'; 'the gestures (which [you] said you didn't have).'"[4] Carmen L. Oliveira's *Flores Raras e Banalíssimas* tells the story of that love, examining a midlife though less than mature relationship that began when Bishop was 40 and Lota 41.

The book incorporates information regarding the protracted episode that would eventually lead to their falling-out in the mid-to-late 1960s. At the heart of their problem was Lota's work, the design and building of a park in a landfill area running along the coastline in that part of Rio de Janeiro called Flamengo, a project Lota undertook at the invitation of the governor, Carlos Lacerda, who was a close friend. Oliveira's extensive research into personal and public correspondence, newspapers, and governmental legislative and regulatory documents makes this the most fully realized account of what Lota was up against in the life she was forced to live increasingly apart from Bishop during those last ten years. It is a sad story of increasing frustration before political intrigue and bureaucratic red tape and just plain bad faith on the part of opponents, enemies, and even Lota's putative allies.[5] This public and personal pressure contributed decisively to the destruction of her life with Bishop. In the 1960s Bishop simply could not help Lota with her political and occupational problems, and clearly Lota became increasingly incapable of meeting Bishop's exigencies. The first lesions in their relationship were marked by some of Bishop's visits to Ouro Prêto, sometimes alone, with Lota occasionally joining her later. In Ouro Prêto she bought an old colonial house on the road to the town called Mariana. It was the only house that she ever owned. It was during this period that Bishop went off to Seattle to spend six months teaching at the University of Washington, as a temporary replacement for the late Theodore Roethke. By this time both Lota and Bishop were in sorry psychological shape. The poet managed to find what she needed to put herself back together. Lota did not. As Bishop moved to reduce her dependence on Lota, the ever more desperate Lota became increasingly dependent on Bishop. Yet Bishop was still insisting as late as 1966 to her American psychiatrist that she was going back to Lota someday: "I couldn't possibly think of anything else — but I feel that lately I have not been managing my life there, and with her, as well as I should and I feel I need advice, quite badly perhaps."[6] Bishop decided to retreat to New York. Still distraught and depressed despite extensive care and treatment, Lota asked for permission to visit, and Bishop conceded. Reluctantly, she later revealed. On her first night with Bishop, Lota overdosed on pills. Rushed to the hospital, she died a week later. For whatever reason, Bishop did not notify Lota's family or friends of her suicide attempt until after her death. Bishop's mishandling of the matter was of course held against her, to the extent that she was denied access even to some of her own belongings back in Rio and at Samambaia. During those first years after Lota's death, Bishop continued the extensive repairs to Casa Mariana that she had started years earlier. Yet she began to feel less and less at home in Ouro Prêto and coincident with her first appointment at Harvard

University she began her efforts to sell her house. When she left Brazil for the last time in 1974, she still had not sold it.

The Brazilian silence after Lota's death on matters pertaining to Bishop lasted more than two decades. Not until the 1990s, in fact, did the recuperation of Bishop's literary reputation in Brazil actually begin. The year 1990 saw the publication of the poet-critic Horácio Costa's pioneering bilingual edition of Bishop's poetry, making a substantial portion of it available in Portuguese for the first time. That year also saw Flora Süssekind's detailed study of Bishop's style, theme and technique, using as a pretext Bishop's friendship with Manuel Bandeira, one of Brazil's premier poets.[7] In 1993, at the Universidade Federal de Minas Gerais in Belo Horizonte, Regina M. Przybycien presented and defended her dissertation, "Feijão Preto e Diamantes: O Brasil na Obra de Elizabeth Bishop" ("Black Beans and Diamonds: Brazil in the Work of Elizabeth Bishop"), a pioneering study that deserves the wider circulation that its publication as a book would give it. In August 1994, the years that Bishop spent with Lota at Fazenda Samambaia were commemorated in Petrópolis by municipal authorities with a seminar, accompanied by an exhibition of books, letters, poems, photographs and memorabilia. The year 1995 was an especially good year for Bishop in Brazil. It saw the publication of Carmen L. Oliveira's *Flores Raras e Banalíssimas*, as well as *Uma Arte: as Cartas de Elizabeth Bishop*, a translation by Paulo Henriques Britto of Robert Giroux's edition of the letters, which includes, as lagniappe, an appendix of hitherto unpublished letters, to May Swenson, Robert Lowell, Ilse and Kit Barker, and to several Brazilians — the poet Carlos Drummond de Andrade, Bishop's friend Linda Nemer, and Emanuel Brasil, Bishop's coeditor of a 1972 anthology of modern Brazilian poetry.[8] Appealing to what Brazilian readers might know about Marianne Moore, in 1996 Companhia das Letras, which brought out Moore's poetry in translation in 1991,[9] published *Esforços do Afeto e outras histórias* (the title is taken from Bishop's piece, "Efforts of Affection: A Memoir of Marianne Moore"), a selection of Bishop's prose translated by Britto. Since then, "The Art of Elizabeth Bishop: An International Conference & *Celebração* in Brazil," May 19–21, 1999, was held in Ouro Prêto, with a volume of selected presentations published as *The Art of Elizabeth Bishop* in 2002. In 1999, there appeared *Poemas do Brasil*, a selection of Bishop's poems identifiably relevant to her Brazilian experience, in Paulo Henriques Britto's translations. *O Iceberg Imaginário e outros poemas*, an ample selection of poems from the whole of the Bishop canon, again translated by Britto, appeared in 2001. In addition to critical essays in the journals, there have been two notable critical books on Bishop. The earlier of the two is *O Jogo das Imagens no Universo da Criação de Elizabeth Bishop* by Sílvia Maria Guerra Anastácio (Universidade Federal de Pernambuco), a richly detailed study of the genesis of Bishop's poetry based largely on archival work with the manuscripts in the Elizabeth Bishop Papers at Vassar College, Poughkeepsie, New York (1999). The more recent one is *Duas Artes: Carlos Drummond de Andrade e Elizabeth Bishop* (2006) by Maria Lúcia Milléo Martins (Universidade Federal de Santa Catarina), an examination of the fruitful interaction of Bishop with Brazil's great 20th-century poet. Both the Anastácio and Martins books are based on dissertations defended at Brazilian universities. That Brazilian interest in Bishop is not restricted to the academy or the poetry-reading public is evidenced by Marta Góes's *Um Porto para Elizabeth Bishop*, a monologue drawing on the poet's letters, poems and interviews. This well-received play premiered at the Festival de Teatro de Curitiba in 2001, toured Brazil's major cities, and in 2006, as *A Safe Harbor for Elizabeth Bishop*, was produced in New York.

That Elizabeth Bishop now has an appreciative audience in Brazil is fitting, especially given the fact that her unique Brazilian experience marked her thinking about herself and helped shape her work while there and later, sometimes in the smallest of particulars, the off-centered use of a word. She rings intercultural changes on a single word — "interior" ("Arrival at Santos"), "ignorant" [ignorado] ("The Armadillo" and "Song for the Rainy Season") and "anniversary" [aniversário, meaning "birthday"] ("Twelfth Morning; or What You Will") — or incorporates a direct, literal, and slightly off-centered translation — "took advantage" [aproveitar, meaning "made good use of"] ("Under the Window: Ouro Prêto").

From her early years in Brazil Bishop talked about "Black Beans and Diamonds," a book she planned to write about Brazil. Always the good traveler, she saw a fair amount of the country. For a few years she and Lota spent winter holidays in Cabo Frio, a seacoast resort town located on a peninsula northeast of Rio de Janeiro. With Aldous Huxley she visited Mato Grosso. She journeyed the great rivers, the Amazon and the São Francisco. She visited and wrote about Brasília. But her Brazilian book was never written, perhaps because the book she wrote for the *Life* World Library series (1962) had diminished the drive and sapped the energy that the writing of "Black Beans and Diamonds" would undoubtedly have required.

Prologue: The Map

Preoccupied with cultivating her impressions, Elizabeth Bishop saw connections and links everywhere, ever stitching together images and statements both within and among her poems. Choosing "The Map" for the first poem of her first collection, *North & South* (1946) turned out to be a harbinger when she put together what turned out to be her final collection. Not by chance does *Geography III* (1976) begin with a lengthy epigraph from *First Lessons in Geography*, a textbook published in 1884. The epigraph is comprised of "Lesson VI" and "Lesson X." "Lesson VI" asks (and answers) several questions: "What is Geography?" "What is the Earth?" "What is the shape of the Earth?" and "Of what is the Earth's surface composed?" "Lesson X" begins with the question "What is a Map?" and provides the answer, "A picture of the whole, or a part, of the Earth's surface." If a goodly portion of Bishop's poetry is dedicated to sketching a picture of parts of the "Earth's surface," "The Map" is a discursive picture of the map that is a "picture of the whole." It is of course impossible to accomplish this task, as the American philosopher Josiah Royce pointed out in *The World and the Individual* (1899). "Let us imagine that a portion of the soil of England has been levelled off perfectly and that on it a cartographer traces a map of England," he writes. "The job is perfect; there is no detail of the soil of England, no matter how minute, that is not registered on the map; everything has there its correspondence. This map, in such a case, should contain a map of the map, which should contain a map of the map of the map, and so on to infinity."[1] The construction of such a map, however, is hardly what Bishop the poet wants her poem to do, for it is her intent to present us with an action — the action of the poet as she reacts to the map before her and absorbs it into her own language.

In *The Library at Night* (2006), Alberto Manguel describes "a tattered atlas which I studied carefully, trying to discover microscopic people in the tiny cities that dotted its continents."[2] One cannot even imagine Elizabeth Bishop thinking about looking for a people-inhabited map. Indeed it is the solitary child (or the childlike poet) who interrogates the "map" in the poem that leads off *North & South*, her first book. Her questions and observations animate the map, such that action and movement take place within it, but it all remains unpeopled. The only indication of a "people" is the poet's surmise that the Eskimo has "oiled" Labrador to achieve its color — yellow.[3] The names on the map show movement: they "run out to sea" and "cross the neighboring mountains." "Peninsulas take the water between thumb and finger / like women feeling for the smoothness of yard-goods." Countries shape out: Norway as a "hare," others as "profiles" (one of them is surely Portugal) that "investigate the sea, where land is." The principal motive of the poem's first ten lines, however, is color: "shadowed green," "simple blue from green," "fine tan," "yellow." And of course the countries have their own colors, but only Labrador's color is named — yellow — and then only to provide the occasion of hypothesizing the painterly actions of the "moony Eskimo." That countries are endowed with colors existing only on maps, unlike the colors assigned to the sea and shore, both of which can be tested by experience, prompts the questions: "Are they assigned, or can the countries pick their colors?" and "What suits the character or the native waters best." Asking these quasi-rhetorical questions leads satisfactorily (at least for Bishop) to the quiet generalization that "More delicate than the historians' are the map-maker's colors."

BRAZIL

1

The Unwritten Elegy

In the early 1950s Elizabeth Bishop reviewed two books on Emily Dickinson, both for the *New Republic*. Her review of *Emily Dickinson's Letters to Doctor and Mrs. Josiah Gilbert Holland* appeared in August 1951, and her review of *The Riddle of Emily Dickinson* a year later.[1] Bishop liked Theodora Van Wagenen Ward's "beautifully edited" volume of the poet's letters to the Hollands. She did not like Rebecca Patterson's book of "literary detective-work," though the book dealt with lesbianism, a subject that was very much on Bishop's mind at the time, according to her biographer.[2] In Dickinson's letters to the Hollands she probably read past those gnomic references to Elizabeth Barrett's poem "Catarina to Camoens" that would have meant more to her a few months later, when, unexpectedly, she decided to remain in Brazil for an indefinite stay, one that would last for close to two decades.

In late 1951 Bishop set out on the voyage that she thought would eventually take her around the world. On November 10, in New York, she boarded a freighter bound for Tierra del Fuego and the Straits of Magellan. Two days out to sea, her mind was on her unfinished review, for the *New Republic*, of Rebecca Patterson's *The Riddle of Emily Dickinson* — that "god awful" book — even though Thomas Johnson had already done such "an excellent job," in "the Times Sunday before last" that "nothing more remains to be said." But May Swenson said something "funny," she remembered, "and I'm going to use it — giving her some sort of credit: 'Kate Scott! / Great Scott!'"[3] Bishop's review did not appear until August 18, 1952 — a delay that prompted her to note on her typescript copy of the review that because there had been a change in editors at the journal the review had never appeared. Her typescript shows that she ended her review: "Or, as a poetic friend of mine better summarized it: Kate Scott! / Great Scott!"[4] The new editor, possibly without Bishop's authorization, dropped this final sentence with the Swenson quotation.

Bishop was unsympathetic to Patterson's "literary detective-work" that

led to the identification of Mrs. Kate Anthon (*née* Scott) as the object of the
Dickinson's "hopeless passion." Bishop did not deny entirely Patterson's thesis:
"The two young women met and fell in love; about a year later Kate Scott
broke it off in some way, and Emily Dickinson had been christened and
launched on her life of increasing sorrow and seclusion.... That her thesis is
partially true might have occurred to any reader of Emily Dickinson's poetry —
occurred on one page to be contradicted on the next."[5]

Bishop's own greatest emotional involvement, though she did not
know it then, awaited her in Brazil where the SS *Bowplate* would make a
scheduled stop. Meeting Lota de Macedo Soares again, falling in love with
her, and deciding to remain in Brazil served to renew her efforts to write
poetry, to turn her intelligence and sensibility toward a new relationship, a
new country, and a new continent. Almost immediately Bishop had begun
to write "Arrival at Santos," the first of her Brazil poems to be published,
early in 1952. She would reprint it as the next-to-last poem in *Poems:
North & South—A Cold Spring* in 1955, and then use it to open *Questions
of Travel* in 1965. In the latter collection, Bishop organized her poems
into sections entitled "Brazil" and "Elsewhere." The second poem in the
"Brazil" section was one she did not finish until just before New Year's
Day 1959. To mark the date for Robert Lowell she sent him "Brazil, January
1, 1502." "Jungle into picture into history and then jungle again," Lowell
characterized it.[6] Bishop's first poem about Brazil, "Arrival at Santos," was
not datelined "January 1952" when it was published in the *New Yorker*
on June 21, 1952. She had actually disembarked in Santos in late November
and was in Rio de Janeiro by the end of the month. When the poem was
published in book form, as the penultimate poem in *Poems: North & South—
A Cold Spring* (1955), it still carried no date, the fate finally appearing in
Questions of Travel, an addition that offers a tenuous link between "Arrival
at Santos," the autobiographical poem placed first in *Questions of Travel*
(1965), and the book's second poem, an exploration into history, "Brazil,
January 1, 1502."

Bishop chose as an epigraph for *Questions of Travel* two lines taken from
a poem attributed to Camões.[7] If in recent years scholars have cast doubt over
the authenticity of Camões's authorship of the sonnet beginning "Quem vê,
Senhora, claro e manifesto," there was no such doubt in Bishop's time.[8] It
appears in such popular collections of Camões's poetry as Rodrigues Lapa's
selection of *Líricas* (in a fifth edition by 1970) and in the small-sized Edições
de Ouro volume available throughout Brazil in the 1960s. In *Questions of
Travel* Bishop quotes from Camões's poem. The poem can be rendered into
English:

If one, my Lady, seeing clearly and manifestly
the fineness of your beautiful eyes,
is not blinded by the very sight of them,
that one has not paid you what is your due.
Such seems fair enough price to me; but I,
having the advantage of deserving them, gave
over even more, my life and soul, for wanting
them, leaving me nothing else besides.
Thus my life, my soul, my hope, all
that I have — all of it is yours —
and the profit taken is mine alone.
Because it brings me such great bliss
giving you what I have and what I may,
the more I give you, the more I owe you.[9]

From this sonnet Elizabeth Bishop took over the last two lines as part of her dedication of *Questions of Travel* to Lota.

O dar-vos quanto tenho e quanto posso,
Que quanto mais vos pago, mais vos devo.
(Giving you what I have and what I may,
The more I give you, the more I owe you.)[10]

As it is amply shown in her work with modern Brazilian poets and her rendering of *Minha Vida de Menina* (published as *The Diary of "Helena Morley"*), Bishop became adept at translating from the Portuguese, but in this instance she chose to invoke Camões only in the original.[11] "The dedication is very simple," she explained to American friends, "it is such a well-known quotation in Portugese [*sic*] that it doesn't sound quite as corny in Portugese as it will to you, maybe, when you get it translated."[12] Most of Bishop's critics seem not to have tried to work out the English meaning of Camões's lines or to have looked into the poem from which Bishop had taken them. In fact, only one reviewer of *Questions of Travel* even mentions the lines from Camões, but that one mention is suggestive. Frank Warnke sees them as linking Bishop to "that earlier poet-traveler" who also "finds in the act of travel an expression of those impossible and deeply human..." — quoting from "Arrival at Santos" — "'demands for a different world, / and a better life, and complete comprehension / of both at last, and immediately....'"[13] Camões as traveler (albeit sometimes a reluctant one) certainly "fits" him to the title of Bishop's book, supporting one of its major themes. That the lines are attributable to Camões establishes this connection, though Warnke's insight might have resulted from his having known the poet when the two of them were at the University of Washington. "He was a professor at the Un. of Washington. Did this as a SURPRISE for me — very nice of him," Bishop noted at the top margin of her copy of Warnke's review.[14] That the lines quoted from Camões are those of a poet-lover no reviewer, not even Warnke, even hints at. But that fact is Bishop's major reason for appropriating them. Moreover, if the two lines quoted were not enough to indicate it, the sonnet from which they are derived goes a long way, in its entirety, toward establishing *Questions of Travel* as a lover's book, one in which the poet performs for her lover, much as jugglers in the Middle Ages performed for the Blessed Virgin, first on Brazilian themes and then on "elsewhere" (largely "northern") themes. The point of Bishop's dedication may be missed if one insists too strenuously that "her published work on the erotic or intimate relationships of her life stopped in *A Cold Spring*."[15] Of course, her decision to print Camoes's lines in the original Portuguese might suggest an exercise in evasion.

It is not unlikely that Camões's sonnet held private meanings for the two of them — Elizabeth and Lota — though such meanings are not evident. In adopting Camões's words, Bishop leaves us evidence of the intensity of her attachment to Lota, that woman — in Elizabeth Hardwick's words — "very intense indeed, emotional, also a bit insecure as we say, and loyal, devoted and smart and lesbian and Brazilian and shy, masterful in some ways, but helpless also," who for 15 years enabled Bishop to have a Brazilian life.[16]

On the dust jacket (back) of *Questions of Travel*, which Bishop thought "rather pretty" though a "bit too chi-chi possibly," appears a reproduction of a drawing of Bishop by the Brazilian artist Darcy Penteado. "I don't think much of that drawing, really," she confessed, "but you know how they insist on photography — and I refused and refused and then it was a choice between this drawing and a lot of blurbs — so I decided this was a bit more impersonal and would also please my Brazilian friends."[17] This disclaimer aside, she liked it well enough to release it to Brazilian newspapers well in advance of the book's publication to be used along with "Dia de Reis," a Portuguese translation of her poem "Twelfth Morning; or What You Will."[18]

Darcy Penteado, as Bishop identified him, was "a very young man who did a lot of society portraits, etc., here a few years ago — now I hear he is doing pop art in Rome!"[19] But Darcy had one other minor accomplishment that might have brought him to Bishop's attention. In 1956 he had illustrated the first collection of Emily Dickinson's poems published in Brazil.[20] That he was thus linked to Dickinson leads to a thought. Bishop said she admired the Amherst poet for having dared to do it, "all alone."[21] Yet she also disapproved of Dickinson's "narrowing of poetic subject to 'love, human and divine,'" a complaint that has led one critic to speculation — "to think that Bishop may have considered a part of her own twentieth-century emancipation from stereotypic womanhood to have been release from that entrapping woman's subject, love."[22] But the release from that "woman's subject," if there was a release, was not apparent in 1965, when Bishop published some of her most closely thought out Brazilian poems in the book she not merely dedicated to her Brazilian lover but so designed as to make a private point.

Questions of Travel contains 19 poems and one story. The first 11 poems are in a section called "Brazil," and the story and the eight poems that follow it are in a section called "Elsewhere." The Brazilian poems include some of her most admired work — "Arrival at Santos," "Brazil, January 1, 1502," "Questions of Travel," "Manuelzinho," "The Armadillo," "The Riverman," "Twelfth Morning; or What You Will," and "The Burglar of Babylon." The work in the "Elsewhere" section of the book has as its predominant setting the Canadian Maritimes. This includes a short story (a longish one, for Bishop) about Nova Scotia, and at least three poems identified with Nova Scotia. These two halves of the book — "Brazil" and "Elsewhere" — stand for the poles around which Bishop organizes her experience as of 1965 — the two hemispheres, north and south (recalling the title of her first volume of poems, published in 1946, six years before she arrived in Brazil — when the poles of her experience were Nova Scotia in the north and Key West in the south). Read from first page to last, *Questions of Travel* can be seen as a statement of where the poet stood at the time, where she had been, and the different place from which, it can be said, she had come. From this point of view, *Questions of Travel* can be seen as a showing forth of her poet's wares and her love for the person to whom she has dedicated her book of poems. Read as a book made public, to be sure, but openly dedicated to Lota, *Questions of Travel* becomes one more of the singular gifts given to illustrate and reaffirm the personal truth of the lines she quotes from Camões: "Giving you what I have and what I may, / The more I give you, the more I owe you."

Questions of Travel was published on November 29, 1965. We now know that by then Bishop was already feeling strong pressures and burdensome demands stemming in large part from Lota's own exhaustion and deteriorating health. We also know that, possibly in reaction to such changes in Lota, Bishop was turning toward at least one "other" — to be named later. With the benefit of hindsight, the attentive reader will realize that the epigraph from Camões can be looked at in a second, more skeptical, way. Besides the possibility of its being read as a direct expression of love, it might also be read as a lover's complaint — that giving one's all is not only not requital enough but that in giving all one actually increases, paradoxically, the remaining debt. Already manifest in 1965 were the signs of the disintegration of Bishop's and Lota's relationship — anger, accusations, unkindness, an affair, even Bishop's quietly defiant assertion of independence in purchasing a seemingly unneeded

house in Ouro Prêto. The almost total disintegration of the Bishop-Lota relationship was imminent, coming to a head at the end of 1966. By the first of
the year, Bishop "had packed a suitcase and had moved out of the apartment
and into a Rio hotel.... Out 'in half an hour,' she complained, 'after fifteen
years with a few dirty clothes in a busted suitcase, no home any more, no
claim (legally) to anything here.'"[23]

It will surprise no one that these contretemps in a sentimental tragedy
should have worked their way into the poet's poetry. But just how Bishop
used her poetry in her quotidian life is not without its curious and strange
interest. That Bishop's two-part scheme for the arrangement of her poems in
Questions of Travel—"Brazil" and "Elsewhere"—was not merely a perfunctory
act of arrangement but might well have carried private messages for Lota gains
support from a Bishop love poem published long after the poet's death.

Among the pleasures in Lloyd Schwartz's 1991 *New Yorker* piece was the
"new" poem he added to the clutch of poems Bishop wrote during her Brazilian life.[24] This untitled work—24 lines in six four-line stanzas—is indis-
putably a highly personal love poem, but it is atypically so in that it treats
erotic content directly. It is a poem of intervention; that is to say, its intent,
chiding lightly as it does, is to persuade. As such, it may have been "too personal to make public," as Schwartz speculates, or "even keep a copy of for
herself." In simple terms the speaker offers an apologia for the Northerner
that she is, as opposed to the Southerner (of the tropics, one presumes). Her
"compass," she asserts, "still points north," to a place where there are wooden
houses, blue eyes, and fairy tales that feature "flaxen-headed" young sons,
lovemaking in haylofts. This North is a land of Protestants and heavy drinkers,
one where crabapples ripen to rubies and cranberries to "drops of blood,"
where hot-blooded swans paddle in icy water. The speaker ends her poem by
proclaiming, saucily, that cold as it was in that land of the north, they would
go to bed early, but never to "keep warm."[25]

Schwartz tells us that he learned of the existence of this poem in 1990
when visiting Ouro Prêto, the small colonial town in the state of Minas Gerais
where Bishop had purchased the house she named Casa Mariana (in part for
Marianne Moore, in part for its location on the road to Mariana). The poem
was shown to him by Lilli Correia de Araújo, the owner of the Pouso do
Chico Rey, a small pension in Ouro Prêto, and Lota's friend as well as
(briefly—probably as early as 1965) one of Bishop's lovers. ("Elizabeth always
had to be in love and she fell in love easily," Lilli said later, but "she also fell
out of love easily."[26]) That affair is perhaps obliquely reflected in the poem
Bishop dedicated to Lilli, "Under the Window: Ouro Prêto."[27] Millier,
Bishop's biographer, seems to imply that it was the appearance of this poem

in the December 24, 1966, issue of the *New Yorker* that brought to the fore what turned out to be the decisive rupture between Lota and Elizabeth.[28]

The "new" poem transcribed from the copy in the possession of Lilli Correia de Araújo may be a part of the story of that break. Its tone is explanatory, with a hint of apology. It is directed to someone identified only as "dear" (a term that, depending on a context the poem does not give us, can hint at either closeness or distance). That the intended auditor of the poem is native to the Southern Hemisphere seems to be indicated by the nature of the speaker's explanation: her compass points North where "Springs are backward." Millier reproduces this untitled poem, preceding it with some enlightening information. "Lilli kept her husband's beautiful paintings of women hanging all around her house and inn," she writes. "Since his death in 1955, she had had only lesbian relationships, thereby preserving his memory, she said. Lilli herself was tall, blond, and Nordic looking," and Lilli and Elizabeth "shared an occasional nostalgia for northern things, especially the spring." Significantly, "among the objects Elizabeth left for Lilli was a poem, framed in her own watercolor illustrations, that speaks to that common nostalgia; the different, yet reminiscent, chill of the mountain air; and the painful compromises their love involved; and the sheer joy of their intimacy."[29] Undoubtedly Bishop and Lilli shared nostalgia for things "northern," but it does not seem to me that this poem is addressed to Lilli. It is more plausible that it is addressed to Lota, as originally intended. If this is so, as I think it is, Bishop's leaving the poem with the (temporary) lover who was originally Lota's friend, suggests something about the nature of Bishop's changing relationship with Lota and Lilli. With the gift of this poem Bishop extended the secret meaning of what Ouro Prêto had come to mean to her. Intended, perhaps, as an intervention to be used directly with a primary lover, the poem is presented to a second lover undoubtedly possessing intimate knowledge of the poet's primary relationship.

What one might now call the Lota-Lilli-Elizabeth poem warrants, therefore, a closer, more formal look. In his *New Yorker* piece Schwartz points to touches that are characteristically Bishop's: "the fairy-tale vividness and coloring-book clarity of her images...; the geographical references — and restlessness — of the world traveller; the delicate yet sharply etched jokes, often at her own expense ('Protestants, and / heavy drinkers': she was both); the apparent conversational casualness disguising the formality of the versification; the understated yet urgent sexuality; even the identification with animals."[30]

It is notable that Schwartz was shown not one manuscript but two: one handwritten, the other typed — both of them "illuminated in the roomy margins with small watercolors by Bishop: a square brown house, an apple tree, a goose, a hayloft with a pitchfork, a swan with its head disappearing in the text of the poem, and a fourposter bed."[31] Even so, Bishop not only did not publish the poem, she virtually "abandoned it in Brazil," writes Schwartz. Yet the poem is also something other than a simple love poem. "With typical obliqueness, it is even *about* Brazil — or, rather, what Brazil is not," notes Schwartz. "She must have been living there for more than a decade when she wrote it, probably in the mid-nineteen-sixties, and of the poems she wrote there it is the only one — at least, the only one that was finished — in which she weighs the world of her childhood in Nova Scotia against the life she chose for herself later, in which she measures not only how far she has travelled from her origins but how difficult it is to escape them."[32]

It is possible to see the matter differently, however. True, Bishop never published the poem and apparently kept no copy of it for herself. And true, Bishop did finally leave Brazil to live out her last years in New England. But the poem does not deal with such matters. It offers an implied comparison of the poet's earlier formative life in the cold north with her "dear" one's warmer south, and it does so for a purpose. The poem strikes the reader as being very private, one not intended for auction or re-collection in a book. Its tone is one of suasion, its intention seduction. It is meant, perhaps, to have its effect, specifically, on one person. Given to that person in handwritten form, it could do the specific work the poet wished it to do. It is not irrelevant that although both the holograph manuscript and the typed version are illustrated apparently with the "same" drawings, as Schwartz tells us, "the images on the typed copy appeared in a different order, but incised pencil outlines suggest that they may have been traced from the handwritten original."[33] Rather than abandoning the poem or even merely leaving it behind when she left Brazil for the last time, Bishop gave away not just copies of the poem, but the ontological poem itself. Her act in this instance recalls, incidentally, those many instances when Emily Dickinson "gave" away a poem, incorporating it into a homespun emblem or weaving it into the text of a familiar letter.

Just how deeply "Portuguese" Bishop had become by the time she composed this lover's poem emerges in a simple detail, a touch no Portuguese reader would need to make a point of. Bishop knew Brazilian culture and the country's language well enough to build her poem around a single Portuguese word that, given the object of her poem as a personal communication to one specific listener, she feels confident enough to omit from the poem. The word is *nortear*. A verb that in the infinitive is literally rendered as "to north," *nortear* means "to guide, direct or lead one's self." Bishop's play on this ultimately nautical word, indicating not merely her bio-geographical origins but her continuing sources of orientation, would seem entirely natural to a Brazilian (or Portuguese) reader. One imagines that the poet, not truly apologizing for her "northern" origin (or, therefore, "northern" orientation), offers her explanations that it is their exposure to northern cold that enables crabapples to "ripen to rubies" and cranberries to turn into "drops of blood," as fortifying facts for her chiding revelation to her southern "dear" that up there, human beings may go bed early, but never to "keep warm."

Unlike Bishop's other poems, this one was intended to share its subject not with the person who now reads it but with the one person who would understand the one "other" about whom it was written. It was in Brazil that this "new" poem meant most — as the poet intended.[34] Yet it also casts light on the secret only hinted at in the Portuguese of Luis de Camões that graces the dedication page of *Questions of Travel.*

This poem, unlike the relationship to which it now testifies, turns out to be something other than still another thing filled with the intent to be lost — like the lost door keys, the hour badly spent, and the three loved houses that went enumerated in the poem "One Art."[35] If "One Art" is both a testament to certain feelings of elegy and loss, it is also intended — in conception, revision, and publication — to be an intervention in her own life. (That the poem continued to have its effect on the poet is apparent in her self-accusation, after she had lost a writing case containing much of her unfinished work, "Oh why did I write that cursed villanelle?"[36]) In this poem about the self's attempt to survive a new or impending loss (that of Alice Methfessel), Bishop refers, too, to Lota; in a strange way, Camões, too, has a ghostly presence in the poem.[37] Lota has become still one more loss — the greatest, perhaps, of such losses — in the litany of loss the poet sets down in "One Art," the villanelle she published in 1976, nine years after Lota's death.

Among the things lost are door keys, badly spent hours, a mother's watch, three "loved houses," two cities, two rivers, and a continent — this in prelude to what would be the devastating loss of her last companion: "Even losing you (the joking voice, a gesture I love)," she writes, "I shan't have lied." For, she concludes, "The art of losing's not too hard to master / though it may look like (*Write* it!) like disaster."[38] The poem's key — linguistic, lexical, phonic — is obviously the insistent rhyming of the words *master* and *disaster.* That the poem is a villanelle enables this rhyme to occur seven times. Indeed, "The repetitions of the key rhyme words, *master* and *disaster*," writes the critic Lorrie Goldensohn, "alternate in the obsessive and tragic dilemma of the grief-stricken speaker, as like a too-tightly wound spring the poem breaks to its conclusion, the painful subversion of language and form by feeling."[39] This rhyme did not appear until the second (extant) draft of "One Art."[40]

Now it is of course possible that Bishop hit on the "master-disaster" rhyme on her own, but it is worth considering the possibility that it is derivative. The possibilities are suggestive. One of them occurs in one of the half-dozen or so most famous poems in the English language. Edgar Allan Poe employs the "master-disaster" rhyme in "The Raven," that great poem of irrevocable loss:

> "Doubtless," said I, "what it utters is its only stock and store
> Caught from some unhappy master whom unmerciful Disaster
> Followed fast and followed faster till his songs one burden bore—
> Till the dirges of his Hope that melancholy burden bore
>   Of 'Never—nevermore.'"[41]

Poe not only anticipates Bishop's master-disaster rhyme but, remarkably, her triple rhyme as well: master-disaster-faster.

A second possible source for Bishop's master-disaster rhyme is "Luis de Camões," a sonnet by the Southern African poet Roy Campbell, celebrating the Portuguese poet's ability to make poetry out of adversity ("fire and shipwreck, pestilence and loss"). The rhyming of "disaster" and "master" occurs in the first quatrain:

> Camões, alone of all the lyric race,
> Born in the angry morning of disaster
> Can look a common soldier in the face.
> I find a comrade where I sought a master
> For daily, while the stinking crocodiles
> Glide from the mangroves on the swampy shore,
> He shares my awning on the dhow, he smiles
> And tells me that he lived it all before.
> Through fire and shipwreck, pestilence and loss,
> Led by the *ignis fatuus* of duty
> To a dog's death—yet of his sorrows king—
> He shouldered high his voluntary Cross,
> Wrestled his hardships into forms of beauty,
> And taught his gorgon destinies to sing.[42]

As Campbell notes, Camões had "lived it all before" ("fire and shipwreck, pestilence and loss"). Indeed, as Bishop undoubtedly knew, it was something more than just the romantic's take on his life that Camões had suffered through the disasters of losing "houses," lovers, and even his work.

It is possible that when in "One Art" Bishop worked at her craft—her "mechanical devising of rhymes"[43]—she did not consciously recall that her poem might be indebted to either Poe or Campbell. But whether or not she was so influenced, there is no gainsaying that she makes the rhyme her own,[44] bringing about its large effect by rhyming "master" with "disaster," over and over again — or, as she said, "This is a villanelle — it repeats & repeats & *repeats*."[45] Marianne Moore had Bishop in mind when she reminded that "an indebted thing does not interest us unless there is originality underneath it."[46] It may be that Bishop's settling on the villanelle — one of her "rare excursions into a complex, pre-existent verse pattern," notes Schwartz — enabled her to focus clearly on the essential elements of her material.[47]

Finally, however, it is the poem's last line that makes the poem. "[T]hough it may look like (*Write* it!) like disaster" is "a parenthetical injunction that is at once confession and compulsion," as J. D. McClatchy describes it, or, in the words of Helen Vendler, "a tenacious interpolation of self-command."[48] It does not detract from her achievement that she may owe the line to James Joyce, for, if so, she has made it her own. Joyce writes: "In the vague mist of old sounds a faint point of light appears: the speech of the soul is about to be heard. Youth has an end: the end is here. It will never be. You know that well. What then? *Write* it, damn you *write* it! What else are you good for?"[49] It's this sudden, angered turning on one's self that she got from Joyce. Of course, what Bishop leaves out of her conclusion to "One Art," in this borrowing from Joyce — "this speech of the soul" — is Joyce's sardonic self-accusation that concludes his words about loss: "What else are you good for?"

It has been said that in "One Art" Bishop "confronts the death of Lota de Macedo Soares with understated but searing directness,"[50] even if it is the fear of losing the one who turned out to be her last companion — not Lota — that the future perfect "shan't have lied" points to. But in any case "One Art" provided no closure to the Lota portion of Bishop's Brazilian legacy, for to the end of her life she planned to write a book-length poem to commemorate Lota. "Only the barest outline of 'Elegy' is left among Elizabeth's papers," according to her biographer, indicating that the poem would be written "'in sections, some anecdotal, some lyrical, different [lengths] — never more than two short pages —.'" The poem would point to Lota's "'reticence and pride'; her 'heroism, brave & young'; her 'beautiful colored skin'; 'the gestures (which [you] said you didn't have).'" The poem would also "investigate specific memories: 'the [door] slamming, plaster-falling — the [cook] and I laughing helplessly'; Lota's 'courage to the last, or almost to the last —'; 'regret and guilt, the nighttime horrors'; 'WASTE.'"[51] It was not to be.

A fitting addition to any account of Elizabeth Bishop and her Brazilian experience is the rehearsal of James Merrill's anecdote. He tells it as having happened in 1970 in Ouro Prêto. "I was her first compatriot to visit in several months," Merrill recalls, but there was another guest, "a young Brazilian painter, in town for the summer arts festival." "Late one evening, over old-fashioneds by the stove," writes Merrill, "a too recent sorrow had come to the surface; Elizabeth, uninsistent and articulate, was in tears. The young painter, returning, called out, entered — and stopped short on the threshold. His hostess almost blithely made him at home. Switching to Portuguese, 'Don't be upset, José Alberto,' I understood her to say, 'I'm only crying in English.'"[52] The sentimental detail that Merrill left out of his emblematic anecdote was that Bishop was crying over the loss of Lota and the Brazilian life they had shared.[53]

2

Unravished Brides

If "Brazil, January 1, 1502" provides reliable evidence of the poet's feelings and attitudes, it is clear that Elizabeth Bishop would have none of Brazil's rather easy and accommodating view of colonial miscegenation in its own history that Gilberto Freyre offered his countrymen and the world in his epochal essay *Casa-Grande & Senzala* (*The Masters and the Slaves*), published in 1933. "No sooner had the European leaped ashore than he found his feet slipping among the naked Indian women," he wrote. "The women were the first to offer themselves to the whites, the more ardent ones going to rub themselves against the legs of these beings whom they supposed to be gods. They would give themselves to the European for a comb or a broken mirror."[1] This historical construction presented Brazil with what immediately became its comforting view of the Indian woman's behavior on first encountering the European male. Bishop's view was that the first Portuguese had "carried off" the Indian girls.[2]

Freyre's book was hardly her first encounter with Brazilian culture. There is evidence to indicate that even before arriving in Brazil in late 1951—where she would make her home for nearly two decades—Bishop had had a taste of Brazilian poetry in English translation. *New Road 1944: New Directions in European Art and Letters*, which reprinted Bishop's poem "Jeronymo's House, Key West" from the September/October 1941 issue of the *Partisan Review*, featured a first-of-a-kind dossier on what was then considered to be modern Brazilian poetry.[3] The poems chosen were by Castro Alves (an excerpt from *The Slave Ship*), Cruz e Souza (one poem), Alberto de Oliveira (one poem), Alfonsus de Guimaraens (one poem), Raul de Leoni (one poem), Ronald de Carvalho (one poem), Menotti del Picchia (two poems), Carlos Drummond de Andrade (one poem), Manuel Bandeira (two poems), Ismael Nery (two poems), Murilo Mendes (one poem), Jorge de Lima (one poem), and Olavo Bilac (one poem).[4] (Four of these poets—Jorge de Lima, Drummond, Bandeira, and Murilo Mendes—would reappear in *An Anthology of Twentieth-*

Century Brazilian Poetry, a collection prepared by Bishop herself, with the collaboration of Emanuel Brasil, and published in 1972.)

The volume *New Road 1944* also contained an essay on "Brazilian Poetry," which summarized several contentious generalizations about Brazil: "Anthropologists and sociologists ... had proclaimed impossible, the existence of civilization in the tropics. Besides, racial theorists stigmatized the coloured people and the mestizos as irrevocably inferior. Iberian decadence sharply contrasted with the vigorous development of Anglo-Saxon populations all over the globe." There was, moreover, "an insidious and pessimistic propaganda which threatened to stupefy and paralyse the energies of the nation, and which produced reasons for a pretended inherent annihilating melancholy of the Brazilian race, as the outcome of the mixture of the Portuguese, Negro and Indian."[5] The poems presented were offered, of course, singly and in the aggregate, as correctives to such easy and familiar canards.

The Olavo Bilac poem included in this 1944 dossier is the nativist-national poem "Brazilian Land" ("O Brasil"), taken from Bilac's collection entitled *The Voyages* (*As Viagens*). Bilac invites the "Mariner," on first encountering this virginal, verdant land to view her as a beautiful woman "standing there, pure virgin who surrenders to your kisses," her breasts "burning with desire," this "fairest of all nature's flowers."[6] Notably, if not surprisingly, Bilac's unnamed translator is cautious or reticent in two crucial places: Bilac's phrase "virgem morena e pura" is rendered as "pure virgin" (dropping the crucial idea of the Brazilian male's infatuation with the "morena" or "mulata") and in the line "Ó desvirginador da Terra Brasileira" the idea of "deflowerer" is replaced, evasively, as "first lover of the Brazilian Land."[7] Bilac's trope — the Brazilian land as dark virgin, awaiting her deflowerer — would have its telling echoes in one of Bishop's own Brazilian poems published a decade and a half later but only after the poet had undergone other experiences and suffered myriad other influences.

"The Portuguese image of Brazil was from the beginning erotic," writes a modern historian, for "as the legendary Portuguese phrase had it, 'beneath the equator there is no sin.'"[8] "Epicurean" was the word Amerigo Vespucci used for the natives encountered in the New World.[9] Gilberto Freyre puts it less evasively, as he states, without qualification, "The milieu in which Brazilian life began was one of sexual intoxication."[10] This, of course, is reflected in Bishop's poem, which finally appeared in the *New Yorker* magazine on January 2, 1960, thus honoring, fortuitously, the month and day the Portuguese expedition, having sailed from Lisbon in May 1501 for the purpose of exploring the Brazilian coastline, is reputed to have reached Rio de Janeiro.[11]

As an epigraph for the poem Bishop chose some words — "embroidered nature ... tapestried landscape"—from Sir Kenneth Clark's *Landscape into Art*.[12] This, I think, was a poet's ruse, intended to throw the reader off the track of the poem's main thrust, at least initially. A more appropriate epigraph, to my mind — one that was closer to her subject — would have been something from Camões. What I have in mind, specifically, are those lines he devotes to the imaginary "Island of Love" in Canto IX. That timeless place, foreign to any chart or map, is imagined by Camões: "Pois a tapeçaria bela e fina / Com que se cobre o rústico terreno ... / Mas o sombrio vale mais ameno."[13] In Leonard Bacon's translation, published in 1950, and thus available to Bishop well before she wrote her poem, these lines read: "There is a tapestry most fair and fine / That covers over all the rustic place ... / Lending to the dark vale a sweeter grace."[14]

In fact, Camões's suitability to Bishop's poem goes beyond its anticipation of the word or two in the phrases the poet chose for her epigraph. It will be recalled that the vision of the fabled "Island of Love" and what will happen there are the rewards Venus bestows on the successful Portuguese mariners. In an episode of free and boundless sex, Vasco da Gama's sailors mate with nymphs in a luxuriously pastoral setting. "He spoke, and forthwith swifter than the hind / The heroes rushed the water-meadows through, / And the nymphs fled through branches intertwined," Bacon renders Camões, "But with less speed than purposeful ado, / Smiling the while, yet raising many a cry, / Till, bit by bit, they let the hounds draw nigh."[15] In Bishop's poem the Portuguese mariners upon arrival found it all "not unfamiliar." Although they saw "no lovers' walks, no bowers, / no cherries to be picked, no lute music," what they encountered, nevertheless, corresponded "to an old dream of wealth and luxury / already out of style when they left home —/ wealth, plus a brand-new pleasure." Their old dream of riches and luxury — the latter as *luxuria* (lust)[16]— would have had its literary source for Portuguese readers in Camões's account in *Os Lusíadas* of Gama's sailors at their lovemaking on the "Island of Love." But history meshes uneasily with imagination, even when romance is incorporated into an historical epic. This is certainly the case with the history imagined in "Brazil, January 1, 1502," which records that the sailors "ripped away into the hanging fabric, / each out to catch an Indian for himself"—yet unable to catch "those maddening little women who kept" retreating, "always retreating, behind" (or into) the fabric.[17]

Always retreating in the sylvan scene — here Bishop nods, perhaps, in the direction of John Keats's "Ode on a Grecian Urn" (1820) where maidens remain forever "unravish'd"— that celebration of the paradox that is an ecstatic stasis.[18] Moreover, one must *assume* that outside of the "tapestry" of Bishop's poem, rapes took place. What the poem does not allow for (recall that "always") is that the Indian nymphs acquiesced in the way Camões's "Does" (since they are "not so Swift as Artificial") allowed the pursuing "Greyhounds" to gain on them.[19] The Indian women in Bishop's poem — if not in history or in the erotic island fantasy of Camões — remain forever unravished like the nymphs on the frieze of the urn considered in Keats's famous poem. In Camões's poem it is all very much different. "And others on that other quarter light / Where naked goddesses a-bathing lie, / Who sudden cry aloud in their affright," Bacon renders Camões. "As not expecting violence so high. / Some, feigning shame a less thing in their sight / Than force can be," while "all mother-naked fly / Into the thicket, yielding to the eyes / What virtue to the lusting hand denies."[20]

"Brazil, January 1, 1502" is among Bishop's least autobiographical, least directly personal poems. Actually, as I have tried to show, it is highly "literary." By that I mean that although Bishop draws on direct experience, as she usually does, that experience comes, as often as not, from written texts and paintings.[21] It is a truism, of course, that the creations of someone else's imagination and art can readily become part of the experience of those who read them or see them. In fact, it can be said that "Brazil, January 1, 1502" was largely derived from Bishop's reading, or, more specifically, perhaps, from the research she did in preparation for *Brazil*, the book she wrote on contract for the *Life* series on world nations.[22] Included in that research were books on the European discovery of the New World, particularly Brazil. In *Brazil* she quotes from the foundational letter written on the first of May 1500 by Pêro Vaz de Caminha to King Manuel describing the land discovered on Pedro Alvares Cabral's voyage of that year.

In her list of sources for her volume on Brazil, Bishop also lists Amerigo Vespucci's spirited accounts of his own attendance on several journeys to Brazil, including the second Portuguese expedition in 1501–1502. It was on that journey that, sailing along the coast from north to south, the various landing places were named for the festive dates on which they were visited, reaching Rio de Janeiro on the first day of the year 1502. Curiously, this auspicious landing, although it is the subject of Bishop's poem, goes unmentioned in her book *Brazil* and does not appear on her list of important historical dates in the same work. "Januaries, Nature greets our eyes / exactly as she must have greeted theirs," begins the first stanza of "Brazil, January 1, 1502": "every square inch filling in with foliage —/ big leaves, little leaves, and giant leaves, / blue, blue-green, and olive." The thick growth and variegated, lush foliage characteristic of tropical Brazil in summer, so evident to the poet in this month of January, as in all past Januaries, including the one in which the Portuguese first laid eyes on the place they called Rio de Janeiro, is offered to us as the reality of the poet's own day in the already very modern city of Rio in 1959–60.[23]

If "Nature greets our eyes / exactly as she must have greeted theirs," it is unlikely that it would do so for the occupants of an 11th-story apartment looking out at the ocean in Leme and Copacabana. Nature's lush show would still be available, perhaps, along the route Bishop would have taken to reach Samambaia in Petrópolis. I do not mean to quibble about this, but it does seem significant to me that a natural setting in modern Brazil should be married in the poet's imagination to the supposed Rio that awaited the Portuguese on their arrival in 1502. Such a marriage is for the sake of the poem, one concludes, and not for the sake of the factual history behind it. In fact, the actual experience of Nature in her fulsome vegetation enables Bishop to fill in the history that is recorded by Caminha and Vespucci, neither of whom possesses the poet's ability to describe nature, or better, to reconstitute nature as if it were a work of human art. Bishop's Nature is "solid but airy; fresh as if just finished and taken off the frame." Whether the frame is the frame on which a tapestry is made or the frame on which lace curtains are stretched, starched, and dried (one suggestion of "fresh"), the language also recalls (to me, at least) William Blake's poem "The Tyger," particularly the lines that ask the question: what power "dare frame thy fearful symmetry,"[24] even as Bishop's lines stress Shakespeare's "airy" nothingness while recognizing that nothingness's "solid" existence.

The claim that there is no Sin beneath the equator it is the burden of the second stanza to deny, for this display of fern, flower, and (now) bird, backed by "a blue-white sky, a simple web," is but the background or scenery (*pano fundo*, if one considers this show as Nature's tapestry or theatrical curtain) for what is in the foreground. For there, up front, is Sin, evidenced in "five sooty dragons" near "massy rocks," "worked with lichen, gray moonbursts / splattered and overlapping, / threatened from underneath by moss / in lovely hell-green flames." (It is not without interest, that this imagery echoes the first stanza of Bishop's love poem "The Shampoo," a personal, sensual poem published in 1955: "The still explosions on the rocks, / the lichens, grow / by spreading, gray, concentric shocks."[25])

Sexuality shows forth in the gaze of the dragons (actually lizards, as it is soon revealed)—"all eyes" "on the smaller, female one, back—to, / her wicked tail straight up and over, / red as a red-hot wire." Bishop here makes the easy identification of sexuality—carnal knowledge—with sin. Surprisingly, this detail of lizards and sex is taken from personal observation. Before finding its place in the poem, this experience was described in a letter Bishop wrote in November 1959: "Watching the lizards' love-making is one of our quiet sports here!" she writes, "the male chases the female, bobbing his head up and down and puffing his throat in and out like a balloon — he is usually much larger and much uglier. The female runs ahead and if she is feeling friendly she raises her tail up over her back like a wire — it is bright red, almost neon-red, underneath. He hardly ever seems to catch up with her, though —"[26]

Bishop's poem suggests that there is an analogy between the lizard's ways of courtship and the recently arrived Christian's sexual pursuit of the little, birdlike Indian women. He may be out to "catch an Indian for himself," but the analogy tells us that he may only be able to do it if the Indian permits him to do so. Pêro Vaz de Caminha had written, "There were among them three or four girls, very young and very pretty, with very dark hair, long over the shoulders, and their privy parts so high, so closed, and so free from hair that we felt no shame in looking at them very well."[27] Indeed, nakedness and shame (or, more accurately, the lack of shame) is a persistent theme in Caminha's account. There is no doubt that, personal voyeurism aside, Caminha knew that these matters mattered to the Court back in Portugal. Consider the following statements in Caminha's letter:

1. They were dark, and entirely naked, without anything to cover their shame.[28]

2. In appearance they are dark, somewhat reddish, with good faces and good noses, well shaped. They go naked, without any covering; neither do they pay more attention to concealing or exposing their shame than they do to showing their faces, and in this respect they are very innocent.[29]

3. And then they stretched themselves out on their backs on the carpet to sleep without taking any care to cover their privy parts, which were not circumcised, and the hair on them was well shaved and arranged.[30]

4. At that place there assembled at once some two hundred men all naked...[31]

5. And then they brought him [the convict] back to us, and with him came the others whom we had brought. These were now naked and without caps.[32]

6. Others wore caps of yellow feathers, others of red, others of green; and one of the girls was all painted from head to foot with that paint, and she was so well built and so rounded and her lack of shame was so charming, that many women of our land seeing such attractions, would be ashamed that theirs were not like hers. None of them were circumcised but all were as we were.[33]

And the final example of Caminha's repetitive observations:

7. There were also among them four or five young women just as naked, who were not displeasing to the eye, among whom was one with her thigh from the knee to the hip and buttock all painted with that black paint and all the rest in her own colour; another had both knees and calves and ankles so painted, and her privy parts so nude and exposed with such innocence that there was not there any shame.[34]

Pêro Vaz de Caminha's account of what the Portuguese saw and did in Rio de Janeiro in 1500 has been widely accepted as objectively factual, at least as objectively factual as could have been expected at the time. Its authority is implicitly acknowledged by Gilberto Freyre, for example, though Freyre goes beyond his predecessor when he writes in *The Masters and the Slaves* (a book that Bishop characterized as "fascinating and depressing"): "It is known to be a fact that even Portuguese men of arms of the fifteenth and sixteenth centuries, possibly by reason of their long maritime crossings and their contact with the voluptuous life of Oriental countries, had developed all forms of lust."[35] In fact, "independently of the lack or scarcity of women of the white race," adds Freyre, wherever he went "the Portuguese always was inclined to a voluptuous contact with the exotic woman. For purposes of racial crossing, miscegenation."[36] The possibly benevolent aspect of this notion has become, in some quarters, something of a commonplace: "Pêro Vaz de Caminha betrays in those words ['de as nós muito bem olharmos'] an attitude that would be, throughout history, perhaps, the basis of the mysterious plasticity of the Portuguese everywhere in the world: that racial co-fraternization that creates the roots of an understanding with the most diverse peoples, in the most eminent Christian sense, such as love for the next person."[37] Needless to say, this notion has also been, no more so than now, vigorously, sometimes ferociously, challenged.

Now Bishop's Indian maidens are not exactly those free, easygoing, pliant, unashamed, unencumbered sexual beings of Caminha's rosy account; but they are not so obviously or unambiguously the clear-cut victims that a parti pris ideological reading of the poem seems to demand that they be.

In her final stanza Bishop completes the structuring simile the poet has been constructing all along—the first term of which appears right off in the opening stanza ("theirs"). These "Christians, hard as nails," came and found it all corresponding "to an old dream of wealth and luxury / already out of style when they left home—/ wealth, plus a brand-new pleasure." This new pleasure erupts "Directly after Mass, humming perhaps / *L'Homme armé* or some such tune, / they ripped away into the hanging fabric," each one "out to catch an Indian for himself,—/ those maddening little women" who keep calling to each other and "retreating, always retreating, behind" the fabric.[38]

Here the Christians behave exactly as if there were no such thing as Sin beneath the equator, though, if we are to believe the poem, Sin is hardly absent from this natural tropical world. There is violation here, but, oddly enough, it is violation of the scenery ("ripped away into the hanging fabric"). Of course, the easy equations are not to be made, for example, that the male lizard equals the Christians, and the female lizard equals one of "those maddening little women." It is the equation between the unspecified, perhaps ambiguous, attitude of the female lizard (is she keeping the other lizards at bay or is she sending out an invitation to one or more of them?) and the "retreating, always retreating" "maddening little women," who keep retreating behind "the hanging fabric." The question is crucial, especially given the tendency on the part of many readers to view this as an incipient rape scene. Of course, to be considered is the fact that in the self-enclosed world of the poem these women will never be caught, whether they wish to be caught or not. In this, they are like the pursuing man and the pursued woman in the sylvan scene of pursuit forever frozen in the frieze ornamenting the urn in John Keats's great ode. It is of course unlikely that these Christians, "hard as nails, tiny as nails" in "creaking armor" will soon catch these probably unclad maidens unless they — the maidens — allow themselves to be caught. (Hence the point of the poet's reference to the 15th-century Masses based on the theme of *L'Homme Armé* and the lyrics of the chanson associated with those Masses: "The armed man is to be feared. / Everywhere has the cry gone out, / That each one should arm himself / With a coat of armour. / The armed man is to be feared."[39]) Still, even the possibility of rape hovering over the scene as Bishop presents it questions the validity of the sweeping assertion by the American Waldo Frank, writing about slavery in Brazil and the growth of "Brazil's mixed population": "There was no rape; almost no case of it is known in Brazil's history."[40]

The historical first and second "Masses" celebrated by the Portuguese in Brazil have had their depiction in art. There is Vitor Meireles's *A Primeira Missa*, a painting now in the National Museum in Rio de Janeiro, in which the Mass is depicted — frozen in medias res — with Portuguese sailors kneeling attentively and indigenous Indians along the edges of the scene, milling about in various poses and strikingly different attitudes toward the unfamiliar behavior of the strangers newly come among them. What is entirely missing in this depiction of the natives is any suspicion or fear of the Christians. A naked Indian holds her child to her breast. Two Indians are perched in a tree, one of whom seems to be watching — expectantly. Another one sits on the ground, watching intently, his chin resting on his folded hands. Several others show surprise, fascination with the unfamiliar ritual playing out before them. The Christians attending the Mass — some of them in full armor — seem almost oblivious to the presence of the curious outsiders — the Indians. Of large national import, this painting has even found its way onto the verso of the 1,000 cruzeiros bill of a generation ago honoring Pedro Alvares Cabral. Since it honors Cabral's voyage in 1500, one that did not take him to the place that the second expedition — not led by Cabral — named Rio de Janeiro, the Mass depicted serves just as well to depict the one described by Pêro Vaz de Caminha as having taken place farther north along the shores of the Atlantic. Still, this famous painting might well have contributed its share to Bishop's imaginary, prompting her to imagine her own version of a Mass in Rio on January 1, 1502.

But while it is highly probable that Bishop was acquainted with *A Primeira Missa*—after all, Vitor Meireles's painting of the first (or at least an early) Christian Mass in Brazil was on display at the Museu Nacional de Belas-Artes as well as reproduced on the nation's currency[41]—it is just as probable (perhaps even more so) that Bishop knew a second painting depicting the arrival of the Portuguese in Brazil, one by a painter with whom she seems to have shared affinities and friends. This 1946 painting by Pedro Luíz Correia de Araújo[42] shows close up in the foreground an Indian woman, head and shoulders, enclosed in tall green fronds that "separate" her and "protect" her from a scene revealing two non–Indians facing at a distance two naked Indian maidens.[43] The Indian woman in profile, obviously attempting to keep herself hidden within a circle of large ferns or fronds, looking out suspiciously if not surreptitiously. Here is something more than the hint of pursuit, capture, and rape. Indeed, while Meireles's painting celebrates the European Catholic arrival in Brazil, Correia de Araújo's painting is monitory in its depiction of Indian wariness and suspicion. He will not have you miss his point. He calls his painting *Conquistadors and Conquest* (*Conquistadores e Conquista*).[44] In making a single Indian woman the most prominent feature of his painting (pictorially foregrounding her — in place and size), Correia de Araújo may have been prompted by Pêro Vaz de Caminha's voyeuristic observation: "Among all those who came to-day there was only one young woman who stayed continuously at the mass, and she was given a cloth with which to cover herself, and we put it about her; but as she sat down she did not think to spread it much to cover herself. Thus, Senhor, the innocence of this people is such, that that of Adam could not have been greater in respect to shame."[45] It is as if Correio de Araújo has taken over this woman and transformed her to make his point.

The argument that this painting is one of the principal sources feeding into Bishop's conception of what the facts must have been on the shores of Rio de Janeiro on the first day of the year 1502 is enhanced, I think, by the fact that it is the work of Pedro Luiz Correia de Araújo, the husband of Lilli Correia de Araújo, Bishop's very good friend and sometime lover in Ouro Prêto. During Bishop's lifetime Mrs. Correia de Araújo was already the proprietor of the Pousodo Chico Rei (Rua Brigadeiro Mosqueira, 90) in Ouro Prêto, the place where Bishop sometimes stayed on her visits to that small colonial city (when she did not stay with Lilli in her own home) before moving into Casa Mariana, her own colonial house, named for her friend, the American poet Marianne Moore, and to acknowledge the fact, as she wrote to Moore, that "the house is on the road to a lovely little town about 8 miles away, called Mariana."[46]

The full particulars in the genealogy of "Brazil, January 1, 1502" will perhaps never be entirely known, but the importance to that project of Pêro Vaz de Caminha's letter and, to a lesser extent, Gilberto Freyre's groundbreaking work, along with the seminal paintings of Vitor Miereles and Correia de Araújo, seems to be undeniable. Of course, it should be pointed out, Bishop's story of pursuit and intended rape — suggested by the title Correia de Araújo gave to his painting — is intended to replace, by way of irony, the conciliatory narrative suggested in Vitor Miereles's painting — replete with unexamined details from Pêro Vaz de Caminha's letter, such as the woman with baby — that he entitled *Primeira Missa*.[47] One suspects that from Bishop's point of view, Caminha's letter to the king, Camões's canto on the nymphs of love, Miereles's painting of the first Christian Mass in Brazil, Freyre's explanations of the first impact of the Portuguese landing in Brazil, even Bilac's allegorized patriotic verses of love encountered by Bishop in 1944 — all these might be collected, in different circumstances, under Correia de Araújo's plain-speaking rubric: *Conquistadores e Conquista*. Writing about Europe's eruptive intervention in Brazil, in "Brazil, January 1, 1502," Bishop is pretty much in agreement with the Amazonian emperor in Mário de Andrade's defiantly exuberant novel, *Macunaíma*, who worries about what would happen to him were he to go to Europe, saying, "Without a doubt, European civilization would play havoc with our unspoiled nature."[48]

In conclusion — it may be, as one of Bishop's readers says, that there is "pathos in these last lines ['those maddening little women ... retreating, always retreating'], a sentiment "that derives partly from our knowledge that the women will not escape their hunters."[49] This is plausible, of course — if we extend them and their situation into the accumulated history we know (or think we know) or back to the mythology of Philomela ("so rudely forc'd," crying "'Jug jug,'" to dirty ears, as Eliot has it in *The Waste Land*).[50] But in Bishop's poem as a thing in itself — as a freestanding artifact — these "retreating, always retreating" women are as safe from history as is Keats's frieze-frozen "unravish'd bride" — no more, but hardly less.[51]

3

Driving to the Interior

In "Cape Breton," first published in 1949, Elizabeth Bishop writes: "Whatever the landscape had of meaning appears to have been abandoned, / unless the road is holding it back, in the interior, / where we cannot see."[1] She did not explore the mysteries that the Cape Breton interior might hold for her. And for some time after arriving in Brazil and long after agreeing to live with Lota in Rio de Janeiro and the far more sylvan Petrópolis, she had little or no interest in exploring the geographically much greater "untamed world of a vast interior" she thought she was already confronting when she disembarked at Santos and, after two days, went off, by train, to Rio de Janeiro.[2] In fact, just getting fully settled in this new place lasted much longer than she had expected. Four years after arriving in Brazil, for example, Bishop complained: "We've been living in the same house, still under construction, since a few weeks after I arrived here and unexpectedly stayed for good."[3]

But there would come a time during Bishop's stay in Brazil when she feared the poet's fear that her poetry was becoming too Brazilian, or rather less American or even, perhaps, less Canadian. "But I worry a great deal about what to do with all this accumulation of exotic or picturesque or charming detail, and I don't want to become a poet who can only write about South America," she confessed to Robert Lowell. "It is one of my greatest worries now, how to use everything and keep on living here, most of the time, probably, and yet be a New Englander — herring-choker — bluenoser at the same time."[4] She became increasingly aware that these contrary pulls posed a problem for her poetry, which, of course, had been there from the start. Just how she negotiated them gives shape to one kind of biographical drama. The reader who would see that drama whole must approach it by looking into the dual questions of "what" and "when." *What* did she know and *when* did she know it? As in all investigations of this sort, not to mention accounts of those investigations such as this one, the routes are seldom linear or direct.

Bishop also wrote, suggesting a different but related route into her work,

33

about what constituted "experience" for the poet. "Think how little some good poets have had, or how much some bad ones have," she writes to May Swenson. "There's no way of telling what really is 'experience' anyway, it seems to me. Look at what Miss Moore has done with what would seem to me like almost none, I imagine, and the more 'experience' some poets have, the worse they write."[5] Yet from the very start life in Brazil was enormously attractive to her. Of the "elegant modern house" Lota was building in Petrópolis, a two-hour drive from Rio de Janeiro, Bishop confided to Alfred Kazin, "It is all very luxurious, and I never felt like Rilke before."[6] That Lota promised to build her a studio apart from the house and next to a waterfall outdid what any patron had ever done for the German poet and, once built, it turned her Rilka-like stay into a permanent removal from her apartment in the United States. Of her writer's studio, she writes, "There is one large room with a fire-place. Lota found a rock somewhere that is gray-blue with mica in it, extremely pretty, and had them make it out of that — whitewashed walls and a herringbone brick floor," and there is "a small bathroom and kitchenette with a pump and a Primus stove for tea, etc." But the best thing, perhaps, was that she now had all her books and all her papers together "for the first time in ten years."[7]

"Coitado" was just about the first Brazilian word to make its way into Bishop's correspondence from Brazil and soon became a great favorite, though she soon got "awfully tired of the endless discussions of the state of everyone's *figado*."[8] During her illness at the outset of her first days in Rio, she would most likely have been touched by the free and easy use of the term that means so much more than does its equivalent in English, especially for a people who seem to "adore sickness" — poor thing or "the poor one."[9] Endearingly appropriate, the word so used seems to absolve a victim of all blame, all responsibility. It became a part of Bishop's working vocabulary. No wonder, as she said exuberantly about her life in Brazil, it was as if she had died and gone to heaven.

There can be little doubt that Elizabeth Bishop's long Brazilian stay affected her thinking about herself and marked her work while there and later, sometimes showing itself in the smallest of particulars, the use, sometimes, of a single, decentered word or brief expression. Knowing some Portuguese will often contribute to one's fuller understanding of the way she, in her poetry, will bring in a single word such as *cachaça*, which appears in "Going to the Bakery," or how she rings intercultural changes on other words — "interior" ("Arrival at Santos"), "ignorant" [*ignorado*] ("The Armadillo") and "anniversary" [*aniversário* ("birthday")] ("Twelfth Morning; or What You Will"). How she coins a bilingual phrase (perhaps) — "Esso — so — so — so" [*é só—só—só—só*] ("Filling Station")— or incorporates a direct, literal, and slightly off-centered translation —"took advantage of" [*aproveitar*, meaning "put to use," "made use of," "made good use of"] ("Under the Window: Ouro Prêto") or — two final examples —"Januaries" [*janeiras*, a New Year's carol or gift] and "'one leaf yes and one leaf no'" [*folha sim folha não*] (both from "Brazil, January 1, 1502"). There are also examples from her letters, say the time she complains about Dona Alice (Al-iss-y) Brant, the original (or perhaps only putative) author of the book known in English as *The Diary of "Helena Morley."* Soon after the book's publication, Dona Alice nags anxiously, "Is it giving any results?" [*da resultado?* or *está dando resultado?*], not a question relating to reviews or critical reception, as one might expect from the wife of a wealthy banker, but "meaning money, of course," as Bishop correctly interprets for her American correspondents.[10]

In the first published versions of "Arrival at Santos"— in the *New Yorker* (June 21, 1952) and in *Poems: North & South—A Cold Spring* (1955)— Bishop (whom I take to be the poem's true speaker) fears that Brazilian customs officers will take away their scotch. When the poem was "*aproveitado*" for *Questions of Travel* (1965)— at a friend's suggestion — the speaker now fears that it is their "bourbon" that might be taken away. At first blush, the reason for this revision defies easy explanation, especially given Bishop's explanation to her friend that the change was "a change from the general to the particular."[11]

What occurs to me, however, is that the change supports and perhaps helps to clarify Bishop's poetic intention. What she wants to convey is that the speaker's original fear had no basis. The change from *Scotch* to *bourbon* reinforces that notion. Let me explain. What the poet probably did not know when she landed at Santos, but would have undoubtedly learned shortly thereafter, was that in Brazil the generic term whisky is synonymous with scotch whiskey. Scotch is called whiskey and the word whiskey always refers to scotch — whether imported or manufactured locally.[12] Whiskey is not employed to mean any of the North American varieties — blended ryes, for example, or straight rye. It is reserved for Scotch alone. In fact, imported scotch whiskey was already quite expensive during Bishop's time in Brazil (and later) and much desired. Bourbon, on the other hand, was not desirable. It was not manufactured in Brazil and, naturally, since there was no demand for it, not imported either. In fact, in a letter to American friends in 1952, Bishop complains that in Brazil "no bourbon is available, unless I cultivate a U. S. Army connection and I guess it isn't worth it."[13]

Thus Bishop's later explanation to Ashley Brown that the change from scotch to bourbon was a change from "the general to the particular" is puzzling since from an American point of view, a change from "whiskey" to either scotch or bourbon would be logical in her explanation, but "scotch" to "bourbon" is not. It is my notion, however, that the change does underline the speaker's Americanness — a fondness for bourbon — and the groundless fear that the Brazilian officials would be attracted to her liquor. The fact would have been, though the callow visitor disembarking at Santos would not have known it, a bottle of bourbon would have held no attraction whatsoever to any honest or corrupt port official. Many Brazilians would be delighted to receive a gift of a bottle of "whiskey," that is, imported Scotch. If given bourbon, however, they would, in all likelihood, serve it to American visitors or give it away. Bishop's change from Scotch to bourbon serves to underline her overall ignorance about Brazil, especially the prevailing Brazilian taste for Scotch whiskey — which, according to sociologist Gilberto Freyre, they sometimes mix with coconut milk.[14] As for the notorious Brazilian Customs, Bishop would soon discover the capricious and frustrating ways of its officers. Three weeks after arriving in Rio, about half of her and Lota's stuff was still in Customs. "We have to make one more trip to retrieve the rest and *pay*," she wrote to friends back in the United States. "Poor Lota and all her lovely cans of tuna fish, dozens of napkins, dishes, etc.," she continued. "All the laws were changed just before we arrived, of course — 'household effects' don't seem to mean what they say any more — just one sample will give you the idea of the Kafka-*puro* we've been through: They *weighed* our Victrola records, pasteboards & all!"[15]

"My Anglo-Saxonism is *really* shocked by the mails," Bishop once confessed to American friends.[16] The hint of this in "Arrival at Santos" reflects not the tourist arriving in Brazil for the first time, but the frustrated sender of postcards from the mainland. "So *that's* where my stamps went to," Bishop wrote to Marianne Moore. "I looked and looked for them, not that it really made much difference anyway because, as you may have noticed, they come almost without glue on them." And because the mailboxes are never collected one has no choice but to go the Post Office with its "glue machines which are frequently incapacitated by their own glue, so that one gives up and goes to the woman who runs a stamping machine, even if the stamps are much nicer. I don't believe that I have made that at all clear," she concludes, "but you'll be able to gather that mailing a letter here is quite an undertaking."[17]

It can be rightfully said that in more than one sense, Bishop's protracted stay in Brazil was one single, long trip into the interior. Her ship, the SS *Bowplate*, put in at Santos, the principal port for the state of São Paulo and located an hour's drive away from the capital city, also called São Paulo, situated on an inland plateau. The poem she wrote about that disembarking, "Arrival at

Santos," was published in the *New Yorker* on June 21, 1952. It seems, at an earlier stage of composition, to have borne the title "To the Interior." The only vestige of that earlier title in the finished poem is in the last line of the poem, which concludes with the phrase "to the interior."

Bishop's use of the phrase is entirely consonant with Brazilian usage, though English-language readers, familiar with the usage of the word in well-known texts such as Joseph Conrad's *Heart of Darkness* and in lesser known texts such as the Southern African Laurens van der Post's *Venture to the Interior*, published in 1951 (the year Bishop arrived in Brazil), usually find nothing peculiar about her use of the term.[18] Indeed, English-language readers are even comfortable with the use of the term to mean, more specifically, "within the self or psyche." (Bishop's biographer, Brett C. Millier, calls attention to "its luminous last line, 'We are driving to the interior,' suggesting an agenda for her future."[19]) When Americans travel away from the sea, they may say that they are traveling inland, but Brazilians say, usually, that they are traveling into "the interior." That Bishop understood this and did not expect most American readers to understand it is clear from a reference in her grant application to the Rockefeller Foundation. Petitioning for a grant to support her while she worked on *Black Beans and Diamonds*, a book about Brazil, she employs the phrase "in the interior": "I have been living in Brazil for almost 14 years now, know the language, have seen most of the better-known sights, and also traveled quite a bit in the 'interior.'"[20] The quotation marks are hers. She is calling attention both to the "foreignness" of the term to her audience and to the flatly denotative sense of the word. She had done the same thing in the earlier poem, though she does not cross the t or dot the i, as she might have, by enclosing the word in single quotation marks. Indeed, "Arrival at Santos" might be glossed by the poet's comment to Anne Stevenson a dozen years after her arrival in Brazil. She was going, in about three weeks, she said, "on a trip 'into the interior' really, this time."[21]

But there may be a further wrinkle in the poem. For a Brazilian knowing what Bishop's destination in the "interior" is as they move out of Santos — undoubtedly the capital city of São Paulo — would see a joke in referring to that journey as a journey "to the interior." For São Paulo at the time, like the seacoast cities — Rio de Janeiro, Porto Alegre, Salvador, Natal — and, perhaps, an inland city like Belo Horizonte or (in an earlier day) Manaus, was too metropolitan to be considered a part of the interior. It is part of the naiveté that Bishop reveals in "Arrival at Santos" that, having already picked up the Brazilian use of "interior," she has not yet mastered its use for herself. She may think she is going "to the interior," but she isn't, at least not in Brazilian cultural terms. Perhaps, in some way, her growing mastery of the term accounts for her change in the title,[22] although "arrival" ("arriving," at last, for a new life in a new land with a new love) suggests much more to the English-language reader than it would to the average Brazilian reader with a little English. That suggestive meaning is lost in the Portuguese of Horácio Costa's literal translation of "Arrival at Santos" as "*A chegada a Santos.*" One last note on the Conradian (or, better, Darwinian) adventure Bishop saw before her upon first looking upon Brazil. Notice how at the end of the 17th line she slips in H. M. Stanley's familiar question, uttered at the moment of facing for the first time the "missing" Dr. Livingstone for whom he has searched far into the interior of the African continent. Perhaps, too, Bishop was recalling Randall Jarrell's description when he contemplated that she was on her adventurous way to Tierra del Fuego, "You really are just like Livingstone; and Stanley too.[23]

Before leaving "Arrival at Santos," I would like to mention two other matters. First, the volume *New Road 1944* that reprinted her poem "Jeronymo's House, Key West" also included a translation of Ronald de Carvalho's poem "Interior," the title of which refers both to the notion of Brazil's geographical "interior" and also to the inner recreation of that geography by a "poet of the tropics"—a task congenial to the American poet who would spend much of the next two decades writing poems that were not dissimilar.[24] And second, the line in "Arrival at Santos" that ends "Glen Fall"—followed by the line beginning with *s* (which anticipates Lowell's similarly constructed lines in "Memories of West Street and Lepke") actually echoes the use of such disjuncture by e. e. cummings in several poems in *XAIPE*, a volume Bishop reviewed in 1950. Here are three examples: (1) "begin to feel of it,dying / 's miraculous / why? be"; (2) "a / long conway / s"; and (3) "—that screech of space)absolutely(my soul / tastes If as some world of a spark / 's gulped by illimitable hell)."[25]

"I wonder who the reviewer was who misunderstood 'Manuelzinho' so—but then I've been accused of that kind of thing a lot, particularly in the social-conscious days," wrote Bishop. "Actually, Brazilians like 'Manuelzinho' very much. I've had several English-reading friends tell me, 'My God (or Our Lady), it's *exactly* like that.' And that's why Lota is supposed to be saying it...."[26] Roughly in the spirit of Bishop's English-reading friends, "Manuelzinho" was described by one reviewer as "Elizabeth Bishop's wry sermon on patience."[27] I agree that the poem can be called a "sermon," and "wry" does come close to characterizing the poet's tone, but that the poem is about "patience" is not quite right—loss of patience comes closer, I would say.

It should be recognized right off that "Manuelzinho" (a diminutive form of "Manuel," often conveying condescension beneath its apparent indication of affection) is a living "descendant" of the fictional and legendary Jeca Tatu, the prototype in Brazilian literature and culture of the unabashed *caboclo* or bumpkin figure of ridicule as he first appears in Monteiro Lobato's earlier work.[28] This bit of information, inaccessible to her *New Yorker* audience, should have helped to reconcile her Brazilian readers to the portrayal of "Manuelzinho," though there is every indication that it did not.

"We were just getting it all more organized when (because of domestic dramas here — none of ours — the cook, the silly girl, was 'carrying on' with another man — although crazy about the one she had)," writes Bishop a decade after her arrival at Santos, "we found ourselves completely servantless. We've made do with a tiny pretty little girl, aged *eleven*, for two weeks now (Manuelzinho's daughter, if you remember *him* — that family certainly is important in my life. I have just written my fourth poem about them)."[29] Significantly, perhaps, Bishop says not "our" life, but "my" life. "I am pleased you said you liked my 'Manuelzinho,'" she wrote to a friend, the poet Robert Lowell. "Somehow when he appeared just now, in *The New Yorker*, he seems more frivolous than I'd thought, but maybe that's just the slick, rich surroundings."[30] Bishop told her aunt Grace Bulmer: "The poem you saw must have been 'Manuelzinho' — about L.'s kind-of-a-gardener — wasn't it? It's all completely true — how he hired the bus to go to his father's funeral, etc."[31]

Who is Manuelzinho and who is saying all those terrible things about him? Bishop makes certain, in her directions at the head of the poem, that the poet is not speaking this monologist's meditation — this speaking in a vacuum, a speaking out loud to the self. It is "a friend of the writer," she insists at the outset, not herself, who is doing the speaking. To the poet May Swenson she wrote: "*The New Yorker* took a long, long poem ['Manuelzinho'] — to my great surprise, it was such an impracticable shape for them. It's supposed to be Lota talking, and I do hope you will like it."[32] But that it is Lota's voice we are hearing is a "fiction," albeit one that is "necessary," for, as Brett Millier points out, "the poem's message has to do with the distance between the tenant and the landowner, and Elizabeth herself owned no land."[33] We know things about the speaker, besides the fact that she is on her own property, not anyone else's, and that Manuelzinho, as her tenant or squatter on her land, is accountable to her. She is also much annoyed at what she takes to be Manuelzinho's shenanigans or bizarre behavior — reactions that clearly establish that she is not a Brazilian since any Brazilian would not only never be surprised at Manuelzinho's behavior (though she might well be annoyed at it or even made angry by it) but she would more than half expect it. That she is an American seems to be indicated when she reveals that she has dubbed Manuelzinho the "Klorophyll Kid," a slurring nickname, she tells us, that amuses her visitors, undoubtedly Americans.

It is an odd world that this "friend of the writer" has fallen into, a world
in which Manuelzinho is "a sort of inheritance." It is the "sort of" that gives
her away, for Manuelzinho is an inheritance, as are his wife and his children
and his father, with preexisting rights and claims. Thus, in that sense, their
tenure on the land does not depend on the present owner, who would have
great enough difficulty in trying to remove from the land these "half squatter,
half tenant" individuals. It would simply not be in consonance with the prevailing mores. The same is true with the cost of medication for his sniffles
and shivering or the cost of his father's funeral. And if he is the "world's worst
gardener since Cain," or a pathetically inadequate bookkeeper whose columns
of numbers "stagger" and who leaves out "decimal points," or the painter of
hats and the grower who has trouble digging up the potatoes but who comes
forth to show off "a mystic three-legged carrot" or the pumpkin that is "'bigger
than the baby'"—evidence, as Bishop says elsewhere, of what is "so Brazilian,"
a land where "Giant vegetables are revered"[34]—what's to be done about it?
He's that paradox of humility and independence, vanity and childlike dependence, whose outlook is more often than not aesthetic if always proper. He
knows the value of a name as evidenced by "Hermosa," the name he gives a
donkey that strikes the speaker as anything but beautiful or handsome. He
knows the value of color, painting his hat green or gold, of garden design,
edging the beds of "silver cabbages" with "red carnations." He is frugal, feeding
himself, in the midst of varied plenty, "boiled cabbage stalks," and wearing
"bright-blue pants," "patch upon patch upon patch" stitched with white thread
until he seems to be draped in "blueprints." Such bizarre aesthetics help to
orchestrate his bizarre existence and provide fodder not for war against him
to be waged by the speaker but for the war stories out of which the poem is
itself stitched. But these are domestic war stories that Brazilians would not
spend very much time telling one another. No, these are stories that non–
Brazilians might well exchange with other non–Brazilians. Not having been
born to the manners and mores of property-owning and house-maintaining
Brazilians, the speaker can tell a good tale to outsiders, to the readers of the
New Yorker, say, where the poem appeared on May 26, 1956, some five years
after Bishop settled in Brazil. Brazilians who could afford to hold and maintain
the sort of property indicated in the poem would not have batted an eyelash
at Manuelzinho's "misappropriation" of his patroness's expense money to pay
for a bus to bring in "delighted mourners" to his father's funeral. And it does
not help much that Manuelzinho says that he prays for his benefactor every
night, as if anyone would think those prayers compensated for the prepos-
terous expenditure incurred, the exasperated narrator — not Lota (pace
Bishop)—clearly implies.

But that very "fact" that Bishop claims it is Lota who speaks in this poem is itself problematical. The speaker may call her portion of land "my property," but the steep paths across it tell a different story. They were made by Manuelzinho or his father or his grandfather, not by the *de jure* owners. It is hard to avoid thinking, rather, that the speaker of the poem, a "friend of the writer," is really either Elizabeth Bishop herself or someone else we might as well call Elizabeth Bishop — who is herself, as the writer warns us elsewhere, at least "an" Elizabeth, "one of *them*," in this case, the landowning outsiders.[35] As Regina Przybycien, Brazil's first major interpreter of Bishop, writes, "Rendered in the condescending voice of Manuelzinho's mistress," the poem "shows the poverty and ignorance of the character as quaint and amusing. Manuelzinho's world is doubly distant from the poet, enveloped in the difference of his social class and of a local culture that she is still trying to figure out. For Bishop Manuelzinho is the exotic other."[36]

Manuelzinho's relationship to the land and to the (current) proprietor of the land is predial, that is to say, he belongs to the land, he is of the land, but he is not, neither de jure nor de facto, the land's proprietor. Indeed, he is responsible for paying predial tithes to the (current) proprietor. He does not in any way "belong" (in the 20th century) to the proprietor, but neither can that proprietor just remove him from the land. His status and the security of his situation (and that of ancestors before him, perhaps) arise from his occupation of the land he farms and the services and products he owes in payment. Manuelzinho is the predial who owes "tithes, etc." to the predialist (who is the friend who owns the land that comes with predials).[37]

More than a dozen years after settling in Brazil, Bishop was still at her complaints, including the extraordinary way "one accumulates a 'family' of dependents in Brazil." "The sewing girl is blue and has to be cheered up; give her the radio and close the door," she writes in resignation. "Then the maid cries, big hot tears, because the horrible TV we keep for her is malfunctioning and makes everyone look like dwarfs, with faces four feet long." Her "second cousin, large and black, who works for Lota in the park but cut his hand badly, seems to be living with us these days and decides he'll 'help' by washing the terrace with floods of water that come in the door of my study." He's joined by his wife, "from whom he's separated," and who "arrives by mistake, has an attack of asthma, gets treated, then has mild hysterics and needs a sedative." Then Bishop has "to read them the plans for the Carnival from the afternoon papers because only the man, Leoncio, can read (but not too well)."[38]

Behind such complaints, however, can be sensed some of Bishop's not unhappy acquiescence — something new to her — in being personally useful

to the individual members of this large Brazilian extended family. In addition
to this, moreover, there was Bishop's scarcely hidden admiration for Lota's
imperial, paternalistic way of dealing with menials and workmen in her
employ. She was not one to suffer fools gladly. For instance, Bishop wrote to
the photographer Rollie McKenna: "We don't need the porcelain stove any
longer, thank you! Lota finally built a large, freestanding fireplace," she writes.
Lota "sat in a safari chair and *produced* it, with Negro boys streaming past
her, each with a rock from the mountainside on his head, just like Cecil B.
DeMille directing *The Ten Commandments*, or the building of the pyramids."[39]
Seemingly born to command, her manner is matter for a mild joke. Lota
"seems to be in very good form" these days, "bossing a crew of fourteen or
fifteen 'mens.'"[40] But Lota's talent for "bossing" would be tested on a much
larger, municipal stage within two years, when the governor of the state, her
friend Carlos Lacerda, entrusted her with the virtually impossible task of
turning a stretch of "useless" land in Flamengo into a park for the people.

Well before Bishop moved into Lota's new house in Petrópolis, where
she was bothered by what she considered to be the shenanigans and outrageous
doings of Manuelzinho, she spent time in Florida. "Faustina, or Rock Roses,"
one of her Key West poems, both in setting and character, appeared in *The
Nation* on February 22, 1947. The poem has an understated but forceful social,
if not explicitly racial, theme. The poem draws on Bishop's acquaintance with
a local seller of lottery tickets. But it is not as a figure encountered in the
streets of Key West that Faustina appears in Bishop's poem, but as a caretaker
of an old, bedridden white woman. The third person in the poem is the visitor,
reasonably presumed to be the poet or someone much like her, since the poem
makes the reader privy to her thoughts (but not those of the old woman or
her attendant).

The title — "Faustina, or Rock Roses" — offers explanatory information
in the form of alternatives. The second half of the title acts as something of
an after- or second thought. In Bishop's poem, whatever else the title may
tell the reader, it names the two efforts at "caring" for the invalid: Faustina's
attempts to divine and answer her patient's requests (barely if incoherently
made known) or the visitor's (perfunctory?) proffering of "rust-perforated"
flowers as a kind of attendance to the patient's spiritual or emotional needs.
But this is a "crazy" house and a "crazy" bed, "frail, of chipped enamel." That
is, it is a place "full of cracks or flaws; damaged, impaired, unsound; liable to
break or fall to pieces; frail, 'shaky'" (*Oxford English Dictionary*). Of course,
Bishop wants these meanings, as well as the suggestion that there is something
mad or insane about the place and the human situation being played out in
the room. Deftly, Bishop presents the two terms of her title at the beginning

and the ending of the opening stanza, though in the case of the "roses" the appearance is figurative as part of a description of the bed which blooms above the sick white woman's head "into four vaguely roselike flower / formations." In this "crazy" room, the floorboards "sag," the table is "crooked," and most of the little pills are "half-crystallized." Everything is at sixes and sevens. The visitor herself is hardly attending to the patient, for she "sits and watches / the dew glint on the screen" while an "eighty-watt bulb" (can't find one of those these days, if one ever could) "betrays us all." In her "stupefaction" the visitor notices things that do not appear to be salient to the poem's overall meaning beyond the fact that they — various kinds of "light" — are the means (complementary to the glow of the eighty-watt bulb) of "discovering the concern" "within our stupefaction."

When Faustina, summoned by the patient's whisper — "Faustina, Faustina" — walks into the scene, her ("sinister") "blackness" has already been prepared for (several lines before we read "her sinister kind face / presents a cruel black / coincident conundrum") in such images as that of "the pallid palm-leaf fan," "bleached flags" and "trophies" ("Rags or ragged garments / hung on the chairs and hooks / each contributing its / shade of white"). There is more than a hint here of the reversal in the servant-master relationship depicted in Herman Melville's 1855 story, "Benito Cereno," the lasting effect of which is revealed in the final exchange between the two captains. When the puzzled American captain asks the liberated Spanish captain, "What has cast such a shadow upon you," the reply is "The negro." The Amasa Delano–Benito Cereno–Babu scenario is mirrored in the story of the narrator-sick woman-Faustina told in Bishop's poem.

Faustina, who tries to determine what her patient wants by exhibiting, in turns, the medical accoutrements on the crooked bedside table — talcum powder, pills, cream, and "farina" — also expresses her own need — for "coñac." She also complains about "the terms of her employment," the details of which the poet refrains from detailing. It is at this point that the poet introduces a "social" fact — that might well have led another writer (or Bishop at an earlier time) to pursue such themes as the exploitation of the worker or the pernicious relationship of the exploited one's opportunity for revenge against her exploiter — the black woman "bends above" the "other" — but the poem seems to go another way. Like an oxymoron, Faustina's "sinister kind face presents a cruel black coincident conundrum." What revelation is there in the face that is at once "sinister" and "kind"? If the situation recalls that of the mistress and her slave or the "haves" and "have nots" or the caretaker and the (always vulnerable) patient or the reversal of the oppressor and oppressed, it is not in any of those terms that the alternatives are expressed. The conundrum is less a social matter than an emotional (psychological) one. The alternatives for reading Faustina's "sinister kind" face are not entirely divorced from "cruel" blackness, perhaps, for they are put: "is it / freedom at last, a lifelong / dream of time and silence, / dream of protection and rest" or is it "the unimaginable nightmare / that never before dared last / more than a second"? The poet does not have the luxury to entertain the question beyond the moment, for it "forks instantly," and in "a snake-tongue flickering" becomes "helplessly prolifera-tive." She gives up. She despairs of an answer. Faustina's eyes "say only either." She beats a retreat from the scene but, more importantly, she, to all intents and purposes, deserts the "proliferative" "problems." She "rises," "awkwardly proffers" her flowers, and "wonders"—not about the black woman and white woman but (a new interest)—"whence come / all the petals." Of the choices in the title—"Faustina" or "Rock Roses," what has come to occupy her mind at the last is unmistakable. Late in 1947, some ten months after publishing "Faustina, or Rock Roses," Bishop told Robert Lowell that she was "working some on another poem called 'Faustina,'" but it is hard, she admitted, "to choose among the various versions she gives of her life."[41] While no such poem was published in Bishop's lifetime, it might be inferred (rightly, I think) that "Faustina, or Rock Roses" was not conceived as, or intended to be, one of those "various versions."

　　If "Faustina, or Rock Roses" remains one of Bishop's most socially con-scious poems, it is also notable that she swerves away from its (possible) direct political or social import by having the "visitor" transposing the opposed answers—dream or nightmare—into her own personally proliferating prob-lems. In an article written while she was still a student at Vassar College, Bishop wrote that what particularly interested in the poetry of Gerard Manley Hopkins was "the releasing, checking, timing, and repeating of the movement of the mind."[42] She herself wanted "to portray, not a thought, but a mind thinking," for "the ardor of its [an idea's] conception in the mind is a necessary part of its truth; and unless it can be conveyed to another mind in something of the form of its occurrence, either it has changed into some other idea or it has ceased to be an idea, to have any existence whatever except a verbal one."[43] In "Faustina, or Rock Roses," the mind that Bishop chooses to depict is the visitor's (the poet's), not that of the white old woman or the black and bare-footed Faustina of the poem's title. As the expression of the speaker's own thinking, this poem can be seen to exemplify Bishop's own version of Wallace Stevens's famous desideratum, as asserted in the poem "On Modern Poetry": "The poem of the mind in the act of finding what will suffice."

　　Moreover, while it cannot be said that Bishop ever demonstrates a poet's rage for order, there is always in her work the sometimes anxious desire to find at least the semblance of order. In this she resembles Dr. William Carlos Williams, whose experience was not entirely alien to her. When he encountered a cluttered, confused, deranged kitchen in the house of one of his nearly improvident patients, the artist he was saw in it not hopeless disorder but a new order — an artistic order. "I have seldom seen such disorder and brokenness — such a mass of unrelated parts of things lying about," the good doctor marveled. "That's it! I concluded to myself. An unrecognizable order! Actually — the new! And so good-natured and calm. So definitely the thing! And so compact. Excellent. And with such patina of use. Everything definitely 'painty.' Even the table, that way, pushed off from the center of the room."[44] Yet attracted as she was to the "definitely 'painty'" quality of shabbily built houses and genuinely primitive paintings, such Williams-like experiences of a "new" order are rare in Bishop's work, the main exceptions occurring in her essay, "Gregorio Valdes, 1879–1939" (1939), and the poem, "Jeronymo's House" (1941), published in the then still leftist *Partisan Review*.[45] Although she had been trying to contribute to the *New Yorker* since her early days in the city, there is no evidence that she offered either of these works to the magazine that would become her principal place of publication.

4

Rainbow, Rainbow, Rainbow

In one of those coincidences that the temporal logic of change brings out, a seasonal vacationer to Cape Breton, with Bishop's poem "Filling Station" on his mind, noticed on his return several years ago that the familiar Esso station on Cape Breton was no longer there. "I drive across the causeway to my rented summer house on the west coast of the island," he writes, and "I remember Elizabeth Bishop's poem 'Cape Breton,' in which she describes the island's 'ancient chill,' its 'dull ... deep peacock colours' and 'little white churches ... dropped into the matted hills / like lost quartz arrowheads. // Whatever the landscape had of meaning appears to have been abandoned.'" By the 1960s, when Bishop wrote the poem, he continues, "most of Cape Breton's coal mines had shut down.... Abandoned farm land was turning to brush. Nearing my house, I notice that the old Esso station where I bought my gas last summer has gone out of business, recently enough for there still to be bottles of Coca-Cola in the unplugged soda machine."[1]

How long this particular gas station had been doing business on Cape Breton is not important, but it would be a nice coincidence if Bishop, who, in "Cape Breton," left a record of her considered impressions of the area while skirting "the interior, where we cannot see," had seen this particular Esso station. It would open up the possibility that "Filling Station" owes something to Bishop's visits to Cape Breton, though the poem was not published until some four years after she first set foot on Brazilian soil, betraying the fact that memory conspires with present circumstance to make up the contents of a poem.

There is an epiphany — of sorts — at the end of "Filling Station." The poet infers that there must be "somebody" or something — force or mover — behind the order that she finds in the filling station. The existence of the product implies the reality of a producer. And the motive of it all is love, for somebody has "embroidered the doily" and watered the plant, as well as arranged the cans "so that they softly say: / ESSO — SO — SO — SO / to high-

46

strung automobiles." And when Bishop decides "Somebody loves us all," her intentions apart, she echoes the words of Robert Browning's Pippa, when the young woman exults: "I may fancy all day — and it shall be so —/ That I taste of the pleasures, am called by the names / Of the Happiest Four in our Asolo! / See! Up the hill-side yonder, through the morning, / Some one shall love me, as the world calls love." Yet, unfortunately, the world is not at all how Pippa sees it, let alone how she would see it. There's scheming, anger, perfidy, and violence beyond the surface that is visible to the Candide-like Pippa always from afar.

But the sentiment of the last line of "Filling Station" is undercut in a second way. To the poet-anthologist John Frederick Nims, Bishop wrote in opposition to the need for explanatory notes to her poems. But there might be exceptions. "One of my few exceptions is the Esso-Exxon note to 'Filling Station,' because I'm not sure how long ago now that happened, but a good many years," she explains. "Also, I'd let students figure out — in fact, I TELL them — the cans are arranged to say so-so-so, etc., so I don't think *that* has to be explained. However — most of them might well not know *that* so-so-so was — perhaps still is in some places — the phrase people use to calm and soothe horses."[2] She did not choose to explain, however, either to the anthologist or to the readers of his anthology, that what was behind that row of Esso cans would be clear to Brazilians (even though Bishop chose to place the poem not in the "Brazil" section of *Questions of Travel* but in the "Elsewhere" section, thereby suggesting that the poem was not "an especially Brazilian poem" and could "be equally true of an out-of-the-way filling station anywhere."[3] Behind "Station #2," as the poem was called when it was submitted to the *New Yorker*— the station described was on the Rio to Bahia road[4] — was the reality of Standard Oil's formidable presence in the Brazilian economy (as Bishop learned), and thus a considerable force to be taken into account in the country's politics. The rallying cry for development in Brazil that emerged from the Aliança para o Progresso (Alliance for Progress) was soon parodied as "Aliança para o Progresso da Esso."[5] Here then is the hidden meaning of that now "historical" progression of cans designed by, ironically, "somebody who loves us all."

Oil, gasoline, and two trucks — a brand-new Mercedes-Benz and a brandless old truck with "a syphilitic nose" — make their appearance in "Under the Window: Ouro Prêto," published in the *New Yorker* on December 24, 1966. The older truck grinds up in a cloud of burning oil. Into the margins of a "ditch of standing water" before a single iron pipe that has attracted the trucks, along with specimens of the town's populace, has seeped oil. That oil "flashes or looks upward brokenly, / like bits of mirror — no, more blue than that: / like tatters of the *Morpho* butterfly."[6] Italicizing the name of the butterfly indicates that she has resorted to referring to it by its name in Portuguese. (In another instance, however, there is no such indication. The scrap of conversation overhead on the spot, "'For lunch we took advantage / of the poor duck the dog decapitated," translates, in the phrase "took advantage of," the Portuguese word *aproveitar*, which might have been more naturally translated, as we have already seen, as "made use of" or "made good use of.") The colors the poet sees here are not those of the rainbow but the single color blue. Nor is there, at the close of this poem, any suggestion of an ending or epiphany, as there is, rather forthrightly, in "The Fish" or, satirically, in "Filling Station." The "mote" painted on the Mercedes-Benz bumper mocks the messianic desire for the Second Coming: "HERE AM I FOR WHOM YOU HAVE BEEN WAITING." The driver of the old truck offers passersby either a bromide to those who are dissatisfied, perhaps, with their share of the world or a reassuring slogan for those who are good-humoredly resigned to their lot: "NOT MUCH MONEY BUT IT IS AMUSING." Such is the wisdom emanating from the knights of the road.

The poem is replete with signs that do not have any significance or at least not the expected significance. The place is called "Ouro Prêto," meaning "black gold," but the only oil here drips from the truck with the "syphilitic nose." For instance, "Mercedes-Benz" combines names that suggest the Portuguese *mercê* (grace) or *merecedor* (deserving) and *bença* or *benzer* ("blessing" or "to bless"). Feet are washed but the act, carried out by truck drivers on their own feet, seems to have nothing to do with the Scripture it may evoke in a reader sensitive to Christian images and meaning. Babies, "muffled to the eyes" despite the heat, are brought by their mothers and given drinks of water, not from a (baptismal) font, but "lovingly" out of dirty hands, from "a strong and ropy stream" coming from a single iron pipe. The *madrinha* ("'godmother'") who is present has nothing to do with baptism. She is the lead donkey, decorated with "a fringe of orange wool," "wooly balls above her eyes," and bells, followed by six other donkeys. Any meaning that the reader might extract from the fact that the women with the babies wear "red dresses" is dissolved by the second fact that they all wear "plastic sandals." The potentially votive burning here is nothing other than the older truck's "blue cloud of burning oil."

It is different, however, when the poet notes that around this water pipe gather what she, recalling Jacques in Shakespeare's *As You Like It*, calls "the seven ages of man." If representatives for some of the ages are not singled out and named, they are present — the baby, the schoolboy, the adult truck driver, the "old man with the stick and sack." "All the world [*todo mundo*] still stops" here, at the place where water is to be found, where, as Melville says in *Moby-*

Dick, all ways lead: "Face a man in any direction and he will walk toward water." Even the donkeys "veer toward the water as a matter of course" until they are driven away. The "old man with the stick and sack" does not drink from his own cupped hands, but has an "enamelled mug," like the broken cup at the source of waters in Robert Frost's "Directive."

The minor epiphanies of these poems — "Filling Station" and "Under the Window: Ouro Prêto"— are anticipated in Bishop's once much-anthologized poem "The Fish." Reflecting her experience in Key West, the poem serves nicely to flesh out in particulars a much earlier poem by William Butler Yeats. "The Fish" by Yeats is devoid of all descriptive details concerning "the fish" the poet addresses as it hides in "the ebb and flow / Of the pale tide when the moon has set."[7] What strikes one right off is that Yeats has no interest in describing any particular fish but in recording his complaint, for the benefit of "the people of coming days," that the "hard and unkind" fish has time and again frustrated his attempts at capture, provoking him to assign blame and utter "bitter words."

Elizabeth Bishop's poem "The Fish" is altogether different. Published in the *Partisan Review* in 1940 in its March/April issue, "The Fish" soon became not just Elizabeth Bishop's signature poem but virtually her only widely recognizable poem. Challenged in its popularity only by "The Man-Moth" and "Roosters" (the latter published in the *New Republic* on April 21, 1941), "The Fish" made its way into nearly all the anthologies devoted to modern American verse. Not surprisingly, the poem eventually became something of an albatross around her neck. As late as 1970 she was still complaining, to Robert Lowell: "I think I'll try to turn that damned FISH into a sonnet, "or something very short and quite different." "I seem to get requests for it every day," she continues, "for anthologies with titles like READING AS EXPERIENCE, or EXPERIENCE AS READING, each anthologizer insisting that he is doing something completely different from every other anthologizer."[8]

To Marianne Moore, in February 1940, Elizabeth Bishop wrote about "The Fish," the poem then in hand: "I am sending you a real 'trifle.' I'm afraid it is very bad and, if not like Robert Frost, perhaps like Ernest Hemingway. I left the last line on it so it wouldn't, but I don't know."[9] The poem that begins "I caught a tremendous fish" ends with the line "And I let the fish go." Santiago's quite different treatment of the tremendous fish he has caught need hardly be invoked for any reader of the poet and fiction writer to perceive the difference between Bishop and Hemingway here. That Bishop's speaker releases her catch back to the water sufficiently differentiates her view of things (at least this once) from that of the "hunters" who populate Hemingway's world, from Nick Adams of "Big, Two-Hearted River" to the author himself in *Green Hills of Africa*. Some might explain this difference as a matter of sensibility not unrelated to gender. (It must not be ignored, however, that Bishop referred to herself, only half-jokingly, in 1949, as once again "being the female Hemingway." She was being taught pool and was about to go to "the cockfights."[10]) That the difference between Hemingway and Bishop on the matter of their relationship to the animals that they hunted might be cultural, however, is suggested by Margaret Atwood's formulation of the difference between the American hunter and the Canadian hunter as presented in each country's characteristic literature. "American animal stories are quest stories, with the Holy Grail being a death — usually successful from the hunter's point of view, though not from the animal's."[11] Canadian animal stories are different in that the hunter sympathizes with the dead and the dying animal, choosing to write from within the victimized animal's point of view. Sometimes there will be a moment of recognition that the hunter and his prey are one, as in Gabrielle Roy's *The Hidden Mountain* when "having hunted down a caribou," the hunter "finally kills it and it turns upon him a gaze full of resignation and suffering. This gaze exchanged between a hunter and an animal either dying or threatened with death — and it's usually a deer, moose or caribou — is a recurring moment in Canadian literature; in it the hunter identifies with his prey *as suffering victim*."[12] A variant on this gaze between fisherman and fish occurs in Bishop's poem. "I looked into his eyes / which were far larger than mine / but shallower, and yellowed," she writes. The irises were "backed and packed / with tarnished tinfoil" as "seen through the lenses / of old scratched isinglass." The eyes "shifted a little," but not to return her stare. Holding her "tremendous" fish, the poet describes a situation conducive to an epiphany, a moment of charity. The whole of "the little rented boat" turns everywhere into a rainbow. As she has stared, the oil from "the pool of bilge" has spread a rainbow around "the rusted engine / to the bailer rust orange," the "sun-cracked thwarts, / the oarlocks on their strings," and "the gunnels," until everything was "rainbow!" — stated, iterated, and reiterated. What any fisherman with even limited experience would know is that the boated fish, dying before the fisherman's eyes, would itself turn into the hues of the rainbow. It is the fish's death, still only imminent, that is foreshadowed in rainbows spreading out in the poet's sight from the oil and bilge in the bottom of the boat. It is a moment of wonder that presages disaster — an apocalypse — for the hunted. The poet cuts the fish loose. There will be no final rainbow this time.

It is not far-fetched to think that at some level Bishop's poem is also about poetry, more precisely, the words in a poem, composition as analogous to fishing. Edwin Arlington Robinson, who died in New York in 1935, just about the time Bishop moved to the city, used the metaphor, as the *New York Times* noted at the time of the poet's death. Recalling his early struggles in his "search for words," Robinson had written in *The Colophon* in 1930: "In those days time had no special significance for a certain juvenile and incorrigible fisher of words who thought nothing of fishing for two weeks to catch a stanza or even a line, that he would not throw back into a squirming sea of language where there was every word but the one he wanted.... He wanted fish that were smooth and shining and subtle, and very much alive, and not too strange; and presently, after long patience and many rejections, they began to bite."[13]

The same fish-poetry conceit is appropriated by João Cabral de Melo Neto, the modernist Brazilian poet Bishop translated for the anthology she coedited with Emanuel Brasil. Notice how in João Cabral's poem "On Elizabeth Bishop" the image of the lens of a fish's eye hovers lightly over the idea of the poet's own eye as a lens that "filters the essential" that "we see yet never see" until "we start talking about it." Bishop's essential words, "lit up in a book," writes João Cabral, "preserve" her "glittering famous fish."[14]

5

Fire and Light

One of the late drafts for "The Armadillo"—"a Nature Note," as Bishop called the poem when she submitted it to the *New Yorker*—shows mainly minor differences in the text (marked in ink in the poet's claw-like handwriting)—an "O!" for "O," a "the" for "a," and the word "forsaking" as an alternative to "escaping."[1] But there are important changes, too. She crosses out the title "Owl's Nest," replacing it with "Armadillo," and having underlined the whole of the last stanza, she writes "Italics" next to it. These last two changes were crucial, for the revised title directs the reader to see a key image, the armadillo, turned into the "weak mailed fist" ciphered into the poem's finale, four italicized lines that change the poem, as if it were a music score, to another key.[2]

Much has been written about "The Armadillo," a poem heavily favored by literary critics, anthologists and teachers alike, but there are still things to be said, questions to examine, and points to be made. It was first published in the *New Yorker* on June 22, 1957, most likely timed to coincide with the festivities surrounding the celebration of St. John taking place throughout countries with Roman Catholic populations, like Brazil, where, according to Bishop, it is the country's "second-best holiday," second only to Carnival. [3] Under the full title of "The Armadillo — Brazil" (the "Brazil" added to the title was the *New Yorker*'s signal that the poet was an observer — tourist like — in an exotic country),[4] the poem has been assiduously explicated for its own sake and thoroughly examined for its putative connection to Robert Lowell's equally famous poem "Skunk Hour." We can begin there. That in the most famous poem in *Life Studies* Lowell was influenced by Bishop's poem stems from Lowell's own acknowledgment in the matter: "'Skunk Hour' [is] not in your style yet indebted a little to your 'Armadillo.'"[5] Some months later he confessed (or boasted): "I used your 'Armadillo' in class as a parallel to my 'Skunks' and ended up feeling a petty plagiarist."[6] Yet it is hard at first to be sure about what Lowell got from "The Armadillo," apart from the fact that both poems feature animals — the family of skunks in Lowell's, an armadillo and a rabbit (joined by an owl) in Bishop's.

But the animals are precisely what Lowell found personally useful in Bishop's poem. The clue to that use is in the first of the two quotations given above when he says that he is indebted, not to "The Armadillo," that is, the poem, but to the armadillo, the animal. After telling Bishop that "The Armadillo" is "surely one of your three or four very best" poems, he confesses: "I thought the title mistaken at first, a [Marianne] Moore name — though I suppose the armadillo is a much too popular and common garden animal for her — for an out-of-doors, personally seen and utterly un–Moore poem." Yet, he decides, "'Armadillo' is right, for the little creature, given only five lines runs off with the whole poem. Weak and armored, I suppose he is those people carrying balloons — illegal — to their local saint."[7] What Moore would not do in her poems, Lowell implies — introduce a "popular and common garden animal — Bishop has done, and, as it turns out, so will he. It is almost as if Bishop's decision in this poem has given him license (so to speak) not only to risk writing his revealingly personal poem but to risk incorporating the name of a similarly "common" animal in his title, one with whom he will identify, as revealed in the reference (above) to "Skunks." In "Skunk Hour" Lowell localizes time, names persons and places, even looks to the specifics of animal behavior for clues to his own character. Thus the skunk allegorically objectifies the poet who searches through garbage cans, but it also does so with a difference: the skunk and her column of babies, unlike Lowell, will not scare. What scares the poet is that his mind is not right. It is not only that things are out of joint — they are: the old woman on the hill is dotty, the first selectman, rather than being a patrician worthy to lead, is a tenant farmer on the property owned by the old woman, who buys up eye-sore property only to let it fall down (creating other, even more disturbing eyesores?), the "fairy" who runs the antiques shop paints everything orange and wants to marry (to better his financial situation) — but the fact is that the poet is himself out of joint. If Marlowe writes, "Why this is hell, nor am I out of it," Lowell declares (echoing Marlowe and Milton), "I myself am hell." The 20th-century poet would spy on lovers but there are no lovers there (he says). Fearing an even more grievous bout of insanity, perhaps, he dare not contemplate inviting someone (in the words of Marlowe's celebrated lyric) to "come live with me and be my love." More in kind, he would be the mother skunk boldly supping on cream that has soured, for that, in a sense, sums up what the poet resorts to doing — plumbing and draining the memories of a life gone sour. If the skunk out at night nosing into garbage is an objective correlative for himself — "I'm a skunk in the poem," he confessed to Bishop[8] — he, too, will continue to prowl, his nose burrowing into his and other people's garbage, taking whatever heart he can from the skunk that will not scare. In fine, Lowell wants to convince his readers that in "Skunk Hour" he has made public some very personal behavior. The skunk out at night nosing into garbage is the poet's (Lowell's) alter ego. Yet, skunk that he is, he'll thrive, we suspect, by continuing to write his poems.

"The Armadillo," on the other hand, does not reveal much about Bishop's personal behavior. In fact, it can be argued, the poem draws only a little on direct personal observation, if anything at all. I say this despite the largely successful effort on Bishop's part to come to some greater, perhaps universal, meaning in the italicized lines that close out the poem: "*Too pretty, dreamlike mimicry!*" she begins. "*O falling fire and piercing cry / and panic, and a weak mailed fist / clenched ignorant against the sky!*" These are lines that might have been spoken by the figure, one fears, of THE American poet, "St. Elizabeth of Petrópolis," as she was sometimes called (somewhat good-naturedly, one presumes) in the circles into which she was introduced by her partner Lota. Indeed, it is with prophetic voice that the narrator of "The Armadillo" speaks the italicized lines to bring into the poem a larger, near-apocalyptic perspective on the scene of bursting fire-balloon, scurrying rabbit, and rushing owl that has just been described as a bit of action against the mountain setting, presumably in Rio.

Of course, in "The Armadillo" Bishop had taken over a large portion of an unpublished comic poem about a rabbit and an owl — comic in tone, but not so comic when one notices that the owl in the abandoned poem clutches the rabbit as prey. The situation of the earlier poem would become useful to Bishop only when she introduced the fiery balloon and a concluding striking cry — this last a message made congruent, I take it, because the poet's fancy has allowed her to metamorphose the armadillo's carapacelike appearance into the mailed fist she names in her message. It was just this fancy that posed the problem for Bishop when she got to the end of her description of the fire-caused panic among owl, rabbit and armadillo. The basic structure of "The Armadillo" is not unlike that of emblematic poems of an earlier century, poems by poets such as William Cullen Bryant ("To a Waterfowl"), Ralph Waldo Emerson ("The Rhodora") or Henry Wadsworth Longfellow ("The Cross of Snow") in which the imagistic expression of a specific individual experience is followed by a symbolic explication of the moral found in the experience experienced or the image observed. That the attack that the Imagists — led by Amy Lowell and Ezra Pound — mounted was against this sort of poetry was not lost on Bishop. Italicizing the "message" was her way of disguising the fact that her poem actually belongs with the moral-based emblematic poems of her predecessors.

That the "personal experience" treated in "The Armadillo" is actually a poet's construct comprised of several experiences — not a single one — is made apparent when one considers "The Owl's Journey," which she failed to place. When she did show it to a friend, Loren MacIver, in 1950, she offered it with a caveat: "This scarcely counts, as poetry, but I thought you might like it," while promising to send "sonnets next time." The poem tells merely the strange dreamlike anecdote of the owl's riding down a long slope on a rabbit's back.[9] Interestingly enough, in the version of "The Owl's Journey" included by Alice Quinn in *Edgar Allan Poe & The Juke-Box* (2006), it is indicated that several insertions have been made that are not indicated as such in the version Robert Giroux included in *One Art*, particularly the crucial one in line 11 — "not hurting him" — a phrase that appears in earlier manuscript versions of the poem but is crossed out in at least one late draft, a change that supports the implication of pain in the line "the owl's claws lock[ed] deep in the rabbit's fur."[10] This last minute subtraction brings to mind the tenderness for baby rabbits that Bishop expressed in a letter to Marianne Moore from Key West in 1943. Having "discovered a place in an alley here where they raise rabbits — also dogs, puppies, cats, hens, roosters, chickens, bantams, etc. — all loose together in a large shady yard," wrote Bishop, "I went to get a rabbit to *eat*, but changed my mind. They had a litter of gray angora ones, with their eyes just opened. I've never seen anything cuter. They sat up and scratched their ears, which seemed to be just as long as their bodies, with first one hind leg, then the other, and arranged the fur on their chests with their tongues just like kittens."[11]

Bishop's introduction of the armadillo into her poem makes all the difference, as Lowell saw right off. Where did it come from? Well, I would suggest that it came off the label of what was in Bishop's time a much-favored brand of *cachaça — Tatu —* that is, "Armadillo." (Recall, too, that Monteiro Lobato's fictive *caboclo*, a forerunner in some ways of Manuelzinho, is named Jeca Tatu.) Even if she did spot a moving armadillo, it may well have been associated in her mind with the beginnings of "The Owl's Nest," which began as "Old Dream," when she was working on it at Yaddo in 1949–50. As Alice Quinn informs us, the successful poem that Bishop brought to completion at that time was "The Prodigal," a self-revealing portrait of a young drunk (she herself was then "often miserable and drinking heavily"[12]), though the putative "prodigal" of the poem is a Nova Scotia cousin, one of her "aunt's stepsons," as Bishop later revealed, who once, recognizing a fellow drinker when he saw one, offered Bishop a drink of rum at "about nine in the morning."[13]

Long before she described the fire-balloons in Rio in 1957, Bishop had seen the "fire-balloons used for festivities," probably in Gloucester, Massachusetts. In "A Flight of Fancy," a story published in December 1929 in *The Blue Pencil*, the literary journal of the Walnut Hill School in Natick, Massachusetts,

she refers to a plan for those fire-balloons: "'I have a scheme, as yet untried....
I presume, sir, that you have seen those luminous fire-balloons used for festivities? Well, I believe a basket similar to this one could be attached to a fire-
balloon. I think the sensation would be a pleasant one — to float about under
the stars, upborne by something like a large Chinese Lantern."[14] This reference
to fire-balloons suggests the likelihood that she had herself seen them (but
without fanciful passenger baskets) launched by the Portuguese living along
the Massachusetts North Shore during their St. John's Day celebrations.[15]
Bishop attended Saugus High School and the North Shore Country Day
School in Saugus and Swampscott in Essex County, Massachusetts, in the
two years preceding her matriculation at Walnut Hill School in Natick in the
same state. Perhaps it is not a coincidence, when one thinks of the owl in
"The Owl's Nest" and "The Armadillo," that the North Shore Country Day
School's literary magazine, to which Bishop contributed, was called *The Owl*.

When she moved to Brazil — in Petrópolis and Rio — Bishop was again
witness to the launching of such "luminous fire-balloons." In a letter dated
June 24, 1959, Bishop describes the St. John's festivities in Rio the previous
evening, "bonfires all up and down the beach" and "everyone setting off fire
works, like our Fourth of July," and sending up "fire balloons" — "illegal but
very pretty, all sizes and colors, little paper ones for children and huge ones
for adults — ten feet or so tall." These balloons "drift through the sky for
hours, turning around and around. I'll do a picture of one that landed right
outside the living room window up in Petrópolis — fortunately it fell in the
brook and went out, so it did no damage."[16] Since Bishop was not in Petrópolis
on St. John's night in 1959, the fallen balloon appears to refer to some earlier
occasion. She captions her drawing at the bottom of the letter: "White with
red hearts & streamers — 10 ft. tall." Sometimes, it was said, the balloons were
the means of conveying a message to the Saint himself on his birthday.

At the end, however, there is "the weak mailed fist," which is "clenched
ignorant." Bishop's use of the word "ignorant" here gives the reader pause.
No poet using it after Matthew Arnold can be ignorant of his use of it in the
last line of "Dover Beach" in the reference to "ignorant armies clash by night."
If the "mailed fist" is brought to mind in Bishop's poem through its evocation
in the "mailed" carapace of the armadillo, it is the echo of "armies" — in
"armadillo" — that further suggests battles and "clashes." "Ah, love, let us be
true / To one another!" Arnold begins. "For the world, which seems / To lie
before us like a land of dreams, / So various, so beautiful, so new, / Hath
really neither joy, nor love, nor light, / Nor certitude, nor peace, nor help for
pain; / And we are here as on a darkling plain / Swept with confused alarms
of struggle and flight, / Where ignorant armies clash by night."[17]

Arnold's ignorant armies wage war as they always have even as the poet now can do nothing more than call his lover to a mutual dedication and fidelity before a world empty of what might be called human values. That "Dover Beach" is above all a love poem, however, was not lost on Bishop or on her friend Robert Lowell. As an epigraph to "The Mills of the Kavanaughs," his devastating memorial to his marriage to Jean Stafford, Lowell chose the lines: "Ah, love let us be true / To one another! for the world, which seems / To lie before us like a land of dreams." While in "Song for the Rainy Season," a love poem at one remove, Bishop notices the "ignorant" map the mildew makes on the bedroom wall — with "ignorant" meaning "unknown," as in Arnold's poem as well as in the Portuguese word "ignorado."

It would not have been lost on Bishop that the St. John's Day festivities, originally intended to mark the date of the good saint's birth — "celebrated with rockets, firecrackers, and *vivas*" — also include fortunes told, as the cultural historian-anthropologist Gilberto Freyre reminds us, that "point to a union of the sexes, marriage, and the longing for a love that has not yet been found." "For the functions of this highly popular saint are essentially aphrodisiac," continues Freyre, "and sexual songs and practices are bound up with his rites. He is the marrying saint, *par excellence*," as witnessed in the popular couplet "'Give me a bridegroom, St. John, give me a bridegroom, / Give me a bridegroom, I pray, for I fain would be wed.'"[18] Such associations were formed deep in the poet's subconscious, one would venture, but it is such associations that bring a poem into being and, unstated, hold it together, not to mention the poet's psyche.

Bishop's success in constructing a poem in which she appropriates the substance of the earlier unpublished poem "The Owl's Journey" — depicting the ride taken by the owl on the rabbit's back — and combines it with the armadillo's rush down the mountain after the crash of the fiery balloon against the mountain, lies in the fact that she convinces us of the actuality of the experience; and more: that the experience has brought her to her concluding peroration. In "The Armadillo" we find a clear instance of the successful application — often replicated in her poetry — of the insight she had into her kind of poetry. In 1933, as she quoted to her friend Donald E. Stanford, also a fledging poet at the time, "'Their purpose (the writers of Baroque prose) was to portray, not a thought, but a mind thinking.... They knew that an idea separated from the act of experiencing it is not the idea that was experienced. The ardor of its conception in the mind is a necessary part of its truth.'"[19] Skilled craftsman that she was, she learned — as well as Wallace Stevens ever did, as he put it in "An Ordinary Evening in New Haven" — to bring about the poem that "is the cry of its occasion."

6

Eye of the Sparrow

In 1954, *Anhembi* (1950–62), the Brazilian monthly founded and edited by the journalist-lawyer-academic Paulo Duarte (1899–1984), published in São Paulo over the course of several issues Vinicius de Moraes's *Orfeu da Conceição*. The winner of the prize for drama awarded at the IV Centenário do Estado de São Paulo that same year, Vinicius's verse tragedy (as he called it) would be played throughout Brazil in 1956 and become the basis for the famous movie *Black Orpheus* in 1959. This play about art and love in a *favela* (slum) at the time of *carnaval* was fully consonant with the *Anhembi* mission — to promote social justice. So was "Squatter's Children," Elizabeth Bishop's poem, which was published (in English) in *Anhembi* in 1956, a year before it was first published in the United States in the *New Yorker*. Like Vinicius's play, this poem describing the play of children offers a strongly implied social message regarding *os favelados* (slum dwellers). In the magazine Bishop's poem was accompanied by a note introducing the American poet in its midst to a Brazilian audience unfamiliar with her name, let alone her work. Yet her stay in Brazil, the note's writer claims, had already affected her sensibility toward not only the Brazilian landscape but toward the Brazilian spirit. That this process is taking place, asserts the writer, is notable in "Squatter's Children," the title of which "can be translated as 'Filhos de favelado.'"[1]

"Squatter's Children" has been characterized as both an "ethnographic exercise" and "a verbal primitive, exaggeratedly visual and aural."[2] But this does not seem quite right. The poem is simpler than these characterizations suggest. It describes children at play on the sides of hills, in a mixture of sun and rain. Seen from a great distance, the boy and the girl appear "specklike" and the pup, a "yellow spot." (It was not until three years after the publication of "Squatter's Children" that May Swenson would send Bishop an expensive pair of binoculars, presumably the ones she used from then on.) What the poet says she sees is actually imagined, and if the poem is ethnographic it is sparsely, not thickly, descriptive: if the tools the children handle belong to a father, it is so because the poet imagines it, even as she imagines the heft of a broken haft, the ugliness of the mother's voice, the directness of the puppy's bark, and the "little, soluble, / unwarrantable ark." Of course, the mentions of "ark," "sin," "mansions," etc., signal the reader that the poet, watching these children of the *favela*, has what has been called a mythy mind. But the myth hinted at and fragmentary is employed by the poet for a vaguely applicable social message. Drawing on scripture —"in my father's house there are many mansions"— the poet says, as if to inform the children, who can hardly know of her existence, that there are "mansions" larger than their squatter's house and to which they have lawful rights. They may rightfully choose their mansion from the all-out-of-doors. The "soggy documents" of the world of nature (that is, all things in nature) attest to those rights — the right to a place in the sun or the rain. As one reader suggests, the poem might just as readily be called "Squatter's Rights."[3]

In this poem, as in the more ambitious later poem "The Burglar of Babylon," the observer is unobserved, hidden by distance, too far off to be observed, which was how Bishop usually liked it. There are no binoculars in play here; hence there is nothing seen close up to discipline her imagination, as in "The Burglar of Babylon." Hence she goes off into myth, something she does not do in "The Burglar of Babylon," a poem which does flesh out a fuller story — family relationships and the language of conversation — for the episode as witnessed.

Bishop put May Swenson's expensive gift to immediate use, for Rio, too, like San Francisco, as Bishop reported, was a city of "the *voyeur par excellence.*"[4] A pair of binoculars, "the nicest and most overwhelming present" she had received "for years and years," enabled this inveterate observer to spot out of her bedroom window, by chance, "a little green female something-or-other just sitting, resting, after making the beds and washing the dishes no doubt — yawning from time to time, or examining a toenail. I watched her for a long time."[5] Over time, she seems to have spotted and watched a lot of things, including a police manhunt in a nearby *favela*, an intense watch that led, eventually, to the composition of "The Burglar of Babylon."

"The Burglar of Babylon," Bishop's longest poem by far —184 lines comprised of 46 quatrains — was published in the *New Yorker* on November 21, 1964, and collected in *Questions of Travel* the next year. Three years later it was reissued as *The Ballad of the Burglar of Babylon*, an illustrated volume aimed mainly (but not entirely) at the children's book market. Reviewed as both a trade book and a children's book, Bishop's poem tells the story of the pursuit by police of Micuçú, a real-life small-time criminal in Babylon, a *favela* on one of the "fair green hills of Rio."[6] That this, too, is a "hunt" is telegraphed by Bishop's homage in the first line of her poem to *Green Hills of Africa* (1935), the title of Ernest Hemingway's fact-novel about hunting big game in the so-called Dark Continent in the author's pursuit of various things, including happiness. Marianne Moore thought it her "best" work, Bishop reported to Randall Jarrell, but that was, she added, because Marianne "approves of the moral."[7]

Late in 1968, Bishop's friend and fellow poet, James Merrill, sent her a copy of his poem "The Summer People." Merrill's poem reminisces about a past in Stonington, Connecticut, when those people who spent their summers in that sea-faring town had their easeful way in a community that seemed to be there for their comfort and quiet pleasure. It is an elegy for the passing of their way of life. Like "The Burglar of Babylon," it, too, is a literary ballad. In February 1969, Bishop wrote to Merrill, explaining that she had not written sooner because she had had the flu (twice) and was still not fully recovered. After making her apologies — innocent enough, at least at first blush — Bishop turns to the poem.

> It was nice of you to say I'd suggested the form to you but I can scarcely claim any originality there, and mine is more a pastiche anyway. *You* have done the original thing with the form. I do see how much more fun it must have been to write the story that way than to write a novel (but then I can't imagine writing a novel at all), and it has turned out very surprising and so interesting that I didn't stop reading for a minute. Really, a great success, I think. *Awful,* too, and full of marvelous detail. I kept being surprised, and that is my favorite emotion in poetry these days because so very little of it has any surprises to it. I love the tarted-up church, the cat, the snow-storm descriptions — all the sophisticated details of the lives of those characters put into ballad form, a kind of superior parody that shows up the story better than prose could have done. (That isn't too clear, I'm afraid, but maybe you'll understand what I mean. A Japanese houseboy in the meter of the border ballads, etc., is really pretty complicated and funny....) You have kept it up all the way through, too. — Also, I like your quotation from Mallarmé — I wonder if you got the same pleasure from writing it that I did from my old-fashioned one — the rhymes and short lines seemed to make description easier rather than harder, and very simple, almost cliché, phrases, come out like something brand new....[8]

Whether it is the product of the lingering flu ("just a cough," she claims) or the fact that she is less enthusiastic about Merrill's poem than she thinks she ought to be, this remarkable paragraph strikes me as the product of palpable strain on Bishop's part to say something insightful about "The Summer People" as well as favorable. The closest she comes to bringing it off, I think, is when she calls it "*Awful,* too, and full of marvelous detail." The "awful" here harks back to the "awful" of her depressive poem on her birthday, "The Bight."

If she can celebrate (as one would expect from her) the "marvelous detail"—
and she can name instances here—it is the sense of slow, undeniable loss of
good summer people and their civilized way of life that Merrill achieves in
the poem that Bishop finds "awful."[9]

The most querulous thought she had about Merrill's poem is embedded,
I think, not in the paragraph quoted above, but in the last sentence of the
letter when she asks, "Is Stonington like that, I wonder?" What is embedded
is Bishop's poetic commitment to the real—visual, really—but, at the time
of her writing "The Burglar of Babylon," to the social reality as well. It is as
if Bishop is aware that Merrill has not seen the irony in his Stonington man-
darin's employment of a Japanese as a houseboy (surely this touch recalls, for
some, some 1930s movies) or the submerged clash of the classes as the Azoreans
seem to ascend in the devolving social structure of this old sea-faring town.
In her poem there is even a monitory moment when she writes of the "million
people" nesting in the hills, clinging and spreading "like lichen"—the last
word recalling its use in "The Shampoo" where it is an image of powerful and
permanent growth—"The still explosions on the rocks, / the lichens grow /
by spreading, gray, concentric shocks." So much for Brazilian efforts to erad-
icate the eyesores in their midst by razing and bulldozing the *favelas*, one at
a time.

When "The Burglar of Babylon" was issued in book form in 1968, it was
retitled as *The Ballad of the Burglar of Babylon*. This illustrated volume, aimed
at the children's book market, included a prefatory note of explanation over
Bishop's initials. "The story of Micuçú is true. It happened in Rio de Janeiro
a few years ago," she begins. "I have changed only one or two minor details,
and, of course, translated the names of the slums. I think that actually the
hill of Kerosene had been torn down shortly before Micuçú's death, but I
liked the word, so put it in." She then testifies to having been one of those
who followed the pursuit of Micuçú "through binoculars, although really we
could see very little of it: just a few of the soldiers silhouetted against the sky-
line of the hill of Babylon. The rest of the story is taken, often word for word,
from the daily papers, filled out by what I know of the place and the people."
Her author's note continues with an explanation for the name Micuçú, which
at the time people thought was "short for *Mico Sujo*, or *Dirty Marmoset*, but
finally it was decided that this was wrong and that it is the colloquial name
for a deadly snake, in the north of Brazil." It was logical, she thought, for "a
young man trying to be a real gangster, like in the films," to "prefer to be
called by the name of a deadly snake."[10]

The reference to "films" brings to mind, not the gangster films Bishop
associates with Micuçú, but the 1954 film *Rear Window*, by Alfred Hitchcock,

in which a photographer in a wheelchair, who through his camera watches his neighbors, becomes convinced that one of them is a murderer, not entirely unlike Bishop's watching through binoculars the pursuit of Micuçú by the police who will kill him. This piece of information — that Bishop watched the proceedings through binoculars — would become useful to those Brazilians who questioned her knowledge about Brazilian society. More about that later on. The second matter in Bishop's preface is the indication that Micuçú's roots are in the northeast of Brazil — the great *sertão* notorious for its impoverished people, and known, on an entirely different level, for its *literatura de cordel* ("literature on a string") — the Brazilian form of the popular ballad.[11] More about that, too, later on.

For all of its social and political aspects, or, perhaps, because of those very aspects, "The Burglar of Babylon" is a problematic poem in the Bishop canon — perhaps the most problematic one, if one considers the point of view of Bishop's Brazilian readers. Whatever she thought about the poem as a recording of a slice of life of true Brazilian realism, they are put off by her off-putting, standoffish vantage point. The witnessing poet has witnessed what occurs in the *favela* called Babylon through her binoculars from the back of her socially privileged place on one of the great beaches of the world. Indeed, it is the poet's claim to reporting actuality with its attendant realism that is — sometimes angrily — dismissed. Not all of her Brazilian readers were willing to grant her what João Cabral de Melo Neto defined, as we have seen, as her "special lens," one that "filters the essential / that we see yet never see."[12] One would think that Bishop's unique lens worked even when she was looking through binoculars from the back window of the apartment at Rua Antonio Vieira, 5, Leme, Rio de Janeiro.

Returning to Bishop's letter to Merrill, one notices that she refers briefly to the fact that he has written about his Japanese houseboy "in the meter of the ballads." Of course, she too had employed a version of ballad meter (or common meter of the hymnal) — four-line stanzas in couplets with three stresses to the line rather than four.[13] Moreover, while each of them has chosen to cast his or her poem in traditional ballad form, the subject matter of each poem could not be more different, though they are equally appropriate. In Merrill's case, his decision to parody the border ballad enables him to maintain his distance from the history of the "summer people" town — its slow decline and virtual disappearance, as the dying fall of a kind of local civilization. In Bishop's case, her decision to tell the story of the burglar's flight and demise as a modern ballad enables her to keep her distance — social and spatial — while establishing her as a witness to an actual event. Of course, Merrill's material and theme are a far cry from that of the traditional border ballads, but Bishop's material, while evoking Jessie James and Sam Bass, avatars of the traditional English-language ballad, has its popular Brazilian antecedents in the so-called "literature on a string" (*literatura de cordel*, so called because vendors would hang their wares — the little books — along a stretched-out cord), which is produced by popular poets of the Brazilian northeast (*os nordestinos*) and collected by Bishop herself.[14] In 1960 she sent Robert Lowell some "ballad books," containing, as she explained, folk poetry — "composed by people who can't read or write, and sung to guitars" — in "a form [that] goes back to Camões"; "they sell thousands of them, displays in all the markets ... and people buying all the time."[15]

One subgenre of this literature on a string is devoted to tales of *banditismo* ("banditry"). Among the most famous of these are the poems devoted to Lampião (*"esse famoso bandoleiro"*), one of which contains the following lines on the criminal's proficiency in killing: "With every shot Lampião / dropped another soldier dead / and with a good gunsight / every shot was on target" ("Lampião de cada tiro / deixava morto um soldado / e como bom escopeteiro / só dava tiro certeiro").[16] If Bishop does not duplicate the seven-line stanza or its rhyme scheme (abcbccd), what she does do is marry the common meter to her "urbanized *nordestino*" subject matter. What she has produced is a modern literary ballad, appropriating Brazilian subject matter, adhering closely to the formal dictates of the English-language ballad tradition. Of course, it is what she did with that subject matter, as well as her nerve in taking it on (as an outsider who never achieved an adequate understanding of the native culture or contemporary politics) that annoyed some of her Brazilian readers (and continues to do so). "You'd be amused by the reception of the 'Burglar' poem here," she wrote at the time, " — it has been mentioned in the newspapers and by the 'columnists.' Some think I'm helping Brazil, some harming Brazil — one thinks I'm morbid."[17] What the Brazilians denied was what she claimed for it: writing "last week's news in the form of poetry."[18]

7

Good Times at Cabo Frio

"I'm not much of a Thoreau — all this loftiness is very depressing particularly in foggy weather," wrote Elizabeth Bishop in her travel notebook in 1938, while she was staying in North Carolina.[1] It was not Thoreau's description in *The Maine Woods* (1864) of Mount Katahdin then that would have attracted Bishop, but his descriptions of shore and sea life in *Cape Cod* (1865). "The few wreckers were either going or coming, and the ships and the sandpipers, and the screaming gulls overhead; nothing stood still but the shore. The little beach-birds trotted past close to the water's edge, or paused but an instant to swallow their food, keeping time with the elements."[2] If these observations by Thoreau are not, in some way, in the background of Bishop's poem "Sandpiper," published in the *New Yorker* on July 21, 1962, one is hard put to explain the coincidence. After all, as Bishop noted in a letter to Katherine White, her editor at the *New Yorker*, the beach at Cabo Frio was "almost like a segment of the Maine coast, except that the water is warm, and the cacti, were all in bloom — rocks, islands, a turtle swimming around and raising his head every once in a while, even a small waterfall." "Thoreau," she suggested, "would have felt quite at home and pleased that there *is* a great deal of the world still pretty much untouched, even if it is not in the U.S.A."[3]

Shortly after Bishop settled in Brazil, Cabo Frio, the popular seacoast resort just over 150 kilometers northeast of Rio de Janeiro, became one of her favored places for vacations. In fact, beginning in 1957 and over the next five years, Bishop and Lota often spent their holidays in Cabo Frio.[4] Despite the fact that Bishop chose to place the poem "Sandpiper" in the "Elsewhere" section (not the "Brazil" section) in *Questions of Travel* (1965), I suspect that the poem — one that had been with her for years but not finished or published until the early 1960s — can be viewed, at least in part, as a product of frequent holidays spent in Cabo Frio.[5]

In the sandpiper Bishop saw not only a nervous and fidgety "student of Blake" but a figure for the kind of poet she saw in herself, one perennially at the task of observing (and recording) the minutiae of the circumscribed world before her eyes. If so, the words "he runs to the south" convey a description of Bishop herself running off, as she was wont to do, "to the south" — to Key West, to Brazil. In fact, she embraced the identification when, in 1976, she accepted the Neustadt Prize in Norman, Oklahoma. "Yes, all my life I have lived and behaved very much like that sandpiper — just running along the edges of different countries and continents, 'looking for something,'" she acknowledged. "I have always felt I couldn't *possibly* live very far inland, away from the ocean, and I *have* always lived near it, frequently in sight of it."[6] In 1960, she wrote to Robert Lowell about a recent stay in Cabo Frio, "marvelous as ever." "The sand is mostly amethyst quartz, a deep lavender, streaked with white as the waves wash the other sand up into it," she described a grotto, "the sides full of quartzes and pot-holes with huge stones still whirling around in them as the waves come up — lots of sea-urchins in little niches, like ikons, and huge pure white or black or lavender-ish rocks, very smooth, arranged in the shadows..."[7] It is not much of a stretch to see Bishop the sandpiper-poet at her work here — a trial run, if you will, or preview of "Sandpiper," published in the *New Yorker* in July 1962, picking her words out, like "a student of Blake," one at a time, from the "millions of grains" — "black, white, tan, and gray, / mixed with quartz grains, rose and amethyst."[8]

Mixing minute description with projected mental states, attitudes, and possible motives, Bishop constructs her construct of the "sandpiper-poet." This solitary shore bird is a "student of Blake," the speaker tells, looking closely between its toes in the myriads of grains along the shore — "millions of grains" that are "black, white, tan, and gray, mixed with quartz-grains, rose and amethyst." If in "Auguries of Innocence" Blake sees the possibility of seeing eternity in a grain of sand, in this poem we are taken away from the fact that we know about the sandpiper's quest — it is after food, not glimpses of eternity. In fact, this poem does not tell us that the bird looks for food, just as we are not told that there is "eternity" in a "grain of sand." Put another way, what we are left with in this poem is the fact that the sandpiper-poet is a seeker (after something; we do not know what) but has not yet "found" anything in the elapsed time of the poem. The larger question for the poet (if not the sandpiper) is that if the proof is in the pudding then the fact that nothing yet has been found implies the further possibility that there is nothing there to find. The student of Blake might well come to the conclusion that the "true" vision is anti–Blakean, in that seeing through the eye (and not just with the eye) gives no results. Maybe description of what the eye sees is all; that there is nothing to be "seen" or discerned beyond what the physical-mental eye sees. That is the reality that nothing else is. It is the romantic dilemma: insight into or mere projection that can never in any way be confirmed.

Behind this poem there is a second poem. Robert Frost's "For Once, Then, Something" is also about a poet-seeker, one who looks over the curb at the top of a well to see what he can see. He sees nothing, until for a split second or so he sees a glint. He speculates that it might be from a piece of quartz, but he does not know. That he has seen "something" is to be his portion, and he makes the most of it. It is "something" he has found, unlike Bishop's "poor bird," "obsessed," which, at poem's end is still "looking for something, something, something." Frost's poem finesses the problem of "insight into — projection," or at least, settling for the glint of light, he chooses not to go into it further. At the end Bishop swerves away from it, calling attention, instead, to the varieties to be seen in the grains — varieties of color and, perhaps, consistency and even texture.

So, too, is Bishop a "piper" of sand — if we allow sand to stand, metonymically, for the things and surfaces of the earthling's world. For a time, readers felt that Bishop's minute and singular descriptions of the things of this world were the sum of what could be expected or desired from her work. Unlike the poetry of the modernists or those who came after them, her cohorts (as followers or not), her poems were not fraught with meaning, with significances available after much fretting or profound thought. But, as we have subsequently learned, the matter was not nearly as cut-and-dried as was thought. The romantic problem of insight or projection was still there, except that her poems stopped short of tackling the problem or dilemma head-on, often choosing to escape it by shifting focus at the end to the poet and her way of thinking — in the act of thinking. As a would-be Blake, she would see through the eye, but finally cannot. She meditates on what her eyes see, mediates the object or landscape into a unique objective correlative. Indeed, often her poetry strikes one as a search for the exact objective correlative, not as T. S. Eliot so famously does (he starts out with what Poe called the effect and searches for what will bring it about) but as Ernest Hemingway does — to find exactly what it was that caused the particular or peculiar emotion in the first place. But Bishop had no visions — rainbow, rainbow, rainbows, notwithstanding; she had to be satisfied with keeping up the search — much like those who look out neither far nor in deep in Frost's great poem. There was no angel in a tree for her, not ever.

Of the sandpiper, she will notice, "His beak is focused; he is preoccupied"; the same might be said of the poet. It is interesting that it is the "beak" she speaks of, not just the eye, which "watches" and "stares." The beak is capable of inserting itself, of breaking through surfaces to "discover" what is underneath.

It is not without significance that, in "The Bight," she singles out for description both the working machinery that "dredges," that with its "click," "click" "brings up a dripping jawful of marl" ("something"), and the pelicans, which "crash" like "pickaxes" (though "rarely coming up with anything to show for it"). It is also, oddly and mysteriously, the dead and flattened hen's beak in "Trouvée" that is the exception, in the middle of the street, to the "old country saying / scribbled in chalk." For all that she tries, in this later poem, there is, apparently, no meaning behind the "thing" itself. The poet tries to make the more than unlikely conjunction of hen, city street, and moving vehicle somehow "fraught" but fails to do so. "Trouvée" is not Frost's "Design," in which the unlucky moth, meeting its destiny, perhaps, or just coincidentally, falls prey to the white spider operating, unlikely, from a white heal-all. Bishop's questions of "why," "how," and "where," asked in the opening stanzas, remain unanswered, as they must, at the close of the poem. That there were few answers, perhaps none that was satisfactory, is suggested in the "faint, faint, faint ... the sandpipers' heart-broken cries," that the poet registers in "Twelfth Morning; or What You Will," a second Cabo Frio poem, one published two years after "Sandpiper."[9]

In *Casa-Grande e Senzala* (1933), a book that Bishop recommended to American friends in 1955 as "a rather startling book about Brazil that really gives one some idea what it's like, translated as *The Masters and the Slaves* by Gilberto Freyre — fascinating and depressing,"[10] Gilberto Freyre writes about the role, tolerated by the Church, that the black man has played from the time of his arrival in the country during "the popular feast-days of Brazil." He "cheered the plantation hands, who inspired the *bumbas-meu-boi*, the *cavalos-marinhos* (carnival 'horses' with men inside them), the carnivals, the festivals," writes Freyre. "As a tolerant Church looked on, he filled the popular feast-days of Brazil with reminiscences of his own totemistic and phallic cults: on the eve of the Feast of Epiphany, and afterwards, at Carnival time, with the crowning of its kings and queens."[11] In *Brazil*, her Time-Life book, Bishop singles out the *Bumba-meu-boi* "play" as an example of the survival of folk drama, especially in the rural north and northeast of Brazil: "A little group of men acts out a story about an ox who dances, sings, grows sick, dies and then returns to life amid general rejoicing and additional songs and dances," she writes. "The stylized figure of the ox, with one or two dancers inside, is followed by other types: the cowboy, the horse, the donkey, the doctor, the priest (who comes to give the last rites to the dying ox) and clowns."[12] It is significant, certainly, that, unlike Freyre, Bishop never gets around to mentioning in her account of this piece of folk drama the role the Negro has been made to play.

Bishop's interest in the *Bumba-meu-boi* persisted. She bought postcards depicting scenes and figures in the drama, one of which she sent to Jean

Stafford, Robert Lowell's first wife. Her message is mainly about Stafford's recent book. She is pleased to see the return of Lottie Jump, her favorite character, she says, though she is also very fond of earlier Stafford books, such as *In the Zoo* and *A Reading Problem*. Then she adds an explanation of the picture reproduced on the face of the postcard: "This card is almost appropriate — 'Bumba meu Boi' — Beat my Ox — given on Twelfth Night, in the backlands. This is one of the 'Kings.'"[13] She does not mention that she herself had already published a poem about one of those "Kings," a poem that when it was collected in *Questions of Travel* she signed out of "Cabo Frio." In 1957, as Brett C. Millier notes, Bishop and Lota began what became a "tradition" of spending the Christmas holidays at Cabo Frio, a town northeast of Rio.

In January 1964, after spending the holidays in Cabo Frio, Bishop worked on "Twelfth Morning; or What You Will." She sent the finished poem to Lowell, who had once vacationed with Bishop and Lota in Cabo Frio, describing it only as "a small poem that I'm afraid you will consider what you call 'carpentry work.'"[14] On January 24, Lowell responded, enthusiastically, as he did to virtually every poem or story Bishop sent him: "The 12th Night poem is marvelous. It has the form, tightness and charm of some of your early poems, such as the one about the little horse and rider ["Cirque d'Hiver"], but translated into nature and direct observation. I carry it around in my bill-fold, and it seems comparable to, 'The Armadillo' that I have long cherished."[15] Besides carrying it around in his billfold, Lowell may have secured the poem for the *New York Review of Books*, a publication that he and his wife, Elizabeth Hardwick, had been closely involved with since its inception in 1963. The poem appeared on April 2, 1964, and was included in *Questions of Travel* a year later.

The holy day of the poem is Twelfth Night, marking the Feast of the Epiphany, but Bishop's poem "Twelfth Morning; or What You Will" is about the morning of that holiday and about "the black boy Balthazár," playing the king who, along with the other two Magi, came to greet the infant Jesus, because he — "the black boy" — was born on the sixth of January. "'Today's my Anniversary,' he sings, / 'the Day of Kings.'" Balthazár's "Anniversary" is his birthday, a day for rejoicing, especially as it starts out in the morning: "The four-gallon can / approaching on the head of Balthazár / keeps flashing that the world's a pearl," and he is "*its highlight!*"[16]

Bishop's poem is not entirely about the black boy Balthazár, however, or even about the "pewter-colored horse, an ancient mixture, / tin, lead, and silver" of the *Bumba-meu-boi* that is either "*inside the fence or out*" (the poet can't or won't say). Rather it is about the poet who would have an experience — perhaps even an epiphany — on this the Day of Kings. Through "the thin gray mist" something does show through: the boy, a fence, a horse, and a "foundered" house. And what it finally adds up to is joyous. The four-gallon can on the boy's head "keeps flashing that the world's a pearl" and that the boy himself is the world's "*highlight*." What the poet makes of the flashing is based on what her favorite among the metaphysical poets, George Herbert, would have turned into an elaborated conceit. But there is no elaboration here. For Bishop it is "for once, then, something." There is an epiphany, at least the glimmer of one — maybe. It is not the human soul that is the pearl of great price, but the world itself. Here is where the subtitle part of the poem's title comes into play. What the boy and the flash from the can become "what you will." Meaning or significance is less a matter of perception than of infusion, though the infusion is only possible, it seems, as a function of perception itself.

Yet "Twelfth Morning; or, What You Will" is not simply, of course, a matter of "direct observation." As Lowell discerned, something or other has been "translated" into a poem of "direct observation." In 1962, Bishop acquired a copy of the poet Cassiano Ricardo's *Martim Cererê (o Brasil dos meninos, dos poetas e dos heróis)*. This 11th-edition copy, illustrated by Tarsila and published by Saraiva in São Paulo, is inscribed on the half-title page: "A Elizabeth Bishop — com respeito e admiração, Cassiano Ricardo, 1962." At the bottom of the same page appears Bishop's notation, in pencil: "(bought at the Book Fair, M of AM, July 24th, 1962)." Bishop's markings appear throughout, with checks placed against the titles of four poems. One of the four is about "the magi." Cassiano Ricardo's "*reis magos*" ("enchanted kings") translates the list of traditional gifts brought to the Christ child — Melchior's gold, Gaspar's frankincense and Baltazár's myrrh — into, respectively, "morning," "day" and "night." These three kings are described: "a red one, who brought / the morning for a present; / another, a gentle one, who presented him with the day," and finally, the "black one, his face cut by lash," who brought him "the Night."[17] Tellingly, this "black" king, rather than making "Him" a gift of myrrh, brings him the questionable gift of the blackness of darkness. Eschewing the reference to "Night" in "Twelfth Night" — the usual term — Bishop's poem sees her Balthazár as a figure of "morning" light. In the fanciful, outrageous getup of one of the Kings of the *Bumba-meu-boi*, he celebrates not anyone else's birthday but his own. Notably, Bishop has reached back to Gilberto Freyre's joyous Negro to counteract Cassiano Ricardo's less salubrious (and rather commonplace) view of the "black" (*preto*) as an avatar of the Prince of Darkness. In this sense, the second half of her poem's title — "What You Will" — points to the permission Bishop grants herself to imagine her Balthazár — in direct opposition to Cassiano Ricardo — as a messenger of joy and, importantly, light.[18]

8

An Ordinary Evening

In 1965, Elizabeth Bishop confessed: "We've been living in Rio most of the last three years because of Lota's job, and although we're right on the ocean with a superb view and I can go swimming, or at least dip in the surf, whenever I feel like it, I hate it, and find that poor shabby spoiled city very depressing."[1] Over the next few years, conditions in the city did not get any better for her, on the contrary, and by 1968, when she published "Going to the Bakery," her flat-out depressive view of Brazilian city life, she had clearly decided that Rio de Janeiro, after a stay of nearly two decades, was no longer part of her three-location Brazilian "home."

In the literary and cultural background of "Going to the Bakery" there hovers, among several other shades, the spirit of T. S. Eliot and behind him William Blake. Years before publishing her poem, in 1943, Bishop asked Marianne Moore if she liked T. S. Eliot's *Four Quartets*. [2] Her friend and mentor answered that though "the intensified honesty of this writing of T. S. Eliot's is resolute and helpful," "the quartets seem to me very sad; so unegoistic a precipitate, there is something alarming about them."[3] That "intensified honesty" had led Eliot to conclude in "East Coker," the second of his *Four Quartets*, that "the whole earth is our hospital."[4] Twenty-five years later, Bishop would offer local particulars for Eliot's generalization in one of her last poems about Rio de Janeiro. By the time she published "Going to the Bakery," after 17 years or so in Brazil, the city was no longer home to her. Indeed, Bishop's neighborhood bakery had become an objective correlative for what her life had become in a city that was diminished, adulterated, and sickly. Originally, this poem critical of Brazil was called "Good-bye to Rio." A vestige of this discarded title appeared as a piece of information —"Rio de Janeiro"— given just below the new title assigned to the poem when it was published in the *New Yorker*. It was conceived, perhaps, but definitely executed as her valediction to Rio and, in all probability, to Brazil, even as her salutation had been "Arrival at Santos." It is not a very attractive city — something of a failure — that she delineates metonymically.

Bishop's readers will sometimes refer to this poem, not as "Going to the Bakery," but "Going to a Bakery" — a slip in memory, excusable of course, but the minor inaccuracy offers an opportunity to point to something meaningful in the experience treated in the poem. The poet is not going to *a* bakery so much as she is going to *the* bakery, the bakery where daily she (or her maid Joanna) goes to buy pastries or bread rolls for breakfast. But in Bishop's poem the walk to the bakery (at least this time) has become a parody of a spiritual quest, one in which the "hero" sallies out on a journey into the world, faces various challenges along the way, and returns with a (sometimes questionable) boon. If this poem records what the speaker sees and feels on a short walk to the neighborhood bakery and back to her apartment, it is not the walk of, say, a *flaneur*; after all, there is a destination for her trip and a purpose to her walk. What the speaker singles out for inclusion in her poem and, more importantly, how she views the things she chooses to include are the substance of her poem. It is nighttime and the low-hanging moon, its customary view of the sea cut off by the blocks of buildings out to Avenida Atlantica, which runs along the beaches of Leme and Copacabana, looks down Avenida Copacabana, which is another block away from the ocean. Of course, compared with the glare from the sun, the moon's light is pale, weaker. It fits the speaker's mood and, through the trick in the poem, also the figures, things, and imagery of the poem overall. Nature wears the colors of the spirit, wrote Emerson. But there is enervation (rather than energy) in the situation, enervation and hints of illness and disease. Trolley wires are "slack," the tracks "slither," the colored balloons are "flaccid" and "dying," the bakery lights are "dim" (electricity is customarily if irregularly rationed), bakery cakes look as if about to "faint," tarts are "red and sore," loaves of bread lie like "yellow-fever victims" in a hospital ward,[5] the "sickly" baker's flour is probably "adulterated," a prostitute dances feverishly in the street, and a beggar exhales the stink of whiskey (*cachaça*).[6] Possibly honorific or at least neutral adjectives are attached to unpleasant, sickly or unnatural things. The beggar talks gibberish, his white bandage shows forth from a black shade, and the speaker gives alms that measured against a weak Brazilian currency amount to a pittance of seven American cents. Everything here is rationed, and everybody is being short changed. Even in the beggar's case, there is the implication that his fresh bandage is but a beggar's prop, added to his dress to deceive those passing by into believing that he suffers from some sort of illness or wound, though it is always possible that there is in fact no wound at all. When she goes past the beggar, her departing words are "Good night," but she chides herself for adhering to a "mean habit" — not because of the meanness of giving the man a mere pittance but for the mean (base, contemptible) habit of expressing an empty-of-meaning valediction, one that effectively evades expressing whatever true compassion that she might think she should perhaps feel. Certainly all the evidence given in the poem culminating in the encounter with the beggar suggests that the last thing she should call the night is a *good* one.[7] She has not found a brighter word or one that is more apt. Language has failed her. But the irony remains that even had she found a brighter word, it would do nothing to relieve the malaise, enervation, sickness or disease she sees everywhere on her walk, for there seems to be no way to bring meaningful energy to this city of a night. An old samba, translated by Bishop, laments: "Rio de Janeiro, / My joy and my delight! / By day I have no water, / By night I have no light."[8] But if the city has failed her, she, too, fails the city. Had she stuck to her original title, her valediction would at least have expressed the more benevolent wish of "God be with you." Note, too, that earlier she had asked herself: "Buy, buy, what shall I buy." It is as a consumer with "terrific money" that she thinks this, but her question anticipates as well, I think, the notion of her original title "Good-bye to Rio," along with the possibility of saying "Good bye" to the beggar, which may be translated as "Adeus" ("in" or "with" God). The personal irony is that Rio has not turned out to be such a "good buy" after all.

"Going to the Bakery," besides recalling Eliot in certain other just as significant senses, is, as hinted earlier, one of Bishop's Blakean poems, most nearly resembling, in my view, his explicitly monitory "London," from *Songs of Experience.*

> I wander through each chartered street
> Near where the chartered Thames does flow,
> And mark in every face I meet
> Marks of weakness, marks of woe.
> In every cry of every man,
> In every infant's cry of fear,
> In every voice, in every ban,
> The mind-forged manacles I hear:
> How the chimney-sweeper's cry
> Every black'ning church appalls,
> And the hapless soldier's sigh
> Runs in blood down palace walls;
> But most through midnight streets I hear
> How the youthful harlot's curse
> Blasts the new-born infant's tear,
> And blights with plagues the marriage hearse.[9]

Note the affinities between Blake's poem and Bishop's — "marks of weakness, marks of woe," "midnight streets," "infant's cry," "youthful harlot's curse," and "hapless soldier." The evil and human anguish Blake finds everywhere in London is mirrored in Bishop's Rio de Janeiro, with its rationing, disease and overall enervation. If Blake's more strident tone is toned down in Bishop, the single major difference between the two poems is that there is in Blake nothing resembling the words of self-accusation that close out Bishop's poem.

But there is one last aspect to "Going to the Bakery" as a quest parody that relocates it in a different context: one shared by other poems, particularly "The Prodigal" and "The Drunkard," the latter withheld from publication during Bishop's lifetime. The poem has not been so contextualized previously, perhaps because Bishop left out something that is of major importance to her poem, information that, once considered, modifies significantly our understanding of what has gone into Bishop's poetic achievement here. She never does tell us why she is going to the bakery, especially why she is going to the bakery at night. The acquisition of fresh breakfast rolls would ordinarily occur early in the morning, before breakfast, not during the previous day or evening. Moreover, it is most likely that in Bishop's time in Rio it would be the ubiquitous housemaid, not the woman of the house, who would go to the bakery. Why, then, would the poet be going to the bakery, especially at night? If not for bread or pastries (the maid would be sent for those as well, and earlier in the day, surely, no later than the afternoon, well before dinner), for what, then? Well, for one, to satisfy her need for one of the major ingredients in Bishop's daily diet — alcohol, probably in the form of *cachaça* or *aguardente*. Running out of booze on any given night when Bishop was binging or merely the fear of running out before the night was over may well have sent her to the neighborhood bakery for a bottle of *Tatu*, the best-selling *cachaça* of the day with its realistic image of an "armadillo" on the label. Perhaps this is why the poem makes so much of the beggar redolent of *cachaça* standing outside the poet's apartment building. He images back the wretch — social differences notwithstanding in the case of confirmed alcoholics — that she recognizes herself to be but will deny as slyly as she can, in this poem at least, by zeroing in on the not-me. The poet's quest is for *cachaça*.

9

Promenade

Describing it as a "castaway" poem, the Brazilian scholar Regina Przybycien suggests that in "Pink Dog" Bishop "finally wrote a Brazilian poem."[1]
It was also a good-bye, as indicated in Bishop's working title, "Farewell to
Rio." Yet the strong sentiment expressed in the poem goes nowhere near the
excusable sentimentality of such poetic farewells, for the poet-castaway intends
no favorable tribute to the city celebrated for its great beauty and fabled
amenities. In no way does it express reluctance to leave Brazil, "a Ilha de Vera
Cruz" (Island of the True Cross), as the Portuguese navigators first called the
land that has long since and less grandly been given a more mundane name.

In early 1979, Bishop explained to an American friend, Ashley Brown,
just where she stood on "Elizabeth Bishop in Brazil" as a subject for advanced
academic scholarship. "One thing I wanted to ask you about — and forgot —
was that young man, Paulo Costa Galvão, from Rio," she wrote. "About his
dissertation — I don't think there's too much to say about me *in Brazil* — just
those poems, and a few Brazilian ones since." And he was not the only one.
"There's another Ph.D.-er, an American girl, who has the same idea, I think —
and I've been trying to discourage her, on the whole." This student had spelled
out her plan in greater detail. "Her idea was to go to Brazil (with husband!)
for a year, look up all my 'old friends' (and enemies, I gathered, too) and so
on — this is some sort of translingual (?) project — she has studied Portuguese,"
complained Bishop. "I think it is all very cooked-up and suspect. The few
friends I had are mostly dead — or wouldn't remember me — or have actually
turned against me." She continued: "I really had almost no 'literary' life in
Brazil — and made no *impact*! I have a rather ghastly Carnival poem ['Pink
Dog'] that will be in *The New Yorker* at Carnival time. It may turn out to be
one of a group about Brazil."[2]

She would not get to the point of grouping her poems about Brazil for
publication, but "Pink Dog" appeared in the *New Yorker* on February 26,
1979 — "the closest to Carnival on the one hand and to Ash Wednesday on

the other," wrote her editor, Howard Moss.[3] Within the week she again wrote to Ashley Brown, explaining: "Well, I meant my Carnival poem was 'ghastly' as to subject matter — not such a bad poem! — at least I hope not. I have two or three more equally 'ghastly' I feel I must publish sometime."[4] Whatever the subject matter of the poem, this letter to Ashley Brown tells us something significant about what I would take to be the "subjective" matter of the poem. Bishop, too, has had little impact in Brazil, or is it that whatever impact she has had has been the wrong sort of impact — that is, personal rather than professional. Surviving friends or acquaintances in Brazil will not remember her, or, if they do remember, they will have turned against her. If she had her way, the subject of "Bishop in Brazil" would be off-limits with no exceptions.

"Pink Dog" is comprised of 13 stanzas of Dante-like terza rima. Besides full rimes (blue, hue, avenue), slant rimes (be able, dog-paddle, sensible), and feminine rimes (corners, beggars, rivers and degenerating, something, talking), to maintain its terza rima Bishop resorts to trick eye-rhymes and trick enjambments (*fantasia*, to be a/n eyesore, see a). Dealing with the dark social side of Brazilian culture, the obscured, if not entirely hidden, infernal side of life in modern Rio de Janeiro, it sets up the naked, hairless dog with a case of scabies, its babies hidden in some *favela*, as a metonym for the city's beggared poor. If the "city" fears rabies in a dog, it fears as well "idiots, paralytics, parasites." Like the pink dog, these are the flotsam and jetsam of the city, all of them naked to their enemies, who send them "bobbing in the ebbing sewage" out in the suburbs "where there are no lights." (That the "civilized" city itself is never distant from the darkened suburbs may be implied in the lines from the poem "Going to the Bakery" — the bakery lights, due to the "rationed electricity," are dim.[5]) Like the pink dog, these are the scapegoats of a society marked by the existence of the *esquadrão da morte* (death squad) whose members dispose of their prey (but not the evidence against them) by throwing it into "tidal rivers."

In a soliloquy rhetorically addressed to the pink dog but as readily directed at herself,[6] the poet advises this nursing mother to dress up in a *fantasia*.[7] Decked out in such a costume, the pink dog, like the poor, will look anything but dangerous or discomfiting. *Carnaval*, the opiate of the rich as well as the poor, costuming such an "eyesore" out of sight and thus, at least for a time, out of mind. No "depilated" dog (or person) will look well at Carnival. So dress up today even if, as sure as night and darkness, "Ash Wednesday'll come."[8]

In "Pink Dog" Bishop employs two key Portuguese words — *máscara*, partly because the word fills out the line syllabically (though it also suggests makeup [mascara]) where mask would not, and *fantasía* because of its cognate suggestions of dream, illusion, and fantasy not readily suggested by the English word "costume." Since each one is free to choose the fancy garb it fancies, the pink dog's *fantasia* will be its "life preserver" against having to struggle against the "tidal rivers" of a society that would be rid of its "idiots, paralytics, parasites," along with its beggared poor by throwing them all into waters that flow out to sea. Let the pink dog emulate the Carnaval "Negroes" celebrated by Gilberto Freyre. "Only a year or so ago, at the carnival in the Praça Onze in Rio de Janeiro, I had an opportunity to view these totemistic societies," he writes, "and at the carnivals of Pernambuco I have seen the Negroes any number of times dancing happily behind their banners, some of which are very fine, embroidered in gold, emblems vaguely reminiscent of the trade guilds mingling with totemistic ones." He took note, too, of "the gilded shovel of the Shovel Club, the broom of the broom-makers, the brush of the wall-and-roof cleaners, the dog of the association known as the Cachorro do Homem do Miudo, etc."[9] Freyre's translator, Samuel Putnam, explains the last reference: "The name of the association means literally: 'the dog of the man who sells the internal small parts of an ox.'"[10]

Published late in Elizabeth Bishop's career, "Pink Dog" was a long time in the making, having been begun, perhaps, as early as 1963. When finished it was described by Bishop as "a rather ghastly Carnival poem"—meaning, as we have seen "'ghastly' as to subject matter." If the subject matter is "ghastly," what is one to make of the poet's attitude toward that subject matter as it is expressed in the tone of the poet's voice? Readers have been puzzled by what they have discerned to be an attempt at humor, at looking at the situation and fate of "beggars" in Rio de Janeiro in sardonically comic terms. The triple end rhymes, the playful quadruple rhyme of "fantasia, be a, see a, time of year, Carnival is here," sliding off to "wear." At whose expense is such satirical talk, presented as if directed, helpfully, at the passing dog? Indeed, all the devices, including the end rhymes, are employed to define the Brazilian Carnival and the way its many roles and uses are played out in Brazilian life, joining samba and soccer as two components, long standing, of the opiate of the poor.

There are numerous surviving drafts of "Pink Dog," one of which is reproduced in the *Dictionary of Literary Biography* (volume 169, page 46). There we have virtually the complete poem, save for a few minor changes in diction, and one important exception. Stanza ten appears in this version in the form of two end rhymes: "be a" and *"fantasia."* In the finished poem the tenth stanza reads: "the sensible / solution is to wear a *fantasia.* / Tonight you simply cannot afford to be a- / n eyesore. But no one will ever see a / dog in *máscara* this time of year."

It is readily seen that even after reversing the "be a-fantasia" rhyme, Bishop has still has to trick the reader into what turns out to be an eye rhyme in order to (seemingly) maintain the triple rhyme by an end-of-the line word division of "an" into "a" and "n." Her fealty to the word "eyesore" compels her into this concocted eye rhyme, and her fealty is rewarded by the implication that, perhaps, the sore(s) the dog is suffering from may be more apparent than real, not being the contagious disease (rabies) that the passersby fear but only a case of the much less fearsome case of scabies. Still, despite its appearance (its pinkness), this dog cannot be said to be "in the pink," that's to say, it is not "in the pink of health or condition." Nor do the passersby consider it to be cute or "cunning." Yet, that is exactly what the poet advises the pink dog to do in order to survive: resort to cunning. Dress up in a fantasia, wear a mask, for "no one will ever see a / dog in *máscara* this time of year."

Besides playing with the quasi-proverbial expression "in the pink," Bishop also alludes to one of the American counterparts to Brazilian carnival. The Easter Parade "down the avenue, Fifth Avenue," as Irving Berlin's celebrated 1933 song has it, is echoed in the dog's "trot[ting] across the avenue." In this case, if the poem is autobiographical, the avenue would be the Princesa Isabel, running along the Copacabana and Leme beaches. This dog displays no end-of-Lent finery, being pink, bare, and hairless, unlike the paraders on New York's Fifth Avenue. Of course, in Brazil the "true," more spectacular, finery comes out not on Easter Sunday but during Carnival, just preceding Ash Wednesday and the advent of Lent.

Other song lyrics are echoed. After pink has suggested red — the red of rosacea — "the red, red robin comes bob-bob-bobbin' along" is, perhaps, echoed in Bishop's reference to beggars — idiots, paralytics, parasites — that "go bobbing in the ebbing sewage, nights out in the suburbs."[11] Lines from Irving Berlin's "Blue Skies" — "Blue skies / Smiling at me/ Nothing but blue skies/ Do I see" and "Never saw the sun shining so bright" are echoed in Bishop's opening line, "The sun is blazing and the sky is blue," as well as, perhaps, in the line "never have I seen a dog so bare!" As for Bishop's triple rhymes, compare "When the Red Red Robin Comes Bob, Bob, Bobbin' Along": "Wake up, wake up, you sleepy-head, / Get up, get up, get out of bed / Cheer up, cheer up the sun is red."

If the dancers of each samba group (*escola de samba*) who parade down the avenue and all those who dance the samba in the streets at *Carnaval* keep from looking unwell by dressing up in their fantasias and dancing, then, too, it can be said, the country and its populace do not look unwell when they are costumed up and celebrating.

But a dancing dog, a dog on its hind legs, presumably, may remind

Bishop's readers of Dr. Johnson's quip about the efficacy of women preachers: not that they did it well but that they did it at all. Bishop's point, of course, is that for the brief period of *Carnaval*, it is all right to be someone that for the rest of the year one is not. Appearance is reality, for the nonce, at least. The pink dog, masked and dancing, is not a pink dog at all, at least not for the duration of *Carnaval*. The implication, of course, is that for the rest of the year the pink dog had better pass itself off as something else, sans scabies, posing no perceived threat to the passersby. It was James Merrill who called attention to Bishop's "own instinctive, modest, lifelong impersonations of an ordinary woman, someone who during the day did errands, went to the beach, would perhaps that evening jot a phrase or two inside the nightclub match-book before returning to the dance floor."[12] A pretty good imitation of a bour-geois middle-class woman? In answer to a question by Ashley Brown about the dramatic monologue as a form, Bishop said: "I suppose it should act as a sort of release. You can say all kinds of things you couldn't in a lyric. If you have scenery and costumes, you can get away with a lot."[13]

In the 12th stanza, Bishop talks about the widely held perception that in recent years *Carnaval* is no longer what it was: "They say that Carnival's degenerating / — radios, Americans, or something, / have ruined it completely. They're just talking." The poet's final statement seems to dismiss the charges, implying, of course, that talk is cheap, that nothing will be done about the Carnival, which — degenerating or not — will just go right on being Carnival. But, almost a decade earlier, Bishop had leveled similar charges. Writing in *Brazil*, the volume she prepared for the Life World Library series, she wrote about the deleterious effect of the Hollywood biblical epic on Carnival cos-tuming: "Commercialism and a false idea of what appeals to the tourist are partly to blame" for the spoiling of Carnival. "Hollywood has had its dire effect, too. For example, a few years ago Carnival seemed to have turned into a movie nightmare. A Biblical epic had recently been popular, and thousands of Davids and Bathshebas samba-ed in the streets in monotonous and uno-riginal groups." But it is "radio and loudspeakers" that have "done the most damage," she concludes. "The virtue of Carnival has always been its spon-taneity and the fact that all the songs, music and dances came directly from the people themselves. When commercial song-writers start composing songs for it, and when these songs are broadcast long before Carnival, all charm is lost," she decides. "Also, when thousands of participants, samba-ing along and singing the year's favorite in unison, are confronted with a loudspeaker blaring the same samba or another one in a different tempo, all singing and dancing naturally stop, and the people shuffle along like sheep."[14]

Of course, the people who object to the Hollywood-inspired costumes and the commercialization of the songs well before they are "introduced" in the Carnival itself are the conservatives who do not wish to accept the conditions and facts that will permit the Carnival to continue to be an aesthetic, ritualized occasion. As the opiate of the poor or even as the illusory social anodyne that the wealthier and more powerful take Carnival to be, let them go on talking. The more things change, the less it seems to matter. So runs the poet's ironic message — "Dress up and dance at Carnival!" The Carnival itself is the pink dog's safety net.[15]

In the late 1960s, the 1970s, and perhaps beyond, there operated around Rio de Janeiro (and other large cities, perhaps) the so-called death-squadrons (*esquadrão da morte*), comprised, it was reported at the time, of off-duty policemen and other vigilantes outside the law who took it upon themselves (but with the tacit approval of the authorities) to rid the city of social undesirables such as drug dealers, addicts, and criminals of all stripe. (Bishop identifies those victims as "beggars," "idiots," "paralytics," and "parasites," though they are obviously the same victims.[16]) Hence the pink dog looks intelligent (to the poet) and lives by its wits, and though it is not an "idiot," it will be taken for one because it begs. Just as its "scabies" (caused by a parasite and therefore not contagious) will nevertheless be seen as contagious by a threatened human populace. The outward sign of her medical condition will be taken as a sign of her lack of inner worth.

Intriguingly, there is, possibly, a trace of "Pink Dog" in "Santarém," a late poem dating from the same period and the last poem published in her lifetime. Bishop describes the traffic on the river ("that conflux of two great rivers, Tapajos, Amazon") as "lots of *mongrel* riverboats skittering back and forth / under a sky of gorgeous, under-lit clouds" (emphasis added).

"Pink Dog" also shows traces of the poetry of e. e. cummings as well as the popular work of Vinícius de Moraes. First there is cummings, a Greenwich Village neighbor at one time whose *XAIPE* Bishop reviewed for the *United States Quarterly Book Review* in 1950.[17] In disgust cummings talks about misfits, outcasts, and mongrel dogs, as Bishop would do later: "this is a rubbish of human rind / with a photograph / clutched in the half / of a hand and the word / love underlined / this is a girl who died in her mind / with a warm thick scream / and a keen cold groan / while the gadgets purred / and the gangsters dined / this is a deaf dumb church and blind / with an if in its soul / and a hole in its life / where the young bell tolled / and the old vine twined / this is a dog of no known kind / with one white eye / and one black eye / and the eyes of his eyes / are as lost as you'll find."[18]

Vinícius, a recognizable Brazilian influence on Bishop, is represented in the collection of 20th-century Brazilian poetry coedited by Bishop and

Emanuel Brasil. "Vinícius de Moraes (commonly known as just 'Vinícius'), famous for his film-script for *Black Orpheus* [1959] and more recently for his popular songs," write the editors of the anthology, "performs in night-clubs, produces musical shows in Brazil and other countries, and makes recordings in Europe — all ways of augmenting his income." Bishop's friend and convivial drinking buddy in Ouro Prêto, this modernist poet who turned to the writing of popular poetry and song lyrics, not only had his unsentimental script about the human flotsam and jetsam of the Rio *favela* filmed for popular consumption but also wrote the wistful lyrics to accompany Antonio Carlos Jobim's music in the greatly successful popular song "The Girl from Ipanema" ("Garota de Ipanema").[19]

And this returns us to Dante, for both the "Garota de Ipanema" and "Pink Dog" have a place in the line of what might be called "the spectator poem celebrating the passing woman," a line initiated by Dante in his *La Vita Nuova*. In Dante Gabriel Rossetti's translation, Dante's sonnet reads:

> My lady looks so gentle and so pure
> When yielding salutation by the way,
> That the tongue trembles and has nought to say.
> And the eyes, which fain would see, may not endure.
> And still, amid the praise she hears secure,
> She walks with humbleness for her array;
> Seeming a creature sent from Heaven to stay
> On earth, and show a miracle made sure.
> She is so pleasant in the eyes of men
> That through the sight the inmost heart doth gain
> A sweetness which needs proof to know it by:
> And from between her lips there seems to move
> A soothing spirit that is full of love,
> Saying for ever to the soul, 'O Sigh!'[20]

Dante's own comment holds meaning for both poems, Vinícius' and Bishop's. "This excellent lady came into such favour with all men, that not only she herself was honoured and commended; but through her companionship, honour and commendation came unto others. Wherefore I, perceiving this, and wishing that it should also be made manifest to those that beheld it not, wrote the sonnet here following; wherein is signified the power which her virtue had upon other ladies."[21] If Dante's words resonate wistfully in Vinícius, they resonate differently in Bishop. There is no place for Dantean adulation in the latter's acerbic evaluation of the "depilated" female dog. If Dante's lady (surely) and Vinícius' *garota* (though less surely) can be said to be "blessed among women," there is less or no doubt that Bishop's female outcast, even hiding behind the *máscara* of *Carnaval*, is blessed among nobody.

10

In the Middle of the Road

Among the handful of modern Brazilian poems that Elizabeth Bishop chose to translate herself for *An Anthology of Twentieth-Century Brazilian Poetry*, the groundbreaking collection she and Emanuel Brasil published in 1972, was Carlos Drummond de Andrade's "In the Middle of the Road" ("No Meio do Caminho"), published in 1928. Notable for its oxymoronic abstract specificity, Drummond's short poem remains Brazil's most famous and most influential expression of literary modernism. It begins famously: "In the middle of the road there was a stone / there was a stone in the middle of the road / there was a stone."[1]

In her 1950 review of *XAIPE*, Bishop commented that often the American poet e. e. cummings' approach to verse reminded her of "a smart-alec Greenwich Village child saying to his friends: 'Look! I've just made up a new game. Let's all write poems. There! I've won!' And in front of the wood-and-coal man's basement shop, on the wall of the Chinese laundry, along the curbs of the dingy but flourishing park, appear poems and ideograph poems in hyacinth-colored chalks."[2] Now, faced with the dead chicken out in the middle of the street in Greenwich Village, flattened into a police-drawn chalk sketch, that became her poem "Trouvée," Bishop may have recalled the imagined "ideograph poems in hyacinth-colored chalks" she adduced in her review.

"Trouvée" is not a "found" poem. It is a well-wrought poem about a "found" object. An example of Elizabeth Bishop's "Dutch" painters' "love of curiosities locatable in time and place"— the observation and words are her friend James Merrill's[3]— the poem "Trouvée" was based on an incident in New York, in the Village, in 1967. In *Elizabeth Bishop: An Oral Biography*, her friend and neighbor for that summer and fall Wheaton Galentine tells about the episode on which Bishop based her poem. "Elizabeth arrived late that afternoon, four or five o'clock, and she said she'd just seen the strangest thing": "a chicken that had been run over by a car on Fourth Street in front of Nicola's," a grocery store. "Individually, we all trotted over to see this bird.

There was a lot of jollity about the chicken, conjecturing where it came from. That night she wrote the poem and brought it over the next morning."[4] The poem begins with several questions: Why should "a *hen*" have met its fate on "West 4th Street / in the middle of summer?" "How did she get there? / Where was she going?" The corpse is described: "a white hen /— red-and-white now, of course," her "wing feathers spread / flat, flat in the tar, / all dirtied, and thin"— thin as "tissue paper." The poet goes back to take a look. "I hadn't dreamed it," she writes. There is the dead hen, "turned into a quaint / old country saying," one "scribbled in chalk / (except for the beak)."

When "Trouvée" was published in the *New Yorker* on August 10, 1968, it was dedicated to Wheaton Galentine and his companion Harold Leeds as a sort of bread-and-butter note. As she wrote to them on December 5, 1967, "I can never thank you enough for your kindness and generosity & everything else. I feel quite sure I wouldn't have survived at all without you. (And I shall dedicate something better than the poor HEN at least, sometime, to you, as one other small footnote of gratitude."[5] What Bishop had had to survive that fall was the death of Lota, who had been hospitalized the day after she arrived in New York and died a week later on September 25, 1967. Only hindsight, perhaps, permits or encourages one to see "Trouvée" as a poem reflective of Bishop's fears that summer about Lota's serious illness and its consequences for herself. Coincidentally, it was at Loren MacIver's studio on Perry Street in Greenwich Village in the fall of 1942 that Bishop first met Lota, then in the company of Mary Stearns Morse, their mutual friend.[6]

Dead chickens are not uncommon in the city streets or rural byways of Brazil. They are part of the rituals and spells of folk religion. "Frequently at night, on country roads, along beaches or in city doorways, candles can be seen glimmering," wrote Bishop in *Brazil*, her book for Time Life in 1962. "A black candle, cigars and a black bottle of *cachaça*, or a white candle, white flowers, a chicken and a clear bottle of *cachaça*— these are *macumba* hexes or offerings, witnesses to the superstitious devotion of millions of Brazilians to this cult."[7]

But here in New York, not Rio, was a white chicken (not one of the striding fiery roosters of her earlier poem) flattened by a truck or car. Its whiteness testifies to its innocence but it also links it to the whiteness in Dickinson's poetry, the ending of Poe's *Arthur Gordon Pym*, and Melville's whale. Despite its small size, the hen too has died the death of totem animal, like Clarice Lispector's *galinha* (hen),[8] Santiago's fish, the bears of Faulkner's Ike McCaslin or Bellow's bear in *Henderson the Rain King*. It is Bishop's fish, released; its death put off to another day. It is The Big Bear of Arkansas writ small. What it is not is what Bishop called it (with tongue in cheek?) when she first offered it to the *New Yorker*, "a very, very light poem you might just possibly like for the summer season."[9]

Yet there is nothing light about "Trouvée." Nothing any longer depends on this un-living object of red and white, a chicken bearing the very colors of William Carlos Williams' famous pastoral image. And as in Blake's "London," this poem is part of the cityscape, not the barnyard, a minimal/ miniaturist poem (strangely reminiscent of "Poem," which recreates her uncle's small painting). The flattened chicken — a surrealist's found object, conducive to Bishop's (and Joseph Cornell's) aesthetic practice of making use of, that is, *aproveitar* [take advantage of, to put to good advantage, or, more commonly, to make use of or good use of; the word also appears in the expression *bom proveito*, the equivalent of *bon appetite*] — suffers the fate of Baudelaire's swan and albatross when it could have stayed withdrawn from the "world" (like the Lady of Shalott, whose tentative venture out into the world brings her death too). Like them, the chicken will cross the road — to be seen, of course, to join the flow of things, perhaps. But "how did she get there?" she asks. "Where was she going?" This is New York City, after all, West 4th Street, to be precise, not Key West where there are "free" chickens roaming the streets, protected by law from being herded or in any way penned in.[10] The flattened chicken gives way to the policeman's body sketch, which itself has implications for seeing the "chalk sketcher" as an image for the poet who can only, in words, provide a sketch for the body (flattened) that was the living, functioning body before meeting its killer — a car or truck or bus — in ongoing traffic. In "Santarem" the pharmacist has "aproveitado" the wasp's nest and Bishop will emulate the pharmacist by asking for it and taking it with her.[11] Bishop's love for the word "aproveitar" suggests a link to Joseph Cornell's love for "junk." In "Trouvée" Bishop is able to "aproveitar" the chicken flattened (like a cartoon character) in the middle of the street. Because she could not recoup her found objet d'art and place it among her own pieces (ship's figurehead, wooden birdcage, ostrich egg) or enclose it in a shadow box (her Cornell-like assembly of winged cherub stickers and child's shoe found on a beach)[12] the flattened chicken becomes the source of her meditation, remains at the center of her concern, and sticks there as a symbol, radiating out and gathering back to itself to no final result — "sem resultado" — it may be said, if we discount the poem. But we must not discount the poem, for it is "Trouvée" that enacts recuperation (or "collecting," as James Clifford defines it, "a rescue of *phenomena* from inevitable historical decay or loss").[13] The poem itself can be viewed as itself an inscription of the actual hen's carcass as mapped or outlined by the thinking-feeling poet.

And it all happens "in the middle of summer," in the middle of the street, suggesting Carlos Drummond de Andrade's poem. The poem's connection to that Brazilian poem becomes clearer when one looks at "The Moose." But before moving on to a consideration of "The Moose," I would suggest that "Trouvée" draws on Bishop's Brazilian experience in still another way. This poem, too, echoes Clarice Lispector's parable-like story "Uma Galinha" ("A Hen"). The Brazilian writer's animal-human parable chronicles the somewhat charmed existence of a chicken the household deems "the queen of the house" after she fortuitously lays an egg just before she is fated to become the family's Sunday dinner. Clarice ends the story laconically with the matter-of-fact information, unexpected but all too natural in the world shared by chickens and human beings: "Until one day they killed her and ate her and the years went by."[14]

On August 29, 1946, in a letter to Marianne Moore, Bishop first set down what can now be recognized as the germ for "The Moose." She had planned a longer stay in Nova Scotia but business over the house in Key West called her back to the United States. "I came back by bus — a dreadful trip, but it seemed most convenient at the time — we hailed it with a flashlight and a lantern as it went by the farm late at night," she writes. But "early the next morning, just as it was getting light, the driver had to stop suddenly for a big cow moose who was wandering down the road. She walked away very slowly into the woods, looking at us over her shoulder. The driver said that one foggy night he had to stop while a huge bull moose came right up and smelled the engine. 'Very curious beasts,' he said."[15]

In 1956 Elizabeth Bishop had written to her Aunt Grace about "The Moose": "I've written a long poem about Nova Scotia. It's dedicated to you. When it's published, I'll send you a copy."[16] Two years later, she wrote to an acquaintance, "My aunt has written me a long letter from Great Village describing the autumn colors in Nova Scotia and telling me how she almost bumped into a moose on the road at night — you have to turn off the headlights, you know. This is the subject of my last poem."[17] But the fact is that not until 20 years later did she actually "finish" her Canadian poem just in time to read it before Harvard University's chapter of Phi Beta Kappa. In the finished poem the trip was not remembered as being all that "dreadful" and the visits to the road by two discrete moose had been conflated into a single visit to the bus to sniff at its engine's hood by a cow moose.

In the long interval between starting the poem "The Moose" and finishing it for the Harvard Phi Beta Kappa ceremony, Bishop lived for the most part in Brazil. She also translated Carlos Drummond de Andrade's poetry. Among the poems she translated was "No meio do caminho," which appears in the collection of Brazilian poems edited by Bishop with Emanuel Brasil for Wesleyan Press as "In the Middle of the Road." Drummond's poem — it is a commonplace to see in it the epitome of Brazilian modernism — bemusedly considers (or celebrates) the existence of that stone in the middle of the road. Bishop's "Moose" does not celebrate the existence of the stone but the appearance, as he puts it, "in the middle of the road," of the curious moose. Drummond's stone, of course, takes on a reality — through repetition — similar to that of Gertrude Stein's modernist "rose" ("Rose is a rose is a rose is a rose"). Yet while in Drummond's poem the stone remains an inanimate object, stubbornly refusing to be (or to recall or to suggest) anything else or anybody at all, in Bishop's poem it is a living being that brings together communally those on the bus whose journey is temporarily interrupted.

Behind Bishop's poem lies the strong emblematic tradition of the encounter in the woods or the forest with the huge beast. In "The Old People" Faulkner offers a hunter's view: "Then the buck was there. He did not come into sight, he was just there, looking not like a ghost but as if all of light were condensed in him and he were the source of it, not only moving in it but disseminating it, already running, seen first as you always see the deer, in that split second after he has already seen you, already slanting away in that first soaring bound, the antlers even in that dim light looking like a small rocking-chair balanced on his head."[18] The buck and the moose, specifically, have a place in the traditions of North American literature, not so much the moose as victim as in James Fenimore Cooper's *The Pioneers* or Jack London's story "The Law of Life" or the moose that crashes out of the forest in Robert Frost's "Two Look at Two," but the moose that looms large in the Canadian literary imagination. Once again I am reminded of what Margaret Atwood says about the moment in Gabrielle Roy's *The Hidden Mountain* "where Pierre, having hunted down a caribou, finally kills it and it turns upon him a gaze full of resignation and suffering." "This gaze exchanged between a hunter and an animal either dying or threatened with death — and it's usually a deer, moose or caribou — is a recurring moment in Canadian literature; in it the hunter identifies with his prey *as suffering victim*."[19] Playing off this tradition, Bishop rings some changes. No one is hunting the female moose that appears out of the shadows of the "impenetrable wood" and the gaze takes in not only the poet but a whole busload of passengers. There are no suffering victims here. On the contrary, the whole episode brings only a "sweet / sensation of joy." The driver stops the bus and turns off the lights, for a moose has come out of the wood and now stands there, "looms, rather, / in the middle of the road." It approaches the bus, and "sniffs at the bus's hood," "towering, antlerless, / high as a church, / homely as a house." A man's voice assures the passengers that it is perfectly harmless. The reassured passengers, whispering that these are

big creatures, suddenly exclaim, "'Look! It's a she!'" Slowly the moose looks
the bus over, and then, "grand, otherworldly," it leaves. The poet gives herself
the last word: "Why, why do we feel / (we all feel) this sweet / sensation of
joy?"

Here we have not the embodiment of "Nature as Monster" but Nature
as "she"—placid, benign, and unthreatening. The Canadian "gaze" here is
anything but that of the hunter and his "suffering" victim. The moment of
the gaze is better described as a visitation (leaving behind "a dim smell of
moose, an acrid / smell of gasoline"), as an incident of healing, perhaps, for
this busload of ordinary voyagers, some going all the way to Boston. "The
Moose," in the largest sense, is a poem about the family of humankind. As
for Atwood's notions of the moose's importance to the Canadian's keen
response to the dictates for survival in a hostile world inhabited by animals
hostile to man, Bishop replaces the hunter's collective urge — satisfied, perhaps,
by the mounting of a moose head on the wall of his house or club — by recoup-
ing the entire moose for her poem, the only place to which she could cart off
an entire moose. There it stands — a she — in the middle of her poem.

In Drummond's poem we have a stone in the middle of the road. It is
not rolling. Therefore it might well gather moss, though one doubts it. In
Bishop's mind was there somehow a set of associations stringing out: middle
of the road / stone / moss / moose / middle of the road? Moreover, in Drummond's poem it is as if the stone refuses to be moved or in any way contained,
domesticated, or made to mean or to symbolize. The "rose is rose is rose"
quality of the poem militates against suggestibility. The stone is stone is stone.
It is just there, repeatedly. In this see Bishop's comment on her villanelle "One
Art"—that it is a poem that repeats and repeats and repeats — pounding in a
notion, perhaps, that the poet's lot has been hard, that she has been given
stones to eat, so to speak — grief / loss — acceptable only if "eaten," incorporated, incarnated as in Incarnation. It doesn't happen in "One Art," for the
"stone" sticks in the throat: "*Write* it!"

If one looks at the earliest surviving treatment of the materials that were
finally shaped into Bishop's finished poem, one may well be struck with the
prosiness of a rather long list. There is no rhyme scheme evident and there
isn't the slightest hint that the finished poem will emerge in the form of the
villanelle. It is obvious even in a first reading of Bishop's "One Art" that the
rhetorical strategy employed is litotes. Her assertions on the way to manage
one's emotions in the face of loss, no less than in the memory of loss, confirm
and emphasize the notion that loss is never managed, at least not entirely. In
an escalating list, from lost keys to lost continents (of course, keys is also a
pun — she lost the keys of southern Florida, as well as house keys, etc.), she

ends by grieving over what will be her greatest loss — "you" — who is, by all signs, her most recent partner. Her command to herself breaks both the metric line and the sustained tone of the entire poem — *Write it* (she corrected a typesetter's mistake by removing the italics from the word "it," thereby increasing the emphasis on "write," that is to say the act of writing as a means of coping).

Emily Dickinson's striking poem about the aftermath of loss begins "After great pain, a formal feeling comes." One might alter the sentiment in that line so as to apply to Bishop's "One Art": "After great pain there arises a need for form." Dickinson focuses on the "formalization" of the body, which takes over from the, perhaps overly, sentient sufferer. The poem is a generalized statement focused on the incident of loss and its aftermath. Bishop's poem meditates on the wisdom of such canards as "time heals" or that even in the greatest of losses, grief, too, must pass.

If one practices losing little things and practices it often (like A.E. Housman's Mithridates, who tasted poison every day and thus managed to last to die old), one prepares oneself to brace against the loss of the great things. Or so one may think. But such "good" advice is contravened by the breath-stopping urge of the last line — an imperative to the self to end the poem. And indeed Bishop finishes the poem, brings to a close (at least for the moment) her meditation on pain and grief, and, not incidentally, fulfills the form of her poem. The demands of the villanelle are met, and form — but not without the struggle enacted in the imperative voice in the last line — is fulfilled. "Disaster" has been "mastered," if only in the poet's "formal" performance.

11

Crusoe in the Land of Vera Cruz

On occasion, Elizabeth Bishop liked doing what T. S. Eliot called "the police in different voices," building poems out of monologues, more often than not addressed to no one in particular.[1] In "From Trollope's Journal" she takes over a historical voice already established in a published text, while in "One Art" (couched, strikingly, in the form of a villanelle), she addresses an unidentified "you" as well as herself—"*Write* it!" she commands. In "Manuelzinho," however, she tries something different. She mimics the Portuguese voice of some Brazilian intimate as that voice might sound in English (if she were expressing Bishop's own feelings), just as, in the much earlier poem "Jerónimo's House," she had invented a lyrical "English" voice for the Cuban Spanish of a denizen of Key West. In "Crusoe in England" Bishop rings still another change on the "different voices" that populate her work by imagining the subdued, weary, memorial voice for the eponymous figure in Daniel Defoe's novel who has long since outlived the exhilarations and dangers of his castaway's life.

Defoe's novel places Robinson Crusoe's unnamed island in the general vicinity of the "Brazils," a land that first bore the Portuguese name of "Ilha de Vera Cruz" (Island of the True Cross), so named by Pedro Vaz de Caminha in 1500.[2] It is not entirely coincidental, I think, that Daniel Defoe's castaway hero is a descendant of Germans whose family name is "Kreutznaeur," which in England has become "Crusoe." It is not known whether the Brazilian poet Carlos Drummond de Andrade made the connections among "Kreutz," "Crusoe" and "Cross," but like myriad readers before and since, he was enthralled by *The Life and Adventures of Robinson Crusoe* (1719). He refers to this in "Infância" ("Infancy"), a memorializing poem that records the poet's discovery that his own life is to be his great subject. "Infância" recalls lovingly the details of the young poet's family's quotidian routine as he was growing up, long before he discovered that he was a poet. "And I didn't know that my story," he concludes, "was prettier than that of Robinson Crusoe."[3]

While Drummond describes the Crusoe story as one "that never comes to an end," Bishop decides to imagine Crusoe's sorrowful thoughts about his past life, that part of which he lived as a castaway with Friday, his one human companion. *Robinson Crusoe* "resembles one of the anonymous productions of the race rather than the effort of a single mind," and thus, writes Virginia Woolf, "it still seems that the name of Daniel Defoe has no right to appear upon the title-page." Bishop agreed, to the extent, at least, of feeling perfectly free to consider Crusoe's story to be nobody's exclusive property, an archetypal story that anyone could take a shot at bringing to a personal, intimate conclusion.

In Bishop's poem, Crusoe has been returned to England, to live out his days "at home"—"wherever that may be," as Bishop wonders in "Questions of Travel," a poem published a dozen years earlier. In fact, "Crusoe in England" was called "Crusoe at Home" in earlier, manuscript versions, a title that might have implied to some readers that Crusoe was comfortable with himself as well as with his country, an idea contrary to the poem's overall concern, the crucial meaning that the presence of Friday in Crusoe's memory, lodged in the particulars of the poem, has for the former castaway. Friday arrives just when he thought, Crusoe recalls, he could not "stand it / another minute longer." Friday was "nice, and we were friends. / If only he had been a woman!" He was "pretty to watch; he had a pretty body."[4]

It is of course possible to work over this poem for biographical (or psychological) correspondences to the Bishop-Lota relationship as we now know it to have been. But what is more interesting here is that in this poem Bishop employs details, imagery and language drawn from one of her own earlier texts. In 1958, she found herself, along with a group of other visitors to Brasilia, spending a day with the Uialapiti tribe deep in the Amazons. In her long piece on that singular trip, which remained unpublished until long after her death, she recorded the observations that foreshadow details in "Crusoe in England." For instance, she notices that "every round dusky behind bore a vaccination mark," adding, parenthetically, that "their rounded behinds and childishly smooth legs, in both sexes, are remarkably pretty."[5] She notes, too, that those in charge of keeping an eye on the Uialapiti live "in dread of infections brought in from outside, the one case of measles, for example, that can wipe out whole villages." Recall the last lines of "Crusoe in England," which reveal that the "pretty" Friday died of measles "seventeen years ago come March." Crusoe's red berry, which gave him his drink as well as the dye he used to dye "a baby goat bright red," has its antecedent in the men of Uialapiti who smeared the whole crown of their head "with a bright red, sticky paint they make from the *urucum* tree, the only dye, and color, they possess; some of them were powdered with it, ears, necks, or chests, hot red ... one young girl had a bright red forehead, suggestive of a bad headache."[6]

Perhaps how the Friday of "Crusoe in England" is related to Lota and her situation as Bishop's lover can be brought into greater focus by referring to one of Bishop's favorite sambas. Translated by Bishop, it appears in "On the Railroad Named Delight," a piece she contributed to the *New York Times* on the occasion of the 400th anniversary of the city of Rio de Janeiro in 1965: "'Come, my mulatta, / Take me back. / You're the joker / In my pack, / The prune in my pudding, / Pepper in my pie, / My package of peanuts, / The moon in the sky.'"[7] Apart from acknowledging its evident obeisance to the Brazilian mythology about the deeply sexual attraction of the *mulatta* (therefore making it typically revelatory of one aspect of Brazilian culture), I would like to speculate on how it might be revelatory about the writer herself. It is not far-fetched to think, that Bishop's Brazilian companion and lover was her *mulatta*, her joker, her prune, her pepper, her peanuts, her moon — in short, her everything. Surely, Lota's dark hue and hair (washed lovingly, with references to the samba's moon in "The Shampoo") would only enhance her appeal in Bishop's nordic eyes. In fact, despite the expected differences, there are intriguing similarities to Lota in Defoe's description of the companion Crusoe named Friday after the day he was found. It occurs in the 14th chapter, one aptly named "A Dream Realised":

> He was a comely, handsome fellow, perfectly well made, with straight, strong limbs, not too large; tall, and well-shaped; and, as I reckon, about twenty-six years of age. He had a very good countenance, not a fierce and surly aspect, but seemed to have something very manly in his face; and yet he had all the sweetness and softness of a European in his countenance, too, especially when he smiled. His hair was long and black, not curled like wool; his forehead very high and large; and a great vivacity and sparkling sharpness in his eyes. The colour of his skin was not quite black, but very tawny; and yet not an ugly, yellow, nauseous tawny, as the Brazilians and Virginians, and other natives of America are, but of a bright kind of a dun olive-colour, that had in it something very agreeable, though not very easy to describe. His face was round and plump; his nose small, not flat, like the negroes; a very good mouth, thin lips, and his fine teeth well set, and as white as ivory.

Genetically, "Crusoe in England" works with displacement and replacement: Crusoe (Kreutz) / Bishop; island near Brazil / Island of Vera Cruz; and England / Cambridge (Massachusetts). The Crusoe / Friday arrangements in "Crusoe in England" mirror the virtually fluid details and aspects of the Lota-Bishop relationship. In "Crusoe in England" Bishop demonstrated that she could tell her life by telling it as if it were Crusoe's by concentrating on Crusoe's memories after he returned to England only to endure a painfully meaningless present. As Bishop's "Strayed Crab" is made to say, "I believe in the oblique, the indirect approach, and I keep my feelings to myself." The losses tabulated in "Crusoe in England" flesh out, so to speak, the regrettable losses more famously lamented in "One Art."

12

A Tale of Jam and Jelly

Elizabeth Bishop could not keep herself from boasting. "I am having some poems in English-Portuguese in a literary supplement, here — there are no magazines, so the newspapers cover literature in varying degrees of seriousness," she wrote to Robert Lowell in 1953. "*The* Brazilian poet, a man of about 65, Manuel Bandeira," she continues, "is doing them and doing them extremely well, I think. I have been trying to return the compliment, I've read quite a lot of Brazilian poetry by now, and it is all graceful, and slight, I think, although Bandeira is sometimes extremely witty, like a gentler Cummings."[1] In the months that followed Bishop continued to associate Bandeira with Cummings in various personal and poetic ways. When the popular magazine *Manchette* announced a contest for the best translation of Cummings' sonnet beginning "it may not always be so; and I say" (from *Tulips and Chimneys*, 1923), Bishop sent Cummings the clipping with a letter dated December 6, 1956, adding a postscript: "I forgot to say that I am *insisting* that you be included in an anthology they are getting out here of Eng-American modern poetry!— or rather a new edition of a poor one that stops with Frost, I think." She had got "Manuel Bandeira, *the* poet here," "very interested," she continued. "I'm not sure what he'll do with you but he is an excellent scholar and translator — and his own poems sometimes seem to me like little, faded, faded copies of yours."[2] Bandeira did not figure in the outcome of the contest, as it turned out, but it is possible that he was a contestant, for this sonnet was the one Cummings poem he is known to have translated.[3]

As for the Bandeira translations of Bishop poems, just how many he did and if at the time they appeared in print, no information has surfaced to date. The one exception is his version of the third of Bishop's "Songs for a Colored Singer" (from *North & South*), which he calls "Acalanto" ("Lullaby").[4] On September 9, 1953, Manuel Bandeira wrote to Bishop about his translation and a gift of orange marmalade: "I am well aware that I do not merit your gracious thanks for my translation of your lines. Even less so do I merit the

gift of orange marmalade — a delicacy (when you have more, don't forget me!).
I hope to have the pleasure of seeing you again soon. We may then talk further
about 'Lullaby.'"[5] And the jam kept coming. On October 25, 1953, Manuel
Bandeira wrote (this time in English): "Thank [you] so much for the raspberry
jam: better than [illegible] — definitely! This is the view you may have from
my new apartment in the same building: when are you coming down to see
it? Very soon, I hope." At the top of the page he sketches out the view from
his window.[6] Perhaps as a belated Christmas gift that year, on December 27th
Bandeira sent her "Thank you for the exquisite jam," an English-language
parody in e. e. cumming's characteristic style and manner.[7]

Further details regarding Bishop's friendship with Manuel Bandeira can
be sketched out from Bishop's published letters. "Did I tell you — I don't think
I did," she gossiped in a letter to Marianne Moore on December 8, 1953,
"how Manuel Bandeira, *the* poet here now, a very nice man about 65 or so —
took me to see his apartment one night?" The apartment, though not as big,
writes Bishop, nevertheless reminded her of Moore's. It made her homesick.
Bandeira admitted that he could "cook nothing except coffee and an awful
sweet much in favor here made of boiled milk and sugar [*doce de leite*]." His
pots and pans he kept in "another very Brazilian arrangement — like a small
Christmas tree." "He is extremely interested in your poetry, too," she tells
Moore, "and I imagine he can really appreciate it because the translations of
his I've seen are excellent — although he refuses to speak a word of English."
Bishop then caps off her account of *the* Brazilian poet with a personal anecdote.
"We left him about 1 A.M. and went downstairs in the elevator. They have a
system of locking the outside apartment-house doors at night, and ... for
some reason or other we couldn't get out. And there was no porter." Finally
Lota decided to get the poet, but neither of them could remember the number
of his apartment or even the floor it was on. "However, after two or three
tries, she found him and the poor man came down in green striped pajamas
and a bright red dressing gown and flapping slippers, to let us out."[8]

They remained friends. Bandeira introduced her to Alice Dayrell Caldeira
Brant (1880–1970), the author of *Minha Vida de Menina* (self-published in
1942) by "Helena Morley," a book that Bishop was then translating. To Paul
Brooks, her editor at Houghton Mifflin, Bishop wrote excitedly on July 28,
1953: "I am going to be taken to see her [Alice Brant] the next time I am in
Rio (I live in the country most of the time) by *the* elderly Brazilian poet
Manuel Bandeira, who knows her well."[9] When, later in the same year, on
December 19, 1953, Bishop published her own first memorial story, "In the
Village," in the *New Yorker*, Bandeira was so taken with it that he brought it
to the attention of his companion — "his elderly Dutch mistress," actually,

who, in turn, as Bishop wrote to Pearl Kazin on February 22, 1954, liked the Nova Scotia story well enough to send Bishop "a large Dutch gingerbread."[10] It was later in the same year Bishop reported to Robert Lowell on Robert Frost's first and only visit to Brazil. On November 30, 1954, she wrote: "Frost put on quite a good show at our fearfully ugly embassy auditorium. Then I asked him to lunch at the house of a friend of mine in Rio — a beautiful old house and garden that I thought he might like to see." As it happened, Bishop's friend invited, among others, "Brazil's 'leading poet,' who's an awfully nice man but who refuses to speak any English at all — Frost refuses to speak anything else — and they are both extremely deaf." Needless to say, lunch was "rather a strain," she admitted, "with me screaming away in any old language I could think of at one end of the table, and Frost's daughter Lesley holding forth endlessly to some poor bored Brazilians at the other end — and Miss Mongan — about her daughter's creditable marks at Radcliffe." It was all capped when Frost asked the hostess "where she got the seeds for the beautiful flowers on the table" and was answered, after she screwed up her courage, with the words, "loud and clear: 'BURPEE.'"[11]

If Frost was wrong about Bishop's being a "public figure," she nevertheless had to admit that she was "a friend of THE poet (at least I keep him provided with marmalade, and he has written me a poem and I have written him one) and he gave me a hammock."[12] The gift took on some sort of personal meaning for her, apparently, for later, on February 22, 1954, in a letter to Pearl Kazin, she once again mentioned the hammock: "Manuel Bandeira sent me a hammock for Christmas — and since then I've seen pictures of him writing in one, so I guess that's the Brazilian spirit in literature."[13] Bandeira also provided her with a striking example of what she considered the special treatment accorded poets in Brazil. "Poets — even when they're bad, as they mostly are — are much more highly thought of here than in the U.S., a nice old-fashioned romantic idea of the *Poet*," she wrote to Marianne Moore. When Bandeira was annoyed by the view from his window — " a dismal courtyard which had never been paved and was full of mud and garbage, etc." — he complained to the city by way of a poem. "Someone, no one knows who, wrote a beautiful poem right back, and the courtyard was promptly fixed! (I doubt the Dept. of Sanitation in Brooklyn would do that — but maybe they would now for *you*, after what you have said about Brooklyn.)"[14]

Six months later, Bandeira went public with his admiration for the American poet and her work. Published in the *Jornal do Brasil*, "Parabens, Elizabeth!" ["Congratulations, Elizabeth!"] may well have been the first important notice in Brazil of the American poet living in Rio, with the possible exception of the note in the São Paulo journal *Anhembi* that accompanied her poem,

"Squatter's Children," in April 1956. On May 21, 1956, Elizabeth Bishop complained to Pearl Kazin: "Manuel Bandeira wrote a little piece titled *Parabéns, Elizabeth!* and relating, all wrong, the story of the caju poisoning."[15] This "crônica" (as such pieces are categorized in Brazil or Portugal) was published five days later in the *Jornal do Brasil*. Although Bishop had seen it before its publication, Bandeira's account of Bishop's poisoning and its aftermath remained unchanged, apparently.

Later, Bishop would account for the Brazilian poet's visits to Samambaia differently: "Manuel Bandeira used to come up to sample tidbits," she told Beatriz Schiller in 1977. "He had a weakness for sweets. He even wrote me a poem, the only one he ever wrote in English: 'I wish I had two bellies / because of your good jellies.' He told me that those two lines were so good that he could think of nothing that could follow them."[16] Of course, as we have seen, this couplet was not Bandeira's only venture into English verse. She seems to have forgotten his take-off on Cummings. She, too, concocted a poem, not in Portuguese, but in English. Though "To Manuel Bandeira, with a Present" is really little more than an example of the sort of doggerel Bishop was capable of on rare occasions, she did labor over the poem as the several versions surviving in a notebook at the Houghton Library indicate.[17]

Manuel Bandeira's name disappears from Bishop's published letters for several years. But on April 26, 1962, she reveals to Robert Lowell that "the" poet — Manuel Bandeira — has lost ground in her estimation to his chief rival as *the* modernist, Carlos Drummond de Andrade. She writes: "I like Drummond (pronounced Droo-Mond) better than Bandeira, I think," she wrote. "Bandeira & I were fairly friendly for a while. I used to make him marmalade — but it was a friendship that has dwindled, although I'll try to take it up again for your visit. He is old and *very* spoiled & deaf. His apartment reminds me of Miss Moore's — very similar."[18] Yet, later on in the same letter she seems to signal still another change in her ranking of the Brazilian modernists. "No one's ever heard of Tate or Ransom or Randall or Roethke," she writes. "Hart Crane is vaguely familiar, maybe," but Cummings, "strange to say, seems best known. Not so strange, maybe — that sentimental side of Cummings, in love and 'social comment,' is sort of the stage they are at here — Bandeira and Drummond — oh, all of them practically —(except Cabral [João Cabral de Melo Neto])."[19] Noteworthy, too, is the observation about Cummings' "sentimental side." Already in 1958 she had begun to have reservations about Cummings' poetry. About *95 Poems*, just published, she wrote to Howard Moss, poetry editor at the *New Yorker* on October 29: "I have Cummings's new one. Well, I find him hard to judge, you know, he is such an institution — but I do like some of them as much as ever. You have to pretend you've never seen a Cummings poem before, and that's difficult."[20] The next day she wrote to Robert Lowell, damning with faint praise: "I just got Cummings' latest, and a lot of it is very good Cummings."[21] Fifteen years later, struggling to prepare for a class, the teacher Elizabeth Bishop complained to her musician friends Arthur Gold and Robert Fizdale in a letter dated April 25, 1973: "I must concentrate on E. E. Cummings for half an hour or so — and I don't think I really like him a lot."[22]

As for Bandeira, it is noteworthy that in 1972 Bishop and her coeditor, Emanuel Brasil, dedicated their work, *An Anthology of Twentieth-Century Brazilian Poetry*, "to the memory of Manuel Bandeira." And of the four poems by Bandeira with which the collection begins, the translations of "My Last Poem" and "Brazilian Tragedy," are by Bishop. Still, in the case of "*The* Brazilian poet," along with that of Cummings — a friend dating back to the early 1940s in Greenwich Village — Bishop's judgments had followed her changing taste in modern poetry.

13

"A Miracle for Breakfast"

In his day Oswaldino Ribeiro Marques (1916–2003) was a well-known and highly regarded literary critic, poet, playwright and translator — in the last instance, of English-language poets, mainly from the United States, including Walt Whitman, Langston Hughes, Ezra Pound, and T. S. Eliot, but also earlier British poets such as Shelley and William Blake. Not widely known is that he numbered among his translations versions of two Elizabeth Bishop poems, "The Man-moth" and "A Miracle for Breakfast," both of them published, the latter accompanied by Bishop's own Portuguese version of the poem, which she based on Oswaldino Marques's own.

Oswaldino Marques first mentions Elizabeth Bishop in 1956 in *Teoria da Metáfora & Renascença da Poesia Americana* when he notes that among the notable poets appearing in the United States in recent decades there is Elizabeth Bishop, a Pulitzer Prize winner and follower of Marianne Moore, who is presently living in Rio de Janeiro.[1] It is not clear when or how Elizabeth Bishop first learned about Oswaldino Marques. What is certain is that it occurred sometime before 1968, the date of his *Ensaios Escolhidos*, a collection of essays that includes a piece on Bishop.

It is also not clear just when Bishop read Oswaldino Marques's critical study, *O Laboratório Poético de Cassiano Ricardo*, though that she was familiar with the book is clearly established by his reference in the second edition of the work, published in 1978, to Elizabeth Bishop and her help. Her name — the only non–Brazilian one — appeared in a list of those who recognized his work for the pioneering study that it is.[2]

Published in 1976 by Civilização Brasileira in Rio de Janeiro, Oswaldino Marques's study has as its subject the 20th-century poet whose major work, *Martim Cererê* (1928), was represented in Bishop's library by a copy of the 11th edition of the work. That volume of Ricardo's famous poem is inscribed to the American poet on the half-title page: "To Elizabeth Bishop — with respect and admiration, Cassiano Ricardo 1962" ("*A Elizabeth Bishop — com respeito e admiração, Cassiano Ricardo 1962"*). On the same page, at the bottom, Bishop has added, in pencil: "(bought at the Book Fair, M of A M, July 24th, 1962)."[3] Two of Ricardo's poems — "O Canto da Juriti" ("The Song of the Wild Dove") and "Anoitecer" (Nightfall) — are included in *An Anthology of Twentieth-Century Brazilian Poetry*, the collection Bishop coedited with Emanuel Brasil in 1972, but neither poem is translated by Bishop.[4] The biographical note for Ricardo in the anthology includes the information that "his poem *Martim Cererê*, an epic vision of Brazilian history and a search for a national mythology, is considered by many to be a classic of modern Brazilian poetry."[5]

Oswaldino Marques's name does not appear in Candace MacMahon's bibliography of Elizabeth Bishop, not as critic or translator. Appearing shortly after the poet's death, the bibliography does list two translations into Portuguese of Bishop poems published during the poet's lifetime — "The Burglar of Babylon" ("O Ladrão da Babilônia") in *Cadernos brasileiros*, 6 (Nov.–Dec. 1964), pages 61–67, and "Under the Window: Ouro Prêto" ("Debaixo da Janela: Ouro Prêto") in *Visão* 35 (Aug. 1, 1969), page 51.[6] To those may be added translations, also from the 1960s, of "A Miracle for Breakfast" ("Um Milagre Como Café da Manhã") and "The Man-moth" ("O Homem 'Bruxa'") by Oswaldino Marques, along with a slightly reworked version of Marques's translation of "A Miracle for Breakfast" done by Bishop with the aid, undoubtedly, of Lota, since Bishop, given her inadequate Portuguese, was not capable of the subtle changes Marques's translation suggested. The intention of the suggestions was to restore an end-rhyme scheme — proper to a sestina — that Bishop follows in the original.[7] "Translators are very strange," often failing to pay attention to details, she confided to Howard Moss, her editor at the *New Yorker*. "The prize example was a man here who translated a sestina of mine, infinite labor, *without repeating a word*. (They're taught not to, in school — not for two pages, or hours, or something.) And yet [I have] come to find out he knew all about sestinas and could recite some old Portuguese ones —"[8] As Oswaldino Marques admitted, he had not noticed that Bishop's poem was a sestina.

14

The Brazil Book

"My one news item," Elizabeth Bishop reported to Robert Lowell on June 25, 1961, "is that I have taken on a job that maybe I shouldn't have, but anyway — writing a small book about Brazil for *Life*'s series in The World Library." Persuading herself that she knew what the editors at *Life* wanted from her — the book would be made up of "mostly pictures, the ones I've seen — superb photographs, of course, and a superficial text of 35,000 words or so, a little of everything — but not *too* LIFE-y" — she had accepted the munificent offer of $10,000. After all, she had "plenty of material, and I think Lota and I can have quite a lot of fun using up our favorite jokes, putting in our favorite people, etc." Her idea was "to do it *fast*, and just accept it as pot-boiling and a sort of penance for my years of idleness. (No one will ever read the text anyway, probably!)"[1] The book would not be the book about Brazil that Bishop longed to write. Years earlier, in 1956, she was talking about her plans for such a book. "I think maybe I'll stick to *Black Beans and Diamonds* [as a title for the *Diary*]. At least I'll see what the publishers think."[2]

Unfortunately, the project did not turn out satisfactorily — at least not from her point of view. The editors made too many changes in her wording, inserted their own material, and made what she considered to be indefensible cuts. That Bishop could tolerate editorial suggestions and changes even to her poems is clear from her published correspondence with her editors at the *New Yorker*. But copyediting by the *Life* editors she considered outrageous and certainly insulting to her intelligence and skill as a writer of American prose. She promptly disowned the book on its appearance in 1963, and when *Life* invited her to help update the text for a second edition, she turned down the offer. She had other plans. She was thinking of a very different sort of book "about the country — memoirs, places, churches, popular music, and one or two life stories."[3] Unfortunately, although she continued to mull over its contents for years, *Black Beans and Diamonds* — her working title — never materialized.

Although Bishop did not originally intend *Black Beans and Diamonds* to be such, certainly not when she first thought of the idea in the 1950s, after the publication of *Brazil* it would have served her as a more personal account of her Brazilian experience, something, of course, that was inappropriate to the text issued by Time Incorporated in 1962. Ultimately, her "own" book" could also have served, one imagines, as a corrective to the skewered account, as she complained in letters to friends, that the *Life* editors produced. So disappointed at the editorial changes in her submitted text was she, that Bishop complained bitterly that the book was not "hers." Not only did she disavow any major responsibility for the published book, she tried hard to dissuade friends and acquaintances from buying it or even reading it. Those "gift copies I have to hand out here," she wrote, "I am correcting, in green ink — a futile job, but I can't stop doing it."[4] However, since she did not usually quote chapter and verse to back up her assertions — an exception is when she writes, "they have messed up what I said about it [Brasília] pretty much, in that book, but the general idea is still there"[5] — that the *Life* editors had virtually ruined her book, rendering it valueless as a book about Brazil, her word about the finished product has been accepted at face value. Fortunately, however, her copy of *Brazil* (containing her signature "E. Bishop"), line-scored and annotated, survives among her books and papers at the Houghton Library, Harvard University.

It is both surprising and enlightening to peruse its pages. Not all of the markings are Bishop's — hers are in green ink, as she indicated; others — in pencil — are, in all likelihood, attributable to Lota de Macedo Soares. There are annotations challenging or contradicting assertions interpolated into Bishop's text by her editors at Time Life. Other annotations constitute objections to stylistic and tonal changes. Others, especially line scorings alongside the text, made without commentary, also register objections — unspecified and unexplained — but undoubtedly clearly enough indicated to convey meaning from Bishop to Lota and vice versa. There are sentences and passages crossed out. There are substitutions of a word or a phrase. And finally, indicating, as I see it, that she sometimes thought about the possibility of preparing a "correct" edition of the book, she sprinkles the text with the simple imperative: "Cut." All this suggests to me that at some point Bishop actually had made some commitment to claiming the book as hers in (possibly) a revised second edition. As it turned out, however, she seems not to have been involved in any way with the edition of the book published in 1967.[6]

Making good use of the occasion of the Elizabeth Bishop centenary, her publishers brought out new, enlarged volumes of her poetry and her prose. Edited by Lloyd Schwartz, *Prose* runs to more than 500 pages and includes stories, memoirs, essays, reviews, blurbs, tributes — even a handful of letters. One of its most striking features is that it prints for the first time the surviving portions of Bishop's manuscript for *Brazil*. Because the manuscript, though substantial, is incomplete, the editor of *Prose* has rounded out his text with material from the published book, altered in accordance with the markings for corrections and changes made by Bishop in her copy of *Brazil* now at Harvard University. It is acknowledged that changes have been made in the text but they are not, in individual cases, identified as such. Notably, however, it is not noted that not all the markings for changes are by Elizabeth Bishop. Some of them are by Lota de Macedo Soares — Bishop's are made in green, Lota's in pencil. The result is that some of the changes incorporated in the text published in *Prose* are not by Bishop at all. It is also the case that some passages are marked with a cross, but appear in the "new" text in *Prose*.

A comparison of the "new" *Brazil* text with the 1962 text published in *Life*'s "World Library" series makes it obvious to me that Bishop's marked copy at Harvard was intended in all probability for a second edition of the book, for she did not try to restore her original manuscript. Why she turned down the Time people's invitation to collaborate in the preparation of a second edition of *Brazil* I cannot answer beyond the probability that she would only be letting herself in for more meddling on their part and that was something she did not want to go through again. Besides, it was difficult to take credit for *Brazil* as a book of her own. One need look only at the large and small print of the book's title, copyright, and contents pages. The title page credits *Brazil* to multiple authors — "Elizabeth Bishop and The Editors of *Life*" — while the copyright page asserts that "Elizabeth Bishop [is] the author of the interpretive text for this volume of the *Life* World Library," information repeated on the verso of the "Contents" page, with the statement "The text for the chapters of this book was written by Elizabeth Bishop, and the picture essays were written by Walter Karp." But in her copy of *Brazil* Bishop, after her name, inserts the phrase "more or less."

Manuscript Changes in Bishop's Copy of *Brazil*

The author of each manuscript change or suggestion in the text is identified as either (B) for Bishop or (L) for Lota de Macedo Soares.

On the "Contents" page Bishop writes: "I am not responsible for chapter headings or captions — although I tried to correct captions." Throughout, she crosses out most of her editors' chapter titles and restores her own:

Chapter 1: "A Warm and Reasonable People" (B: no alternative given)
Chapter 2: "Undeveloped Land of Legend" (B: "The Land of Dye-Wood")
Chapter 3: "Century of Honor and Pride" (B: "The Only Western Empire")
Chapter 4: "Shifting Centers for Government" (B: "Three Capitals")
Chapter 5: "The Slow Awakening of a Giant" (B: "Animal, Vegetable and Mineral")
Chapter 6: "Graceful and Popular Skills" (B: "The Unselfconscious Arts")
Chapter 7: "A Merited Respect for the Arts" (B: "The Selfconscious Arts")
Chapter 8: "A Changing Social Scene" (B: "Groups & Individuals")
Chapter 9: "Struggle for a Stable Democracy" (B: no cross-out, no alternative title)
Chapter 10: "A Nation Perplexed and Uncertain" (B: no cross-out, no alternative title)

Chapter 1

(Page 9) Under a picture of visitors to Brasilia, (B) adds "Day of the open[n]ing."

(Page 11) (B) places a question mark to the side of the sentence: "During the three days when Conceiçãozinha was hidden in the washerwoman's shack, and survived, it is a safe guess that more than 60 babies died in Rio."

(Page 11) In the sentence "Most of this tragic waste of life is due to malnutrition, which weakens a person's resistance to disease" (B) brackets the clause "which weakens a person's resistance to disease" and adds an exclamation point in the margin to the left of the text.

(Page 11) In the phrase "there are many good free clinics" (B) replaces the word "good" with "worthy."

(Page 11) In the sentence "life expectancy has gone up considerably in the last few decades" (B) brackets the words "has gone up considerably in the last few decades" and adds a question mark in the margin.

(Page 11) In the sentence "Cut it back to a stump above ground, and in a matter of days it sends up a new shoot and starts unfolding new green leaves" (L) comments in the margin: "[hours]."

(Page 11) In the phrase "a widespread lack of refrigeration" (L) brackets the words "a widespread."

(Page 11) To the phrase "combined with bursts of energy" (B) inserts the words "asceticism &" before "bursts of energy."

(Page 12) (B) changes the sentence "Brazil is very big and very diverse" to read "Brazil is very diverse."

(Page 12) (L) line-scores the sentence "In fact the Portuguese regard Brazilian Portuguese as 'effeminate'—charming when women speak it, but no language for men." And (B) adds "(Cut)."

(Page 12) (B) cuts out the words "or a sufficient degree of prosperity" in the sentence conveying the information that men are addressed "by 'Doutor' if they have a university degree or a sufficient degree of prosperity."

(Page 12) In the sentence beginning "Even today one occasionally sees an elegant lady out walking" (B) inserts the word "old" between the words "elegant" and "lady."

(Page 13) (L) line-scores two separate sentences without comment: "In fact, in the spirit of mollification the courts more than two decades ago ruled that henceforth no one could be legally termed illegitimate" and "That is the perfect statement of the Brazilian belief in tolerance and forebearance: everyone should be allowed to descend from the *bonde* in his or her own way." To a statement "that a speaker of Spanish would not understand Portuguese if he were hearing it for the first time" (L) crosses out "if he were hearing it for the first time" and adds an exclamation point in the margin.

(Page 14) In the sentence "Values are simple and realistic in Brazil" (B) crosses out the words "simple and."

(Page 14) (L) places a question mark next to the sentence "Outside of fashionable circles, the poor are thin and the rich are fat, and fat is a sign of beauty, as it has been since the ancients."

(Page 14) (B) marks "(Cut)" next to the sentence "Yet if anyone asks naively, 'But why not have lunch at one o'clock every day?' she will reply, 'Oh, well — this isn't a factory.'"

(Page 15) (B) marks "cut" next to the sentence "Perhaps because Brazilians are usually as indifferent to cooking as they are to physical comfort, the food is very bad," underscores the clause "the food is very bad" and places a question mark in the margin next to this clause.

(Page 15) (B) line-scores and writes "cut" against the sentence "There is a popular notion that famous beauties should have a drop or two of such [Negro] blood in their veins: it is supposed to make them more vivacious," and places a question mark in the margin against the next sentence: "Since everyone also wants to be as *claro*, or white, as possible, this is another of those contradictions that seem to bother no one."

(Page 15) (B) places the word "mercurial" within parentheses and writes "cut" in the margin against the clause "Brazilians are mercurial."

(Page 15) (B) writes "(Cut)" next to the sentence "A man's speeches, his moral and physical courage, are admired, but actual violence is going too far."

(Page 20) (B) In a photo caption (B) crosses out the word "Colonial" in the sentence "Colonial Houses lining a hillside street in Bahia were built in the days when the sugar-exporting city was a thriving center of wealth, learning and political power."

Chapter 2

(Page 25) (B) places an "x" in the margin and crosses out the words "a skirt" in the sentence "In one of the parks of Rio stands a fine, flamboyant example of Latin American park sculpture, a much-bigger-than-life-size man dressed in a costume-pageant outfit with wide fur-trimmed sleeves and a skirt, holding onto a ton or so of undulated bronze banner."

(Page 26) (B) places an "x" in the margin and circles the word "hundred" in the sentence "Pedro Alvares Cabral was supposedly on his way directly to India in command of a fleet of 13 ships; if so, he was off his course by several hundred miles."

(Page 26) (B) crosses out the phrase "the history of Brazil" and writes "Brazilian history" in the margin.

(Page 27) (B) changes "the red caps" to "a red cap."

(Page 28) (B) line-scores with an upward arrow the sentences "Early Brazilian history abounds in fascinating personalities: condemned convicts, devout Jesuit missionaries (St. Ignatius Loyola's order was founded in 1540) and Portuguese noblemen, often younger sons, who became the 'great captains' appointed by the crown and given almost kingly powers. But this oddly assorted crew had found no gold." (B) also crosses out the phrase "in fascinating personalities."

(Page 28) (B) places an "x" next to the sentence "Everyone today seems to know at least two facts about this half-a-continent that became Brazil: it is bigger than the United States was before Alaska became a state, and the seasons there are the reverse of those in the northern hemisphere" and crosses out the words "today seems to."

(Page 28) (B) line-scores the sentences "In the cooler regions to the south, frosts rarely occur. Altogether, the seasons are a bit lacking in variety."

(Page 28) (B) replaces the word "still" with "often" in the sentence "the warm climate is still blamed by Brazilians for the country's lack of development and for almost everything else wrong with it," and line-scores the next two sentences: "It is held responsible for the 'laziness' they regard as their greatest defect (although on occasion laziness is considered an attractive failing too). But what Brazilians call laziness may well be due more to bad health, poor food and boredom than to climate." She also crosses out the word "Brazilians" in the latter sentence.

(Page 29) (B) places an "x" in the margin beside the sentence "Another big geographical handicap is that although there are great and navigable rivers, they have never served to open up the country or help its economy to any great extent," and crosses out the words "any great extent."

(Page 29) In the sentence beginning "From the palm trees alone come oils and waxes" (B) crosses out the word "alone" and places a question mark in the margin.

(Page 29) In the sentence beginning "There is not much coal or oil," (B) inserts the words "& probably not much" after the word "coal."

(Page 29) (L) line-scores the sentences "But all this treasure was hidden from the 16th Century explorers and merchants — hidden in the future as well as underground. They kept on risking ships and lives rounding the Cape of Good Hope for spices from the East. From Brazil came only wood and curiosities: dyewood, animals, birds, skins and a few Indians." And (B) moves the word "dyewood" as a replacement for "wood."

(Pages 29–30) (B) rearranges the words in the sentence "The Indians did not make good slaves; accustomed to life in the forests, they simply gave up and died when set to work in the fields" to read (adding the phrase "in the hot sun"): "The Indians did not make good slaves, accustomed to life in the forest, when set to work in the fields in the hot sun, they simply gave up and died."

(Page 30) (B) crosses out the word "diminished" in the sentence "Undoubtedly, the missionaries did save thousands of them from slavery or slaughter, but the Indians died off anyway, from smallpox, measles and inanition, and their primitive but unique culture and their skills and art diminished with them, or blended gradually into the culture of the Portuguese and the Negro slaves."

(Page 30) In the sentence "After almost a century of rumors and occasional lucky finds, gold was discovered in good quantity in what is now the state of Minas Gerais (General Mines) in 1698" (B) crosses out the word "gold."

(Page 30) In the sentence beginning "They [the famous *bandeirantes*] came from around São Paulo, most of them descendants of the Portuguese and Indian girls" (B) crosses out the words "most of them."

(Pages 30–31) In the sentence "They discovered the more glamorous items of Brazil's mineral wealth — diamonds and semiprecious stones as well as gold — and, incidentally, made the young country conscious of its unprecedented size and its forbidding geography" (B) crosses out the word "young," placing a question mark in the margin above it.

(Page 31) (B) places a question mark in the margin next to the sentence "Most particularly they [the *Inconfidência Mineira*] were excited by the recent successful American Revolution, which became their inspiration."

(Page 31) (L) places a question mark in the margin next to the sentence "The young envoy who talked with him died on the way back to Brazil, but the conspiracy in Minas, perhaps acting under false expectations of American help, went ahead, and grew overbold."

(Page 32) In the caption "Leading a massive ox team that pulls a small cart, a boy treads through a village in Minas Gerais" (B) replaces "a village in" with "Congonhas."

(Page 32) (B) places an "x" against the caption "Floating on the Rio Negro, the raft-houses lining the city of Manaus are safe against the seasonal floods. Some of the inhabitants ply the river as petty tradesmen," and crosses out the word "lining."

(Page 32) In the sentence "Men have been here for centuries, clearing the forests and planting crops" (B) underlines "clearing the forests" and places an exclamation point in the margin below the words.

(Page 32) In the sentence "Where the rainfall is heavy, the Amazon forest rises, inhuman and repellent, an appendage of wilderness occupying almost half the area of Brazil" (B) crosses out the word "appendage" and adds an exclamation point in the margin.

(Page 37) (B) places a question mark against the caption line "In a hammock, a device invented by South American Indians."

Chapter 3

(Page 42) (B) places a question mark against the sentence "Meanwhile, Pedro, the nine-year-old heir apparent, discoursed learnedly on Virgil's Aeneid with his tutors, supposedly comparing his father's plight to that of Aeneas," and in the next sentence underlines the name "Octavio Tarquinio de Sousa."

(Page 43) (B) places an "x" in the margin against the sentence "In 1814, with Napoleon defeated, Portugal was rid of the threat from France, and in 1816 Dom João invited a French mission of architects, musicians, painters and sculptors to visit Brazil."

(Page 43) (B) places an "x" against the sentence "His departure was the first of several Brazilian abdications or 'renunciations' of power, which are often discussed in terms of João VI's unhappy career. Not all the abdicators have filled their pockets as liberally as he did…"

(Page 43) In the sentences "Dom Pedro had been badly brought up. He had led the luxurious but slovenly life of the small upper class of Brazilians of his day; he had been friendly with slaves and stableboys, and from his teens his love affairs were notorious. A fascinating character, he was a brilliant, energetic, spoiled and dissipated neurotic. He suffered from occasional epileptic fits. He was fundamentally kindhearted, generous toward his mistresses and devoted to his children, legitimate and illegitimate alike" (B) crosses out the words "small," "of," "a" and "toward." (L) Underlines the word "teen." (B) places a question mark in the margin to the right of the paragraph.

(Page 43) In the sentence beginning "He conceded the crown to his daughter, Maria da Glória" (L) underlines the word "daughter."

(Page 44) (L) places a question mark in the margin against the sentence "Dom Pedro I had been a high-minded ruler, very much superior to João VI, and well intentioned. Ruling Brazil had been beyond his powers. And the Ruler that Dom Pedro left behind him was only five years old." (B) places parentheses around the words "well intentioned" and writes "(cut)" in the margin next to the paragraph.

(Page 44) (L) places a question mark in the margin next to the second half of the sentence "Dom Pedro II was not a genius, but he was a remarkable man for a member of the Braganza line, and in most respects he was much in advance of his countrymen."

(Page 44) (L) line-scores the lines "freedom of speech and of the press. There was taxation according to wealth."

(Page 44) (B) line-scores and places an "x" in the margin against the words "[Dom Pedro] had corresponded with John Greenleaf Whittier, one of whose poems he translated into Portuguese. It was called 'The Cry of a Lost Soul.'"

(Page 45) Against the sentences "The eagerly grasped-at foreign influences, the attempt to adopt the inappropriate and the neglect or ignorance of resources at home — the old photograph suggests all of these. Dom Pedro was the owner, so to speak, of a waterfall even higher than Niagara and almost as spectacular, but few people in Brazil paid very much attention to it. Nevertheless, it was during Dom Pedro's long reign that Brazil's material expansion really began" (B) placed two separate "x's" in the margin, changed the phrase "a waterfall even higher than Niagara and almost as spectacular, but few people in Brazil paid very much attention to it" to read "a waterfall higher than Niagara and more spectacular." (B) also crosses out the word "nevertheless" and places both an exclamation point and a question mark next to it.

(Page 45) (B) line-scores the paragraph beginning "Dom Pedro created many titles, principally baronies. Most of the new barons were landed proprietors who had grown rich on sugar or coffee — for by this time coffee was the leading crop and Brazil was supplying the world. One exception was Ireneo Evangelista de Sousa, the Baron Mauá, later Viscount Mauá, who was the J. P. Morgan of Brazil," adds the injunction "(cut)" in the margin, and adds what seems to be a note: "Indian names — all except one[.]"

(Page 45) In the sentences "There had been two foreign wars, the first undertaken in 1851–1852 partly to get rid of the brutal Rosas regime in Argentina. The second was Brazil's one real war, fought against Paraguay. It lasted from 1865 to 1870 and is still regarded by Brazilians with a mixture of pride and shame," (B) circles the word "shame" and places a question mark in the margin.

(Page 45) In the sentence beginning "But even though Argentina and Uruguay had been Brazil's allies during the conflict," (B) crosses out the words "even though."

(Page 45) In the sentence beginning "The Emperor loathed slavery, believing it to be a shameful blot on his beautiful, beloved country," (B) underlines the word "blot."

(Page 46) Against the sentences "In 1887 Dom Pedro again went to Europe, leaving Princess Isabel as regent. He was exhausted and diabetic and looked far older than his age" (B) places an "x" in the margin.

(Page 46) In the margin next to the sentences "The day was May 13, 1888. There was a week of celebration" (B) writes "followed by."

(Page 46) Against the sentence "There was also widespread suspicion of Isabel's husband, the French Count d'Eu" (B) places both an "x" and a question mark.

(Page 46) (L) line-scores the sentences "In many ways Dom Pedro failed to accomplish much. Brazil was still almost empty, almost completely illiterate and divided between the few very rich and the many miserably poor" and adds a check mark to the line-scoring.

(Page 46) (L) places a question mark in the margin next to the sentences "In spite of the Emperor's respect for education no universities had been founded. Enrollments in schools of higher education were small and the teaching was inferior." (B) underlines the word "universities" and changes it to "university."

(Page 46) In the clause "but if there were more monarchs like him, world history would make more edifying reading," (B) circles the word "world."

(Page 47) In the caption reading "a trio of patricians," (B) underlines the word "patricians."

Chapter 4

(Page 54) (B) places an "x" in the margin next to a sentence containing the words "necklaces and sometimes, at the waist, a *balangandā*, a jangling collection of silver charms on a silver loop."

(Page 55) (B) places both a question mark and an "x" in the margin next to the sentence "Because it was so far south of Europe the settlement called itself, ambitiously, 'Antarctic France,' and its leader was Nicolas Durand de Villegaignon, a religious tyrant who dreamed of founding a Utopia there." (B) also crosses out the words "of Europe" and "tyrant," replacing the latter with the word "fanatic" and adding another question mark in the margin.

(Page 55) In the sentence "Between 1930 and 1960, the outlying section of Copacabana grew from little more than a suburb, with a half-deserted beach, to the currently overpopulated 'south zone' with its 10-story-high apartment houses," (B) crosses out the words "little more than" and circles the word "suburb." In the margin (B) adds "distant?"—a word that is to be inserted, perhaps, before the word "suburb."

(Page 55) In the sentence "The 100-foot-tall figure of Christ the Redeemer by French Sculptor Paul Landowski was placed on top of the Corcovado in 1931 to commemorate the first century of Brazilian political independence" (B) circles "1931" and places a question mark in the margin.

(Page 55) In the sentence "Now, however, modern sanitation has changed that, and enormous suburbs have spread out to the north and northwest" (B) inserts the word "working-class" between "enormous" and "suburbs."

(Page 56) (B) crosses out the word "groups" in the sentence "... it is only during the last 20 years or so that these hills have become covered with the groups of shacks called *favelas*, most of which are inhabited by immigrants from the northeast of Brazil. It is roughly estimated that 700,000 of Rio's 3.3 million inhabitants now live in these slums, thereby creating the worst of the city's many problems." Next to the sentence beginning: "It is roughly estimated that 700,000 of Rio's 3.3 million" (B) writes "over a million)."

(Page 56) In the sentence "Nevertheless, as soon as a housing project draws a thousand or so *favela* dwellers to better quarters, the same number of immigrants from the northeast mysteriously appears, ready to move into the vacated shacks" (B) crosses out the word "draws," lines-scores the sentence and places an "x" next to it.

(Page 56) In the margin (B) characterizes as "'induction'" the entire paragraph, seemingly, that follows: "For there is no denying the attractions which city life, even at its worst, holds for these people. In the small towns or villages of the interior there is the same poverty, plus boredom and isolation. In the city there are the bright lights, radio and television (it is surprising how many antennas appear above the *favela* shacks), *futebol* (soccer football), the lotteries, the constant excitement and the sense of participation — even if only on the lowest level — in the life of a great city. All this offsets the misery and filth, the standing in line for water and the frequent visits of the police." (B) also crosses out the words "For there is no denying" and changes "attractions" to "attraction."

(Page 56) In the sentence beginning "Old buildings and even hills are continually being removed to make way for new structures and new developments, and although the limits of the colonial town are still indicated by the oldest churches..." (B) crosses out the word "limits," adding a question mark in the margin below.

(Page 56) (B) crosses out the words "going on" in the sentence "A couple returning one night to their eighth-floor apartment on the Morro da Viuva (Widow's Hill) heard a terrific bumping and crashing going on inside and naturally thought, 'Burglars!'"

(Page 56) In the sentence "On a more mundane level, a central capital would offer better living conditions and fewer distractions for government workers, and it would help to develop those great empty spaces that have haunted Brazil for so long" (B) adds the word "supposedly, between the words "would" and "offer" and changes the phrase "haunted Brazil for so long" to "haunted the Brazilian."

(Page 57) (B) changes the sentence "Bonifácio may even be responsible for the name 'Brasilia'" to "Bonifácio may have been [word illegible] for the name."

(Page 57) (B) places an "x" next to the sentence "The first constitution under the Republic, in 1891, specified the marking out of a quadrilateral on the central plateau of Brazil where the future Federal District was to be situated."

(Page 57) In the sentence "When President Juscelino Kubitschek came into office in 1956, he wanted to distinguish his term by a never-to-be-forgotten public work" (B) changed the word "wanted" to "was determined."

(Page 57) The sentence "One of his first acts as president was to announce that the capital long dreamed of was to be built at last..." (B) changes to read: "One of his first acts as president was to announce that the dreamed of capital was to be built at last..."

(Page 57) In the sentence "As a site for the capital, the government decided on a bleak, almost barren plain where Brasília is now" (B) changes the second "a" to "the."

(Page 57) In the sentence "It is of course to Kubitschek's credit that he had remarkably sophisticated tastes in architecture for a head of state" (B) removes the words "remarkably" and "for a head of state."

(Page 57) (B) changes the beginning of the sentence "The world-famous Brazilian architect Oscar Niemeyer had for many years been a close friend of his and had previously designed buildings for him..." to read: "The world-famous Brazilian architect Oscar Niemeyer was a close friend and had previously designed buildings for him..."

(Page 57) The beginning of the sentence "The site plan, giving the city the shape of an airplane or bird..." is altered by (B) to read: "The city plan, that gives the city the shape of an airplane or bird..."

(Page 57) (B) changes the two sentences "There was no railroad to the site and only dirt roads. The Brazilian economy was already in a bad way, but Kubitschek embarked on his monumental plan anyway, and construction was begun" to read "The Brazilian economy was already in a bad way, but Kubitschek embarked on his monumental plan anyway, and construction was begun. There was no railroad to the site and only roads." (B) also questions the word "site," crossing it out as well as the word "dirt."

(Page 57) In the sentence "A sprawling, ramshackle shantytown, the 'Free City' for immigrant workers, grew up near the site," (B) crosses out the word "site."

(Page 57) (B) writes "5%" in the margin next to the sentence "the legislators and members of some executive ministries are now required by law to live there, at least part time, but Brasília is still only partly finished."

(Pages 57–58) In the margin next to the sentence "To date it has cost the Brazilian people more than 600 million dollars, magnifying the country's economic emergency" (B) writes "3 billion."

(Page 58) (L) writes "good" in the margin next to the sentence "The results of all this expenditure and of three years of round-the-clock work are controversial, to say the least." The phrase "to say the least" is underlined by (B).

(Page 58) (B) inserts the word "already" between the words "have" and "been" in the sentence "Some of the government buildings are too small and annexes have been added, or will have to be."

(Page 58) (L) writes "good" in the margin next to the two "x's" placed there by (B) alongside the sentences "Entirely dependent on electric power for its elevators and on gasoline for its cars, it is a city built for the automobile, where almost nothing can be reached on foot."

(Page 58) (B) crosses out the word "some," adding below it the words "consider it to be — etc.—," in the sentence ending: "...Brasília has been called an 'old-fashioned' city, and is considered at least 35 years behind the times by some contemporary city-planners."

(Page 58) In the sentence "The isolated city is a difficult place to govern from, and legislators so dislike going there that it has often been difficult to achieve a quorum in the chamber" (B) changes the word "difficult" to "impossible."

(Page 58) Beside the sentences "Senators and Deputies fight for places on the planes leaving each weekend for Rio or São Paulo. The course of justice in the federal courts has slowed almost to a standstill, and government business has also slowed down woefully," which (B) has line-scored, (L) writes "good."

(Page 58) (B) crosses out the words "felt" (twice) and "some people feel, such men," writes "cut" (twice) in the margin and places an "x" beside the paragraph "Another disadvantage to Brasília that will be felt for a long time is in the caliber of the men it is drawing to politics. Formerly these were men who felt the attractions of Rio as a place to educate their children, to be in touch with what was going on culturally, to escape from the provincialism of the more remote part of the country. But now, some people feel, such men will not be attracted to Brasília."

(Page 59) (B) crosses out the rubric "A Frontier Capital's Jet-Age Splendors."

(Page 59) In the sentence "For centuries the beckoning hinterlands have been entered many times and hopefully settled many times" (B) underlines the word "beckoning," places an exclamation point next to it and crosses out the words "hopefully settled many times."

(Page 59) In the sentence "In this long story Brasília is the latest chapter, another hopeful plunge into the interior, only more colossal and more splendid than any that went before" (B) underlines the words "more colossal" and places an exclamation point next to them.

(Page 60) In the caption "Hand laborer cleans the broad marble roof of a new building in Brasília" (B) crosses out the word "cleans" and replaces it with "cements" and places an "x" next to the line.

(Page 60) (B) places an "x" next to the caption "Soaring slabs rising 25 stories above the plain (*opposite*) provide a target for tropical lightning. The two connected towers house the offices for the congressmen."

(Page 65) (B) crosses out the word "conical" in the caption reading "Conical cathedral, 108 feet high and 197 feet in diameter, has a spidery frame of concrete slanting beams. In the completed structure the beams support glass walls."

(Page 65) (B) writes the word "small" (underlined) beside the caption reading "Stately image of blindfolded justice (*below*) sits proudly on a stone pedestal in Brasília's Plaza of the Three Powers, the windswept center of the spacious city."

Chapter 5

(Page 69) (B) places an "x" beside the caption reading "Tropical produce is carried to Manaus from tiny outposts along the Rio Negro. The river highways of the Amazon area carry only a small volume of commerce."

(Page 69) (B) crosses out the entire first paragraph, which reads "In the Brazilian national anthem there are lines which Brazilians have for years found amusing. Speak of the giant land 'eternally lying in a splendid cradle.' The lines were true until a very short time ago. But now there are obvious signs that slowly, in spite of great problems and a thousand difficulties, the giant is at last waking up."

(Pages 69–70) "They have a national penchant for skimming off quick profits instead of laying the foundation for solid future earnings. The economic history of Brazil could almost be told in its long succession of spectacular booms. Brazil's economy was dominated by sugar, gold and coffee in succession, with brief interludes devoted to other products." In these sentences (B) underlines the words "skimming off" and "laying the foundation," and in the margin places an "x," an exclamation point, and the word "rubber."

(Page 70) "One of Brazil's earliest occupations was cattle raising, and it was necessarily an imported one. The Portuguese discoverers had been surprised to find that the Indians had no domestic animals, or at least no useful domestic animals. The Indians did keep many pets, referred to by the Portuguese as *bichos de estimação*: dogs, monkeys and birds." Here, in the margin, (B) begins by writing at the outset "beginning=" and, toward the end, places an "x." The phrase "referred to by the Portuguese as *bichos de estimação*" is placed within parentheses and the words "had only" are written in the margin.

(Page 70) (B) circles the word "hence," which starts a new paragraph following the sentences quoted above.

(Page 70) (B) writes "culture" just above the word "civilization" in the sentence "From it came the so-called 'leather civilization' that developed in this whole vast region of Brazil during the first centuries of the country's history."

(Page 70) (B) crosses out the words "which is" in the sentence "At the turn of the 20th Century, zebus were imported into the huge section of fine cattleland in Minas Gerais which is called the 'Minas Triangle,' and which is now the center of the cattle industry."

(Page 70) (B) line-scores the sentence "In the 1920s the fever reached such a pitch that a single good bull brought as much as $7,500, compared to an average price of $250 for bulls of European breed."

(Page 70) (B) In the sentence "Outside the beef-raising Triangle, the cattle of Minas Gerais are dairy cattle, and the products, including the white Minas cheese seen on almost every table at least once a day, are sold everywhere" the words "seen on almost every table at least once a day" are enclosed within parentheses and the phrase "no longer" is written in the margin.

(Page 71) (B) places an "x" in the margin and crosses out the sentences "The buffalo present some small problems on occasion, though. Buffalo like to lean on things and meditate. Sometimes they lean on their owners' frail mud-and-wattle houses, which collapse under them."

(Page 71) (B) line-scores the sentence beginning: "With 72.8 million head, Brazil is second only to the U.S. in number of beef cattle, but not in beef production..."

(Page 71) (L) writes "good" in the margin next to the sentence — which (B) has line-scored — "But commercial exploitation has just begun, and fish still represent one of the greatest undeveloped resources of the country."

(Page 71) (B) places an "x" in the margin next to the sentence "In the states of Pará and Amazonas there is, for example, the *pirarucu*, the 'fresh-water codfish,' weighing up to 500 pounds."

(Page 71) (B) inserts the word "only" between the words "item" and "in," and in the margin places an "x" and writes the word "(cut)" in the sentence "The *pirarucu* is an important item in the diet of the river people."

(Page 71) (B) changes the "One large" to "A," underlines the word "abundant," and places an "x" in the margin next to the same word in the sentence: "One large whale-processing plant has been built at Cabo Frio, a coast town east of Rio. Whales are abundant, and whale meat is being urged on a somewhat reluctant public in the coast markets as the cheapest form of meat."

(Page 72) (L) writes "finally[?]" in the margin next to the sentence "At present the coffee trees are penetrating into the state of Mato Grosso."

(Page 72) (B) crosses out the word "today" in the sentence "The coffee problem has also stimulated the growth of industrialization, chiefly in São Paulo, today Brazil's most prosperous state."

(Page 72) (B) rearranges the words in the sentence "It was a quiet town of 25,000 people only 80 years ago" to read "Only 80 years ago it was a quiet town of 25,000 people."

(Page 72) (B) underlines the words "although" and "white, modern" and places an "x" and a question mark in the margin next to the clause "it has a bustling, cosmopolitan atmosphere, although with its white, modern skyscrapers and many parks it remains intensely Brazilian."

(Page 74) (L) writes *Uisque do Norte* in the margin next to the sentences "One product of the sugar cane is *aguardente*, generally called *cachaça* or *pinga*. A clear, fiery, powerful drink made since colonial times, it is known as 'the brandy of the poor.' *Cachaça* is now being exported."

(Page 74) (B) line-scores the sentence "But Brazil today imports some $49 million worth of Asian rubber each year."

(Page 74) (B) circles and crosses out the word "beautiful" in the sentence "They are beautiful, very tall trees with straight trunks and arched, bare branches terminating in characteristic cup-shaped bunches of needles."

(Page 74) (B) places an "x" in the margin, along with the word "was," next to the sentence "It is used in the manufacture of phonograph records, polishes and varnishes."

(Pages 74–75) (B) writes in the margin the words "there *is* rain" as a corrective to the assertion in the sentence "The carnauba is one of the principal economic supports of the states of Ceará, Piauí and Maranhão, and the people of the dry sertões say that is the compensation given them by God for the scourge of drought — since when the weather turns wet the palm produces no wax."

(Page 75) (B) rewrites the sentences "Tobacco is raised in most of Brazil, and has been for centuries. It was important trade merchandise for the slave dealers" to "Tobacco is raised in most of Brazil, and has been for centuries & was an important trade merchandise for the slave dealers."

(Page 75) (B) changes the sentences "The cashew fruit of the northeast is also processed in the form of syrups and pastes. And then there is the guava. Guava paste, accompanied by white cheese, is the favorite dessert all over Brazil" to read "The cashew fruit of the northeast provides the valuable cashew nut; the fruit is processed in the form of syrups and pastes. And then there is the omnipresent guava. Guava paste, accompanied by a standard cheese, is the favorite dessert all over Latin America." (B) also places a question mark next to the final sentence.

(Page 75) In the margin (B) places both a question mark and the words "*heavy* oil" next to the sentences "But so far only traces of oil have been found. Due to a fear of foreign exploitation, oil exploration and production were restricted in 1953 to a single government monopoly, Petrobrás."

(Page 75) (B) crosses out the concluding sentence "Indeed, the giant is awakening, but before he can exercise his strength he will have to take steps that Brazilians wish had been made long years ago."

(Page 76) In the caption "Coffee workers rake berries (*left*) so that they will all dry thoroughly" (B) crosses out the word "rake" and replaces it with "hoe."

(Page 76) (B) places a question mark next to the caption "Coffee trees set in trim rows on a plantation in Paraná (*opposite*) each yield about a pound of coffee yearly."

(Page 80) (B) places an "x" next to the caption "Industrial scion, Francisco ('Cicillo') Matarazzo (*opposite*) is São Paulo's leading art patron. He and his family own Latin America's largest business empire." Below the caption (B) writes "Bienal?"

Chapter 6

(Page 83) (B) places a question mark in the margin next to the opening sentences of chapter 6, "Popular arts and handicrafts are still flourishing in rural Brazil as they have not in the United States since colonial days. More sophisticated art, of course, comes from the cities. From the cities, too, come the manufactured products, good and bad, artistic or trashy, that a contemporary man buys to satisfy his esthetic cravings, instead of making things for himself as he used to do."

(Page 88) (B) places an "x" and a question mark in the margin next to the sentences "A favorite costume year after year seems vaguely patterned on the costumes worn in the time of Louis XV. Where else in the world could one see a hundred male Negroes, in blue and white and silver Louis XV costumes seeded with tiny white light bulbs, and wearing white curled wigs and plumed hats, dancing down the middle of the main street at 4 A.M.?"

(Page 89) Below the caption "Patchily dressed, Rio neighbors turn out for impromptu Carnival merrymaking. The frenzy is actually good-humored and sober" (B) writes "(from 'Orfeo')."

Chapter 7

(Page 97) (B) crosses out the first sentence of chapter 7, "Few countries show greater respect for the arts and for culture than Brazil — and in few countries is the respect more merited," as well as the words "other of the world's under-industrialized countries" in the second sentence, "For example, there is certainly more good contemporary architecture in Brazil today than in any other of the world's under-industrialized countries." (B) places an "x" in the margin next to the second sentence.

(Page 98) (B) places an "x" in the margin next to the paragraph beginning "The young architects who collaborated to produce the building [the Ministry of Education and Health in Rio de Janeiro] benefited tremendously from the help and advice given them by the French designer Le Corbusier, who was then visiting Brazil."

(Page 98) (B) places an "x" in the margin next to the sentence "The backwardness of Brazil's steel industry, for example, has long prevented the use of steel-girder construction; almost all of the highest buildings are of reinforced concrete."

(Page 99) (B) places an "x" and a question mark in the margin next to the beginning of the sentence "Amid all this misuse of the country's natural assets, a force for the good is represented by the noted landscape gardener and botanist Roberto Burle Marx."

(Page 99) (B) crosses out the words "imitation of the" and "the large formal park in the center of Paris" in the sentence "Until Burle Marx began his work, the average public or large private garden in the tropics or subtropics was an inappropriate, sun-yellowed imitation of the Tuileries, the large formal park in the center of Paris."

(Page 99) (B) "x's" out the "re" in "redevelopment" in the sentence "For Caracas in Venezuela, he is creating a public garden; he is also working on a big urban redevelopment project in Rio."

(Page 99) In the sentence "Mud-and-twig houses with their thatches of straw or grass, little stores and bars with their whitewash or pink- or blue-wash wall, and their heavy shutters and half doors — all have a highly pleasing effect" (B) circles the words "little stores and bars" and crosses out the word "with."

(Page 99) (B) line-scores and adds a check mark next to the partial sentence "and there are always rooms for guests, perhaps with the lock on the outside — for although hospitality was obligatory, it was just as well to be cautious."

(Page 100) (B) crosses out the word "overstated" in the sentence "Unlike the overstated baroque churches seen all over Spanish America, the Brazilian churches are fundamentally simple and solid, even severe, and merely overlaid with decoration."

(Page 100) (B) crosses out the words "almost as" in the sentence "Much of the art and architecture of the 17th and 18th Centuries is almost as anonymous as was that of the Middle Ages in Europe, but two master sculptors and architects, both mulattoes, are known by name."

(Page 100) (B) crosses out the word "Crude" in the sentence (about Aleijadinho's twelve prophets) "Crude, but powerful and dramatic, they gesticulate against the white church with its bright blue doors and against the sweep of bare, ore-filled hills."

(Page 101) (B) places an exclamation point next to the sentence "There is very little money available for such projects, and the average Brazilian, like his counterpart elsewhere, is indifferent to, ignorant or resentful of any interference with property" and revises the sentence to read "There is very little money available for such projects, and the average Brazilian, like his counterpart elsewhere, is indifferent to them, ignorant & resentful of any interference with property."

(Page 101) (B) crosses out the words "a remarkable reflection" in the sentence "Portinari's early pictures are a remarkable reflection of southern Brazil's coffee country."

(Page 101) Above the sentence "There are the blood-red hills, the dark green coffee trees, the Negro women carrying water-filled oil cans on their heads, the children playing *futebol*" (B) places a question mark.

(Page 101) (B) places an "x" in the margin next to the sentence "Among the best abstractionists are Aloisio Magalhães and Iberê Camargo."

(Page 102) (B) changes the word "Italianate" to "Italian" in the phrase "Italianate influences."

(Page 102) (B) crosses out the word "professionally" in the sentence: "But in spite of this fondness for the *idea* of the poet as a man of special charm and privilege, writers in Brazil, unless they are employed in some government department, have professionally an even harder time of it than they would in the United States."

(Page 102) In a sentence ending "endless discussion of the French poets Charles Baudelaire or Paul Valéry, the philosopher Saint Thomas Aquinas, the essayist G. K. Chesterton or the stories of William Faulkner" (B) crosses out the words "the French poets Charles," "Paul," "the philosopher," "the essayist," and "the stories of."

(Page 103) In the sentence "The poets of the *Inconfidência Mineira* sang of such un-Brazilian creatures as cupids and swans" (B) changes "creatures" to "fauna."

(Page 103) In the clause "The *sabiá*, a rather fat thrush, is to Brazilian poetry what the nightingale is to English verse" (B) changes the word "verse" to "poetry."

(Page 103) (B) writes the word "(cut)" in the margin next to the paragraph "Brazil's most famous abolitionist poet was Antônio de Castro Alves. Lines from his long dramatic poem entitled "'The Slave Ship' retain their significance and dignity to this day: 'Exists a people whose banner serves / To hide such infamy and cowardice! ... / My God, My God, what a flag is this?'"

(Page 104) (B) adds the words "& respectable" after the word "respected" in the sentence "He [Machado de Assis] grew famous and was highly respected and in 1897 founded the Brazilian Academy of Letters, remaining its president until his death 11 years later."

(Page 104) (B) writes "40 yrs later" in the margin next to the sentence "The other great writer, Euclides da Cunha, was the author of one of the world's strangest books, *Os Sertões*, which was published in English as *Rebellion in the Backlands*."

(Page 104) (B) substitutes "the" for "or" and crosses out the words "all of" in the sentence "Antônio Maciel, known as *Conselheiro*, or 'Counselor,' who had fortified himself and all of his followers in the little settlement of Canudos, far in the interior of the state of Bahia."

(Page 104) In the margin next to the words "(see Chapter 8)" (B) writes "(Cut)."

(Page 104) In the sentence "Brazil's veneration for the arts is due not only to the European tradition but also to the fact that upper-class Brazil is one big family" (B) crosses out the word "veneration," places a question mark in the margin, and places an "x" next to the phrase "upper-class Brazil is one big family."

(Page 104) In the clause "many of the writers and artists do come from the educated and interrelated upper class" (B) replaces "many" by "most" and crosses out the word "do."

(Page 104) In the paragraph "Although Brazilian writers and artists are spared the abrupt and cruel fluctuations of reputation that artists experience elsewhere, they probably suffer from lack of competition and serious criticism even more than from the relatively limited audience for Portuguese literature or from the deadening effects of facile journalism. A favorite way for Brazilian writers to have their pictures taken is pleasantly supine, in a fringed hammock. Too many genuine Brazilian talents seem to take to the beds too early — or to their hammocks" (B) crosses out the word "probably" and places an "x" in the margin, crosses out the word "facile" and places an "x" in the margin, and rearranges the last sentence to read "Too many genuine Brazilian talents seem to take to their beds — or to their hammocks too early."

(Page 105) In the caption "On a balcony in Rio, the late composer Heitor Villa-Lobos experiments with the sounds of a crude native percussion instrument" (B) places the word "crude" within parentheses and places an exclamation point just below the word.

(Page 105) (B) crosses out the sentence "Only in the past 50 years has their work [Brazilian artists] become truly Brazilian in spirit."

(Page 106) (B) crosses out the word "Stark" in the caption "Stark abstractions are painted by prize-winning Manabu Mabe (left), a self-taught immigrant from Japan."

Chapter 8

(Page 114) In the sentence "The old upper class — the landed gentry, the intelligentsia, the diplomatic set and a few other groups — resents the small, pushing new upper class — mainly first and second generation immigrants who have made their fortunes in business and industry" (B) underlines the word "upper," writes "middle" in the margin, and places quotation marks around the words "mainly first and second generation immigrants who have made their fortunes in business and industry."

(Page 114) (B) crosses out the words "liberal-minded South" and "North," and inserts an "x" in the margin followed by the words "person who has lived in S.A. or the N. Am. South —"

(Page 114) (B) places an "x" beside the sentence "with each new census, an increasing proportion of the total population is classified as white."

(Page 115) (B) crosses out "who had lived in Brazil and had returned" and replaces it with "Brazilian."

(Page 115) (B) crosses out the word "dominated" and places a question mark in the margin.

(Page 115) (B) writes the words "state now" in the margin besides the sentence "today there are occasional news stories of land-greedy men who cheat or murder the Indians and of sad publicity stunts involving them, but Rondon set a high standard of behavior toward primitive man."

(Page 116) (B) underlines the words "what seemed like" and writes "some times" in the margin.

(Page 117) (B) cosses out the word "teenage" and writes "young" above it.

(Page 117) (B) crosses out the word "otherwise" and places a question mark in the margin.

(Page 117) (B) crosses out the words "where so much is changing, another new development is mass spectator sports."

(Page 117) (B) crosses out the words "lose all sense of team play."

(Page 117) (B) replaces the word "a" by "the."

(Page 121) (B) underlines the words "at its best" in the caption "Schooling at its best is excellent, although over-all progress remains spotty[.]"

(Page 123) (B) places a question mark after the caption "Catholicism is the prevailing faith, though the Church is not a powerful establishment[.]"

(Page 123) (B) places a question mark after the caption "Humble offerings of candles are made on All Souls' Day at a church grotto in Rio. Despite its 65.5 million adherents, the Catholic Church perennially lacks priests."

Chapter 9

[No markings.]

Chapter 10

(Page 145) (B) places an "x" in the margin next to the clause "although everyone, of course, had theories."

(Page 145) (B) places a question mark besides the words "not a demagogue but as a man with a reputation for honesty who did not make false promises." (L) also inserts a question mark next to the same words.

(Page 146) (B) crosses out the words "Central and South America" and replaces them with "the Americas."

(Page 146) (B) writes "and other things!" next to the sentence beginning "the old capital of Rio, because of its tremendous population increase."

(Page 146) (L) writes "Brasilia é pior" next to the sentence "Recife has a slum problem almost as bad as Rio's, as have all the larger cities."

(Page 146) (L) writes something unintelligible next to the sentence "the one from Rio to Brasília has already been the scene of numerous washouts and other disruptions."

(Page 146) (B) places an "x" in the margin next to the sentence "in Brazil's case they are qualities which will undoubtedly help guide the country through any crisis that lies ahead."

(Page 146) (B) crosses out the words "for example" and "what is called" in the sentence "for example, the Brazilian people have a genius for what is called human relations."

(Page 146) (B) crosses out the words "free, simple" in the sentence "other countries that are not endowed with the free, simple attitude toward other races and cultures that the Brazilians have had for so long, or with the innate Brazilian respect for other peoples, may never be able to solve their racial problems in the Brazilian way."

(Page 147) (B) places an "x" in the margin next to the sentence "even though there is no sizable middle class — usually a prerequisite to national stability — and though the country has been divided between the very few rich and the many poor for so long, the way of life seems more democratic than that of many other countries."

(Page 147) (B) places a question mark in the margin next to the sentence "the *Integralistas*, the country's one pseudo-Fascist party, existed only briefly more than 20 years ago, and the Communist party was made illegal in 1947," while also crossing out the word "pseudo."

(Page 147) (L) linescores this passage and writes "good" in the margin: "the antiforeign nationalist is almost always one of two types. The first type comes usually from the newly rich class and is generally a first- or second-generation immigrant. (Most of the big new fortunes in the country have been made by immigrants.)"

(Page 147) (L) linescores this passage and writes "good" in the margin: "his business has probably been granted government privileges and strong government protection. Naturally he is afraid of foreign competition, particularly of American large-scale competition, and particularly if he is an inefficient producer, or if his profits are out of proportion."

(Page 147) (L) linescores this passage and places a question mark in the margin: "but since the United States actually means very little to the ignorant and poor in Brazil — that is to most of the people — the blame for all ills is more often put on a local politician or simply on the government."

(Page 148) (L) writes "good" in the margin along the sentence "for what Brazil lacks above all else is a good, sound government, and this can be achieved only by raising the level of society as a whole through education and through increased material well-being."

(Page 148) (B) places an "x' in the margin and crosses out the words "government would then be a reflection of a healthy body politic" in the sentence "if that can be done, there would be no problem in Brazil that good government could not resolve, because the government would then be a reflection of a healthy body politic."

(Page 148) (B) places an "x," followed by a question mark, besides the sentence " one should not make exaggerated cultural or social claims for Brazil; still, politics aside, it has done remarkably well."

(Page 148) (L) places an "x" besides the sentences "everyone who visits Brazil agrees that the ordinary, average Brazilians are a wonderful people, cheerful, sweet-tempered, witty and patient — incredibly patient. To see them standing in line for hours, literally for hours, in lines folded back on themselves two or three times the length of a city block, only to get aboard a broken-down, recklessly driven bus and return to their tiny suburban houses, where like as not these days the street has not been repaired, nor the garbage collected, and there may even be no water — to see this is to marvel at their patience."

(Page 148) (L) linescores the sentence "other people undergoing the same trials would surely stage a revolution every month or so."

(Page 149) (B) crosses out the word "Indians" in the caption "In the Mato Grosso, Indians receive inoculations at a rural clinic" and replaces it with the word "Brazilians."

Appendix

(Page 153) (L) linescores an entry in the section entitled "For Further Reading": "Kubler, George and Martin Soria, *Art and Architecture in Spain and Portugal and their American Dominions.* Penguin Books, 1959."

(Page 155) (B) adds, in the section titled "Famous Brazilian Cultural Figures and Their Principal Works," the words "aguas" and " Quaderna" to the entry "Poetry: *Cão sem plumas, Duas aquas[.]*"

In Robert Wilson's copy of *Brazil*, Bishop "corrected the title page so that it reads: 'some by Elizabeth Bishop; and more by The Editors of LIFE.'"[7] But the evidence suggests that this is not entirely accurate. For there is more of Elizabeth Bishop in *Brazil* than she was willing to acknowledge when she thought about the changes her editors had made in her text. That she was inclined to overstate her criticism of the book as published — when one knows just how little, comparatively, she would have restored, added or deleted in the text — is made quite clear in the exaggerations in her letter to Robert Lowell: "The BRAZIL book IS awful; some sentences just don't make sense at all.

And at least the pictures could have been good ... Maybe, if you can read it at all, you will find a trace here & there of what I originally meant to say."[8] Perhaps it is going too far to think that she might have said more accurately, as we say for her, "you will find more here & there than I can stand of what the editors have changed in what was supposed to be *my* book."

One last word. In the version of *Brazil* that appears in *Prose*, published in 2011, as the editor states, the changes marked in Bishop's copy of the 1961 edition now in the Houghton Library, Harvard University, were incorporated, along with the restoration of her original text for the final chapter of the book, thus creating a hybrid text.

15

Scenery, Storms

By "stroking" his cat Jeoffrey, Christopher "Kit" Smart (1722–1771) tells us in *Jubilate Agno*, he "found out electricity," for he "perceived God's light about him both wax and fire." If Elizabeth Bishop's Tobias was not the source for such divine knowledge — that "the Electrical fire is the spiritual substance, which God sends from heaven to sustain the bodies both of man and beast" — he was nevertheless capable of putting on quite a good show. But more about Tobias later.

Bishop concludes "The Map" with the wisdom of a final line — that the colors of the mapmakers are "more delicate" than the colors of the historians. Nature's colors, however, are a thing apart, especially, as she learned, in Brazil. In "Arrival at Santos," she points to a coast, to a harbor, and, "after a meager diet of horizon," to some "impractically shaped" scenery, capped by mountains that are "sad and harsh beneath their frivolous greenery." The third poem in *Questions of Travel*— after "Arrival at Santos" and "Brazil, January 1, 1502"— gives the volume its title. Published in the *New Yorker* on January 21, 1952, the poem contains a prepostional phrase —"in another country"— that echoes both T. S. Eliot and Ernest Hemingway — Eliot's epigraph for "Portrait of a Lady" (a quotation from "The Jew of Malta") and Hemingway's short story "In Another Country" (which itself pays homage to Eliot). Elsewhere Bishop echoes Hemingway's famous passage in Chapter 27 of *A Farewell to Arms*, in which Frederic Henry recalls, "We had heard them [words], sometimes standing in the rain almost out of earshot, so that only the shouted words came through." In "Questions of Travel" Bishop characterizes Brazilian rain: "to listen to rain / so much like politicians' speech: / two hours of unrelenting oratory."

Bishop is deservedly celebrated for the close descriptions of nature and place in poetry, often to the extent of shortchanging her generous reliance on other texts by writers as disparate, in most ways, as Charles Darwin, whose *Voyage of the Beagle* was one of her great favorites, and Richard F. Burton, who traveled extensively in Brazil. The latter, to focus on just one instance, offers a useful example of just how dependent on the writings of others Bishop could sometimes be. Burton's *Explorations of the Highlands of Brazil* (1869), especially the chapters on the colonial *mineiro* (mining) towns of Ouro Prêto and Diamantina, provided her with the background for a reading of *Minha Vida de Menina* (1942), a book Bishop translated as *The Diary of "Helena Morley"* (1957). In 1953, from Samambaia, she writes to friends about Burton and his book: "Faber & Faber [publishers] ... have several books on cat raising I am going through (because of Tobias) and we are now reading Burton's travels here, which are absolutely *marvelous.*" (She hadn't realized that Burton had been in Brazil, as well as Arabia.) Burton's "knowledge of languages is fantastic," she marvels. "Lota says she hasn't found one mistake yet in his Brazilian Portuguese, Negro dialects, slang, place-names, Indian names, etc.— and they are almost impossibly difficult — and he has explained a great many words to her that she never knew about before." Moreover, he took the same trip to Ouro Prêto that she and Lota did. "He explains all the place-names, etc.— things we had tried and tried to find out about and failed." "Of course he hates the baroque and admires above all a good straight wide main street," she continues. "He says of Ouro Prêto —'What they will do when they come to put in gas and water mains?' (everything's so crooked). Lota said 'Ha-ha, Mr. B., they knew perfectly well they never *were* going to put in gas & water mains.' But in general it is an extraordinary & fair book to have been written 85 years ago."[1]

It was not lost on Bishop, however, that Burton was a master at descriptions of natural scenery, though, as she notes, he is "prolix." Yet his descriptions convey sentiments that anticipate Bishop's own sentiments regarding Brazilian scenery: "the wildly beautiful, the magnificence of virgin forest, the uniform grace of second growth, begins to pall upon us; we are tired of grand mountain, picturesque hill, and even of softly undulated prairie." And when he writes "I cannot but hold that green is the most monotonous of colours, and that in a warm, damp climate its effect is a peculiar depression,"[2] the affinity of his observation with the sentiments expressed in the opening lines of Bishop's poem, "Questions of Travel," is unmistakable. She complains of "too many waterfalls"—"crowded streams" that "hurry too rapidly down to the sea"— and the pressure of "so many clouds on the mountaintops," spilling "over the sides in soft slow-motion," making them into "waterfalls under our very eyes."

Burton's notion of the depressive effect of Brazil's permeating and pervasive "green," that "most monotonous of colours," is transformed in Bishop's writing into "scenery" that is "unbelievably impractical." "Lota has lots of land here [Petrópolis] & is in the middle of building herself a large and elegant modern house on the side of a black granite cliff beside a waterfall — the scenery is unbelievably *impractical*," she wrote in 1952,[3] and a week later, to Marianne Moore, "My friend Lota's country place in Petrópolis ... is a sort of dream-combination of plant & animal life.... Not only are there highly *impractical* mountains all around with clouds floating in & out of one's bedroom, but waterfalls, orchids, all the Key West flowers I know & Northern apples and pears as well."[4]

If traces of Burton's sentences are present in "Questions of Travel," moreover, the poem also echoes Rudyard Kipling. In *Brazilian Sketches*, the British writer describes his arrival at Santos in the late 1920s "beneath the brassy glare of a West African sky." We "loafed up a Dutch-like river that twisted through too-green flats; and tied at a wharf where all the world's steamers were unloading goods of luxury, mechanism, and apparel, or taking in coffee-bags that slid along furlongs of moving floors, and decanted themselves, like headless Gadarene swine, into their proper holds"; and later he talks about "the crashing (colours hit here) green of its cut lawns and the raw grasses and clumps of flowers."[5] In Rio, writes Kipling "the Gardens cried aloud — just like politicians — that they could produce everything man requires between certain degrees of latitude."[6] Yet it was not just the "outsider," such as Burton, Kipling and Bishop, who remarked on the excesses of scenery, of color, in the Brazilian landscape. Brazilians did, too. Take Vinícius de Moraes's "Soneto de Intimidade," which states that "Nas tardes da fazenda há muito azul demais," which Bishop herself translated as "Country afternoons, there's much too much blue air."

Then there was the Brazilian storm. The most spectacular electrical storm I can remember is the one I witnessed from a top-floor apartment of a highrise building in São Paulo decades ago. Lightning shot through the sky all around, including, it seemed, below me. Bishop, too, found the Brazilian electrical storm notable, as evidenced in her poem titled, simply enough, "Electrical Storm." But before we take up Bishop's poem, let us take a look at a description of such a Brazilian storm written a century earlier than Bishop's, that of Isabel Burton, the wife of Sir Richard Burton.

> On the 17th of January, 1866, we had an awful storm, worse than any known for twenty-five years; there was an awful blackness, the lightning was red, the wind drove in the windows, the hail was jagged pieces of ice one inch in diameter, sharp and long, and made round holes like a bullet, there was a network of flashes, rain from all quarters — a regular cyclone. It drove through the room fronting north, which was like a ship's cabin in a gale. We saw the cathedral struck, the cross knocked off, tiles blown away; the hotel room was like a shower-bath, with a continuous stream of rain. Several houses were struck, some of the doors split, and the streets quite flooded; people were frightened, and lighted candles, and brought

out the Madonna. There were sharp rattlings like earthquake; it blew a clock against the walls away; the people all met as after a revolution in Paris. The windows were everywhere broken, and the water looked black.[7]

Bishop's "Electrical Storm," first published in the *New Yorker* on May 14, 1960, and subsequently collected in *Questions of Travel,* tells the story of Tobias's prudent withdrawal in the face of a storm at dawn that strikes at Samambaia. "*Cra — aack!* — dry and light. / The house was really struck." "Tobias jumped in the window, got in bed — / silent, his eyes bleached white, his fur on end." Hail falls, "the biggest size of artificial pearls. / Dead-white, wax-white, cold." Tobias? The cat "stayed in the warm sheets," and the "Lent trees had shed all their petals; / wet, stuck, purple, among the dead-eye pearls." We "got up to find the wiring fused, / no lights, a smell of saltpetre, / and the telephone dead."

Leading up to its final suggestions of Ezra Pound's "In a Station of the Metro" ("petals on a wet, black bough") and *The Tempest* by Shakespeare ("those are pearls that were his eyes") are several suggestive coincidences with Isabel Burton's description. The religious: denuded "Lent trees" / "cathedral struck." The hail: "Dead-white, wax-white, cold" / "jagged pieces of ice." There may even be a veiled reference to Isabel Burton, the wife of a diplomat serving in Santos and São Paulo in Bishop's little poke at "diplomats' wives' favors / from an old moon party" — "Dead-white, wax-white, cold."

As for the frightened Tobias — "handsome, and a brilliant cat intellectually, of course"[8] — who prudently ensconces himself in a warm bed, he needs no literary precursor. But if he had one, it surely wouldn't be Isabel Burton's Brazilian cat, who was dispatched by a native — "about four feet high, but perfectly well proportioned, as black as a coal" — who, despite "roasting my favorite cat at the grill," as she put it, continued to serve as her "right-hand man" for the remainder of her time in Brazil. On one occasion, she later complained, this man Friday "roasted" her cat because, he explained, "all the little negroes were taught to be cruel to cats," for they were tools of the devil, "and that he *had* done atrocious things to cats."[9]

16

Different Hats, Different Folks

A description of the gestures and actions of the incipient, secreted bisexual or sign-giving transvestite, the poem "Exchanging Hats" did not make it into the *New Yorker*. But through the good editorial offices of the poet John Malcolm Brinnin, it was accepted for publication in *New World Writing*. Between the time of its acceptance and the proof stage, she "improved" her poem and made it more explicit by substituting the word "Anandrous" for the *New Yorker*–friendly word "Pajama'd."[1]

"Exchanging Hats" appeared in 1956. But for some so far unexplained reason it was never reprinted. Bishop chose not to include it in any of the selective or collective volumes that she saw through the press in the last two decades of her life, not even in her *Complete Poems* in 1969, which she enlarged with prose pieces and translations. About "Unfunny uncles who insist / in trying on a lady's hat" and "Anandrous aunts, who, at the beach" keep "putting on the yachtsmen's caps," this poem constitutes a genial if sly foray into the world of gender-blending and transvestite twists and "sex exchanges," laying out a virtual litany of socially acceptable, if temporary, experiments. Listed are "unfunny uncles" — "funny uncle" is a code word for homosexual — who try on ladies' hats, aunts who try on yachtsmen's caps, and others who put paper plates on their heads or don the Indian's feather bonnet or opera hats. Then there are these lines in which "he" is "the hatter": "And if the opera hats collapse / and crowns grow draughty, then, perhaps, / he thinks what might a miter matter?" The spelling "miter" is an old form for "metre" (a unit of measurement) so does the reduction in size of opera hats matter much or at all? But "miter" is also a less common spelling for "mitre" (ecclesiastically, according to the *Oxford English Dictionary*, a mitre is "a head-dress forming part of the insignia of a *bishop* in the Western church" — emphasis added). In this way the poet inserts into the poem a reference to herself.

What are we to make of Bishop's sly insertion of herself into the poem? She, who in school was often known as "Bishop" and "The Bishop," might well affect the real thing, a bishop's hat. What would it matter, then, if this poet named Bishop were to work in a bit of transvestitism by placing "a mitre" on her own head? But a mitre might also be "a headband or fillet worn by ancient Greek women; also, a kind of head-dress common among Asiatics, the wearing of which by men was regarded by the Romans as a mark of effem- inacy"—*OED*). Or as Samuel Johnson has it, in *A Dictionary of the English Language* (1755): "Mitre — 1. An ornament for the head. 2. A kind of Episcopal crown." Bishop, too, may be numbered among all those "hatters" whose mad- ness is natural.

Long after Bishop had composed her controversial poem on hats, the *New Yorker* published a poem titled "Hemingway's Hat."[2] It is by the British Vicki Feaver, who, in an essay entitled "Elizabeth Bishop: The Reclamation of Female Space," links Bishop's "The Fish" with Hemingway's *The Old Man and the Sea*, but does not mention "Exchanging Hats."[3] But like Bishop's poem, Feaver's poem toys with the idea of playing at gender. Not needing to be evasive or unsuitably subtle — the times have changed since Bishop feigned and occluded her sexual preferences — this poet starts out wondering about what she would be like as a man, as she sports "a copy of the canvas / leather- peaked cap Hemingway wore / at the Finca Vigia" that her mother gave her to make her "look dashing, nerveless" but which makes her feel "like a Shake- spearean heroine / dressed as and played by a boy." Reminded by such play at changing hats, she thinks back to the sexual games of the previous night: "me riding you," and a shared penis, a "glistening pillar" sliding between them, and, the next morning, "you washing me, soaping and rinsing / with a woman's tenderness." If "Hemingway's Hat" begins its homage to Bishop by invoking "Exchanging Hats," it completes it by recalling the woman's ten- derness of "The Shampoo," Bishop's great love poem to her Brazilian com- panion.

"Here is the little poem Mrs. [Katherine] White couldn't understand," wrote Bishop of "The Shampoo." "I have changed three words, though, since she returned it. I wonder if I am in honor bound to return it to them because of the three words before I send it someplace else? [published in *The New Republic*, July 1955] & do you remember those tin basins, all sizes, so much a part of life here?"[4] "The Shampoo" was the last poem in the collection *Poems: North & South—A Cold Spring* (1955). "Arrival at Santos" was the next-to- last in the same collection. Then Bishop chose to begin her next book of poems *Questions of Travel* (1965) with "Arrival at Santos." Curiously, she did not choose to reprint "The Shampoo" even though that one, too, can be con- sidered a "Brazil" poem.

It begins with a description of lichens — "still explosions on the rocks" that grow "by spreading, gray, concentric shocks"—and ends with a reference to the basin in which her lover's hair is washed—"this big tin basin, / battered and shiny like the moon"—neatly echoing the image evoked by "concentric" introduced in the third line of the poem for those who have seen the concentrically placed, nested tin basins—smallest to largest—for sale at any weekly fair in Brazil. The still—the unchanging—nature of rocks and moons and stars are belied by the adjectives used to describe them: explosions, shocks, shooting. No wonder there are "shooting stars" in the black hair in a poem that was first called—a false start because too explicit about the trace of irony in Time's being "nothing if not amenable"—"Gray Hairs."

As for the reference to "lichens" as "still explosions on the rocks," consider Bill Bryson's spirited popular account: "Lichens are just about the hardiest visible organisms on Earth, but among the least ambitious. They will grow happily enough in a sunny churchyard, but they particularly thrive in environments where no other organism would go—on blowy mountaintops and arctic wastes, wherever there is little but rock and rain and cold, and almost no competition." Bryson also notes that lichens are slow growing, sometimes taking "more than half a century to attain the dimensions of a shirt button," he writes. "'Those the size of dinner plates' (he quotes another source) are therefore 'likely to be hundreds if not thousands of years old.' It would be hard to imagine a less fulfilling existence. 'They simply exist, testifying to the moving fact that life even at its simplest level occurs, apparently, just for its own sake.'"[5]

In Bishop's vaguely metaphysical poem, the relative permanence (or at least longevity) of the lichens when considered in the context of the brevity of human life is a source of both discouragement and hopefulness. For the poet will console her lover with cold comfort: though attending so long (as the lichens) on the heavens, "the heavens will attend as long on us." So carpe diem is the order of the day. In its curiously inverted argument, "The Shampoo" takes its place alongside Andrew Marvell's "To His Coy Mistress," a poem of seduction, which opens wistfully—"Had we but world enough, and time, / This coyness, Lady, were no crime"—but closes bravely: "Thus, though we cannot make our sun / Stand still, yet we will make him run."[6]

17

Village Matters

"I am a little embarrassed about having to go to Brazil to experience total recall about Nova Scotia; geography must be more mysterious than we think," wrote Elizabeth Bishop to Katherine White, her editor at the *New Yorker*.[1] But, perhaps, as the old advertisement for the Pall Mall cigarette proclaimed, "distance lends enchantment." For safely distanced, nested away in a different hemisphere, Bishop found herself writing about her childhood in Nova Scotia. Delving into family memories, she wrote poems and stories. Among the most soulful of these ventures are the poem "Sestina," to be taken up first, followed by the story "In the Village" and the poem "First Death in Nova Scotia."

"Do I have a poem called 'Early Sorrow'?" puzzled Elizabeth Bishop in a letter to Lloyd Frankenberg on March 22, 1960. "I thought it was just called 'Sestina,' if it's the one I think it might be..."[2] The poem *is* called "Sestina," and it draws on the poet's childhood in Nova Scotia, exploring a vein of rich memories of a child's life in Nova Scotia. Written in Brazil and published in the *New Yorker* on September 15, 1956, the poem emerged from the same memories that went earlier into the marvelous story "In the Village." In fact, "Sestina" is itself anticipated by the story, especially the paragraph that reads: "My grandmother is sitting in the kitchen stirring potato mash for tomorrow's bread and crying into it. She gives me a spoonful and it tastes wonderful but wrong. In it I think I taste my grandmother's tears; then I kiss her and taste them on her cheek."[3] In this sense her biographer, Brett Millier, is surely right in noticing that "anxiety" lurks behind the "pastoral" in this poem, even as the grandmother, "stirring," keeps everything going, keeps everything, in a sense, altogether.[4]

"Sestina" is a poem in which everything signifies. The grandmother works at a "Little Marvel Stove," her little granddaughter beside her. And it speaks out, as does everything in this scene, the grandmother laughing as she reads the jokes in the almanac. But the grandmother is all activity: she sits, laughs, talks, thinks, knows, cuts, says, tidies up, hangs up the almanac, shivers, thinks, puts wood on the stove, sings — in short, she busies herself. The child is more passive, but she is taking it all in: What does the child do? She watches, draws, puts (a man in the drawing), shows, and places (a flowerbed).

Nor does the almanac remain silent or the kettle quiet. While the iron(y) kettle sings and dances in the midst of tears, tears, tears everywhere it seems (quite unlike the man-moth of another poem who husbands his one tear and would swallow it), the almanac jokes, foretells, twice hovers, "seeds" the child's drawing, hangs from its string. How conducive to reminiscence, it may be asked, must have been that first encounter with the "literatura de cordel" ("literature on a string") sold by street vendors or at the weekly fair, having been prepared for it by the "clever" almanac hanging "on its string," the "birdlike" almanac "hover[ing] half open above the child," the hovering almanac that says "*I know what I know.*" Here is evidence of the power of words, the force of words written down, natural in Brazil to the "nordestino" (and others), natural to the (Nova Scotia) child who writes and draws, who puts in the missing (father?) into her drawing? And through it all, moves the grandmother, "laughing and talking to hide her tears." "Sestina" is a poem about how the child reacts to what transpires in her little (but all encompassing) world and how that world is reflected in her imagination (as she makes comparisons) and draws a picture and makes art, as what she sees, what she hears, what she feels seeps into her child's drawing, into her poet's poem, where form — sestina — controls sentiment even as it enables (and controls) its proper expression. Wisdom speaks dialogically, as the grandmother says, "*It's time for tea now,*" the stove says, "*It was to be,*" and the almanac — a practical Book of Ecclesiastes for everyday use — follows up "*I know what I know*" with "*Time to plant tears*" — certainly one of the ancient and honorable imperatives for poetry itself.

"You were very right to put your story in," wrote Robert Lowell of "In the Village" when assessing Bishop's third book of poems, *Questions of Travel,* in 1965. "It's one of your finest poems, and bridges the two sections ["Brazil" and "Elsewhere"]."[5] Still within the first year of her long stay in Brazil — which began in 1951, it will be recalled, with her long recuperative stay due to a severe allergic reaction to the cashew — Bishop marveled to friends that "geography must be more mysterious than we realize."[6] Exhilaration at first at the possibility of writing and putting together an entire collection of such stories, the feeling would not last beyond the writing of a story or two. Later, she would play down her ability to write fiction, by insisting (correctly, her biographers have judged) that her first important Nova Scotia story was "*entirely*, not partly, autobiographical" (though she admitted to having "compressed the time a little and perhaps put two summers together, or put things a bit out of sequence — but it's all straight fact."[7] She was even willing to accept corrections to the story (in names and incidents) made by her aunt, her "only nice relative," she claimed, adding "we have equally literal imaginations."[8]

Like so many other writers, Bishop found a radical change in geography to be a stimulus to memory. One thinks of Rilke, who embraced a peripatetic necessity as part and parcel of his poet's life. Or one thinks of Ernest Hemingway's stories about summers spent in northern Michigan, written while he struggled to perfect his style in Paris, or Henry James recovering his Albany cousins after settling in London, or James Joyce recreating Dublin in Trieste and Paris. Joyce, in particular, may have been a congenial model for Bishop. That she knew his writing is apparent in her recognition that her friend and collaborator Emanuel Brasil has been influenced by Joyce's *Portrait of the Artist as a Young Man* (1916) in the writing of his own bildungsroman, *Pedra Fantasma* (1977).[9] So, too, are there affinities between Joyce's famous novel and her story "In the Village," suggesting that the Joyce is an unacknowledged predecessor, in style and, to some extent, technique for her fiction overall, but especially so in "In the Village" and "Memories of Uncle Neddy."

> Once upon a time and a very good time it was there was a moocow coming down along the road and this moocow that was coming down along the road met a nicens little boy named baby tuckoo ... .
>
> His father told him that story: his father looked at him through a glass: he had a hairy face.
>
> He was baby tuckoo. The moocow came down the road where Betty Byrne lived: she sold lemon platt.
>
> > *O, the wild rose blossoms*
> > *On the little green place.*
>
> He sang that song. That was his song.
>
> > *O, the green wothe botheth.*
>
> When you wet the bed first it is warm then it gets cold. His mother put on the oilsheet. That had the queer smell.
>
> His mother had a nicer smell than his father. She played on the piano the sailor's hornpipe for him to dance. He danced:
>
> > *Tralala lala*
> > *Tralala tralaladdy*
> > *Tralala lala*
> > *Tralala lala.*

Uncle Charles and Dante clapped. They were older than his father and mother but uncle Charles was older than Dante....

The Vances lived in number seven. They had a different father and mother. They were Eileen's father and mother. When they were grown up he was going to marry Eileen. He hid under the table. His mother said:

— O, Stephen will apologise.

Dante said:

— O, if not, the eagles will come and pull out his eyes.

> *Pull out his eyes.*
> *Apologise,*
> *Apologise,*
> *Pull out his eyes.*
> *Apologise,*
> *Pull out his eyes,*
> *Pull out his eyes,*
> *Apologise.*[10]

This, the opening section of the first chapter of Joyce's *Portrait*, introduces the dramatis personae of the novel: the child, the father and mother, the aunt and uncle. Much like Bishop's "In the Village," though there the father's presence is established by the mother's protracted mourning. But the focus in both works is, of course, the child. As Dorothy Van Ghent has written of *Portrait*, "In this extremely short sequence at the beginning of the book, the child's sense of insecurity, in a world whose form he cannot grasp, is established — and with insecurity, guilt (he must apologize) and fear (the horrible eagles)."[11] Except for the gender of the child and the demand that the child apologize with its image of the eagles, this sentence can be accurately applied to much of Bishop's story. Van Ghent's next sentence might well describe the motive behind a good deal of Bishop's other work, without ever quite achieving the desired end. "With these unpromising emotional elements established in him, the maturing child will try again and again to grasp his world imaginatively as a shape within which he has a part that is essential to its completeness and harmoniousness and meaningfulness."[12] The creation of that imaginative world, in all its salience, would have been the good work, perhaps, of the novel or series of related narratives that Lowell suggested she write, as will be seen below.

When Lowell first read "In the Village," he singled out Bishop's cow for loving admiration, pining that he "could weep for the cow."[13] If, however, Bishop's cow is an affectionate portrait of an actual cow sharing the writer's childhood in Nova Scotia, its inclusion in the story is anticipated by the appearance of Stephen Daedalus' congenial "moo cow" at the very outset of

Portrait, though, notably, the heroine of Bishop's story leads and guides her cow on a pleasant journey through the village, while the memory in Joyce's novel takes the form of having the baby Stephen met by the cow coming down the road. Bishop follows Joyce as well in depicting events that take place around the heroine that are never explained to her and which she has to figure out later, perhaps much later. In *Portrait* it is the Christmas dinner during which Stephen's father, friends, and aunt argue bitterly about Ireland, her priests, and Parnell, Ireland's fallen leader. Bishop creates the scene in which the heroine's mother is being fitted for a dress that will begin to take her out of her protracted period of mourning as well as scenes in which her grandmother and aunts unpack her mother's belongings. It is clear that in both Joyce's Christmas dinner scene and Bishop's "mother" scenes the reader is expected to infer facts and situations that are not yet apparent to the reflectors — the young Stephen or the young Elizabeth. It was this quality in her work that probably led Bishop to describe "In the Village" as "more a prose-poem than a story, anyway."[14]

Prose-poem or not, however, it would be helpful to know what Bishop was reading during her first months in Brazil — whether or not, specifically, she reread Joyce's *Portrait* at that time (or might even have read it for the first time). In either case, Bishop would not have missed the coincidence that it was a "cachou" that Dante gave young Stephen "every time he brought her a piece of tissue paper." A "cachou," annotates Joyce's editor, is "a silvered aromatic pill or pastille made of licorice, cashew nut, or gum, and used to sweeten the breath."[15] It would not have worked exactly on her as his *madeliene* did on Proust, but the word "cachou," encountered in this fashion, may well have initiated the release of the memories that enabled her to take on the narrative which became "In the Village." Interestingly, in its turn, "In the Village," Robert Lowell claimed, released family memories that enabled him to write much of *Life Studies*, especially the long prose section of this highly influential book published in 1959.

Curiously, Lowell also chose to versify Bishop's "In the Village" (boldly and shamelessly, though less successfully). In "The Scream" he reduces the story to its elements, curtails the narrative flow, and violates Bishop's reticence and emblematic restraint (exercised similarly in Joyce) by identifying, emphatically and excessively, the mother's "scream, the echo of a scream" as the immediate source and perdurable fact of childhood trauma. This, of course, diametrically opposes Bishop's style of reticence and thematic understatement, a style available to her in Joyce's *Portrait*. In Lowell's hands, Bishop's memories of Nova Scotia become not the impetus for a retrospective rendering of what it was like at the past moment but an opportunity to dramatize (in the form of a monologue) an adult's interpretation of those moments. Of these three self-centered artists, Lowell was the one least likely to bring off the literary trick of seeming to disappear before the events of his poems. Even the attempt to write "The Scream" in the voice of his friend and fellow poet fails to hide the operatic pitch (or "now-familiar-trumpet-notes," as Bishop put it elsewhere) that Lowell so much affected.[16] He exclaims: "Back and away and back! / Mother kept coming and going —/ with me, without me!"[17] There are no "adult" exclamations in Bishop when she writes: "First, she had come home, with her child. Then she had gone away again, alone, and left the child. Then she had come home. Then she had gone away again, with her sister; and now she was home again."[18] Sometimes less — and I am talking about the number of words here —*is* less. In Lowell's poem the scream no longer hangs over the story; it *is* the story. And it tells a lesser story.

Exuberant in his reaction to "In the Village," Lowell encouraged Bishop to go on writing up her Nova Scotia memories. "I've been dragging up old conversations with you and wondering just how autobiographical both this ["In the Village"] and that other two little girls story ["Gwendolyn"] are," wrote Lowell. "I feel they are perhaps parts of a Nova Scotia growing-up novel — though of course they are rounded short stories — the second is much more considerable, but somehow it raises the first." He continues his ruminations, thoughts on the fly, if you will: "So I think of some Education of E. B. or E. B.'s Downward path to Wisdom. What K[atherine] A[nne] Porter's childhood stories aim towards, or a super Miss [Sarah Orne] Jewett. But it could be less than a novel — something in three, four or five sections that would go for about a hundred pages."[19]

Encouraged by Lowell, in subsequent weeks and months Bishop did try to write other stories that recover for literature her memories of Nova Scotia. Working more slowly than Lowell, she was writing, at what was, apparently, still an early stage, what she called her "Uncle Artie" materials, when Lowell took the wind out of her sails by rewriting "In the Village" as "The Scream" in 40 lines of Bishop's own voice, beginning "The scream, the echo of a scream, / now only a thinning echo."[20] In April 1962, upon receiving a typescript copy of Lowell's latest volume, *For the Union Dead*, Bishop wrote back, not quite enigmatically: "'The Scream' really works well, doesn't it? The story is far enough behind me so I can see it as a poem now. The first few stanzas I saw only my story — then the poem took over — and the last stanza is wonderful. It builds up beautifully, and everything of importance is there. But I was surprised."[21] Of course, Lowell's poem misses the point, unless its final stanza is meant to be taken ironically. And I don't think that's the case. The fact is that the existence of "In the Village" gives the lie to Lowell's final stanza.

None of it is gone — not the voices, certainly, not the mother's excruciating scream. As David Kalstone notes, "In Bishop's story that last phrase [in Lowell's poem] is part of a question, not a statement: 'Are they too frail for us to hear their voices long, too mortal?' And the voices, apart from the scream, belong not to people but to things: 'clothes, crumbling postcards, broken china; things damaged and lost, sickened or destroyed; even the frail *almost-lost* scream.'"[22]

That Lowell's appropriation of her story did not sit well with her is clear from other things she had to say at the time. In the same letter to Lowell, with scarcely diminished or disguised petulance that either Lowell did not sense or, more likely, refused to acknowledge, she complained: "I don't know why I bother to write 'Uncle Artie,' really. I shd. just send you my first notes and you can turn him into a wonderful poem. He is even more your style than the Village story was."[23] Retitled "Memories of Uncle Neddy," her "Uncle Artie" story was left in manuscript at her death. That it is a lesser story than "In the Village" may have been acknowledged tacitly, in 1984, by Bishop's editor (Robert Giroux) when he chose to place it just before "In the Village," the final story in the volume of Bishop's collected prose. Encountered first, the story leads in nicely to "In the Village." If read afterwards, however, it comes out as a more detailed working out of the implications of the storied "clang" of the much richer, earlier written, story. Unlike Joyce's writing in the first pages of *Portrait*, which serve to foreshadow the novel's full treatment of major themes and concerns, Bishop's writing of "In the Village" came close to exhausting — her poet's way of writing prose largely, if not exclusively, contributing to this — the most fecund of her childhood memories of Nova Scotia, those that so dominated her imagination in the early months and first years of her long stay in Brazil.[24] But the material was still available for poetry, for nine years after the publication of the story "In the Village" Bishop published the poem "First Death in Nova Scotia" in the *New Yorker* in 1962 and then three years later collected it in the "Elsewhere" section of *Questions of Travel*. Its very title, "First Death in Nova Scotia," announces that it is a childhood memory poem, one written in her forties after settling in Brazil. Bishop forecasts that there will be other deaths in Nova Scotia after the first one (a comma between the words "death" and "in" might have suggested something else), and still others elsewhere as well.

In this poem about death, it is not of a beautiful young woman (the most poetic of subjects, as Edgar Allan Poe would have it) that she writes, but of a young boy, one not known, particularly, for his beauty. The death is of a bravely named Arthur, after his father surely, but also an invocation of the King Arthur of legend, perhaps of history, and thus worthy enough to be laid out (a showing of the corpse as well as a display, as in a feast like, perhaps, the feast described in Keats's "Eve of St. Agnes") before the photogravures of Edwardian royalty. For also laid out in display of honor or, perhaps, merit are Edward (Prince of Wales) and Princess Alexandra, his wife, and their son, King George, and Queen Mary, his wife — royal dignitaries all, whose heyday has come post–Victoria, that is, after 1901.

The scene is cold, cold, both outside and inside, characterized by the heatless parlor, and the snow-filled outdoors, a memory sharpened if not exacerbated by the contrast with the steamy, lush environs of Samambaia in Petrópolis, or the balmy seas of Rio, where Bishop wrote her poem. The presence of the "loon" gives a local Canadian touch in two immediate senses: the loon is native to the hemisphere and the hunting of it is not alien to the ethos of hunting underlined in *Survival*, Margaret Atwood's taxonomy of Canadian traditions and mythologies of victims and victimization. Indeed the loon as displayable trophy stands there in place of any putative Canadian dignitaries. That Uncle Arthur fired a bullet into "him" tells us that he has broken the Canadian law against killing the loon (pictured on the Canadian dollar bill — hence its sobriquet, the "loonie"— as well as explaining plausibly why Uncle Arthur stuffed it himself). The white-breasted bird on the table is anthropomorphized (he keeps "his own counsel" as his red eye eyes the "little frosted cake" of the coffin) into an equal of the dead white, not yet old enough to be an Arthurian boy, one who has been cosmetically made-up, but only partly so, by Jack Frost. (Winter's color man and avatar of the Grim Reaper does better by the Maple Leaf, the poet points out, adding the word "Forever"— for emphasis but with some irony — to evoke Canada's ubiquitous symbol as well as the "The Maple Leaf Forever," the well-known 1860s patriotic song celebrating Queen Victoria: "Our Emblem dear, / The Maple Leaf forever! / God save our Queen and Heaven bless, / The Maple Leaf forever."[25]) It is in the child's tale that the adult poet indulges (for the sake of childhood memory) that an invitation to become one of royalty's pages comes from "the gracious royal couples." But it is an invitation that must be turned down by the dead little boy with eyes shut up tight, clutching his lily of the valley (ironically signifying the return of happiness, a resurrection). Outside the roads are "deep in snow," keeping them all inside, in a communal parody of the family in Whittier's "Snow-Bound" that carries on in a renewed if quiet celebration of life, not in the Nova Scotia obsequies of an early, otherwise unremarkable, death, in which the display of boy and loon signals the fact that one of them has a longer shelf life than the other. In the poet's fantasy it is too bad little Arthur cannot accept the royals' invitation to become their smallest page — deep snow is only one factor in precluding his journey — though there was always the saw: "No one will be a knight where he has been a page."

Toward the end of her life Bishop faced another death — a last death. Robert Lowell died unexpectedly on September 12, 1977. Bishop did not speak at the memorial ceremony held in Boston, but she did feel compelled, as some others did, to mark his passing with a poet's considered and more lasting tribute — an elegy. She chose to write about Lowell in North Haven, Maine, the island where Lowell had summered for decades and where she, too, had spent time. Fittingly, the poem took the form of an elegy, rooted (as, classically, an elegy should be) in the natural details of sea and flowers and birds. Its singular turn comes, however, when Bishop brings up the ironic fact that the poet, who, in life, rewrote, repeated, and, above all, revised his work, can no longer, in death, do any of those things. "The words won't change again." The great changer of his own poetry ("*repeat, repeat, repeat; revise, revise, revise*") is now frozen in his tracks. Now his poems are permanent, no longer susceptible to his changing intentions, to any sort of metamorphosis. The poet has indeed "left for good" — a phrase that has its own edgy ambivalence. Bishop's elegy also reads, in words addressed to the poet it would elegize, "You can't derange, or re-arrange, your poems again." The allusion to Lowell's streaks of madness lies only partly hidden in Bishop's choice, I think, as an active verb, of the word "derange," rather than, say, "disarrange." She insists on pounding in the truism that the dead Lowell can no longer "derange" or "rearrange" his poems, or anyone else's (including Bishop's). The poem works best if the reader is familiar with the proclivities of the two poets as well as the ins and outs of their long friendship.

The matter would seem to end here, if not for something Bishop said about the Lowell poem after she had finished it. Writing to the poet Frank Bidart, a mutual friend, Bishop explained that "North Haven" incorporated words and images from other poets. "'Daisies pied' and 'to paint the meadows with delight' are straight from the summer part of the song in Shakespeare — you know the other part, 'When icicles hang by the wall'? … The 'incandescent stars' I'm pretty sure are from Marianne's 'Marriage' — but that isn't too important. (I think I felt the more literary the better!) 'Mystic blue' is I think a steal from Cal, isn't it? — also more or less on purpose."[26] Now here's the thing. An awareness of the sources of the borrowings — especially those to Shakespeare's *Love's Labour's Lost* (5.3) and Marianne Moore's poem "Marriage" — brings us to a subtext for Bishop's poem. Each source brings us words about marriage. In Shakespeare the cuckoo mocks "married men," while in Moore we learn that marriage is "This institution, / perhaps one should say enterprise / out of respect for which / one says one need not change one's mind / about a thing one has believed in." There's that notion of "mind-changing" again, poignantly relevant, it would seem, to an elegy about a man who, at the moment, of death was literally on his way to the New York apartment of his second ex-wife, carrying with him a portrait of his third wife, whom he had apparently just left for his second wife. How interesting it is that that something like all this "revising" so much in Lowell's character should have been embedded in Bishop's otherwise so seemingly innocent imagery of flowers and other natural beings. The possible borrowing from Lowell's own poetry, since I have left off searching for "mystic blue" in Lowell's poetry, I leave to the efforts of others. Yet I would note that "The Mystic Blue" is by D. H. Lawrence, one of Bishop's favorite poets, a fact that leads me to wonder if, in her explanation to Bidart, Bishop's memory has (revealingly) betrayed her.[27]

18

The Art of the Scapegoat

"Elizabeth Bishop has written a charming poem about the prodigal son," wrote Randall Jarrell.[1] "Charming" is hardly the word I would use to describe this trenchant double sonnet about scapegoating. It joins several other poems in the Bishop canon that reveal her penchant for scapegoating others. The caretaker of pigs in this poem is but one in a goodly number of scapegoats and sacrificial surrogates in Bishop's poetry, each one serving, perhaps, a specific emotional function — Manuelzinho, Micuçú, the man-moth, a dead hen in a New York City street, a pink dog in Copacabana, a moose in the road, even her mad mother. These figures are satirized, sympathized or empathized with, even transformed into a source of familial feeling among strangers. The will to scapegoat is only one of the secluded motives behind some of Bishop's best poems.

The composition of "The Prodigal" predates Bishop's long Brazilian years, beginning in December 1951. Published in the *New Yorker* in 1951, the poem appeared, appropriately enough (some would say), on March 17th, St. Patrick's Day. Could the editorial point, made in the city that hosts the largest annual Irish day parade anywhere in the world, have been made any clearer? Smart readers of the magazine were encouraged to see in Elizabeth Bishop's poem a somewhat puritanical commentary on the heavy drinking and boorish public behavior stereotypically associated with the celebrants of this holiday in Irish America. To drive the point home, the magazine also displayed on the page facing the poem a cartoon showing two castaways marooned on an island. The man on the right kneels before a case of liquor that has drifted in to shore. The other one holds up a bottle and says, "I was hoping for a nice dry white wine."[2]

"The Prodigal" is about a young man who tends hogs, living too close to "brown enormous odor" emanating from a sty "plastered halfway up with glass-smooth dung," and from which "moving snouts" and "pigs' eyes followed him." The boy, considerate "even to the sow that always ate her young," is a

140

drinker, one who hides his "pints behind a two-by-four." He thinks sometimes that he almost might endure "his exile yet another year or more."

"But it took him a long time finally," the poem concludes, "to make up his mind to go home."[3]

The title of a literary work may function in various, often tricky, ways. It may announce a theme, name a focusing or centralizing metaphor, suggest an attitude, mood or tone, or even point to the genre to which it pretends. A title may help to determine how a reader will understand a given work. How, one wonders, incidentally, whether Emily Dickinson's failure to give her poems titles was the result of her disdain for titles, or simple indifference to the practice of assigning titles to her poems, or her refusal to permit the exercise of control or power that is the potential for any title. Of course, she often embeds a simple, one-word title in her first line, say, in "Pain has an element of blank" (title: Pain) or "Success is counted sweetest" (title: Success) or "The Brain is wider than the sky" (title: Brain).

For the skillful use of a title, one that Bishop was certain to have appreciated, consider Robert Lowell's "Skunk Hour." It is not called "The Skunk's Hour," which might well lead Lowell's readers away from his main intention, which I take to be the definition of a state of the spirit or a state of mind — his state of mind, if you will, at a given time in his life. The skunk nosing about for food in the dark of night "will not scare" and that fact might serve to encourage the poet who is feeling down and perhaps depressed. But he's acting like "a skunk," a voyeur, insensitive, if not hostile, to the privacy belonging to others. And he's feeling like "a skunk," guilty, inept, inadequate in his response to the exigencies of life. Remove the title "Skunk Hour" (or change it to "The Skunk's Hour") and you have a different emphasis in the voice, a different meaning, if you will. He will not say, colloquially, that he is a "skunk," but he will say that he feels "like a skunk." Of course, in another sense, it is possible that the poet is "skunked" as well — that is, drunk — as only a solitary drinker, perhaps, can be "skunked."

The physician-writer Richard Selzer tells us that his first piece of serious writing was a retelling of the story of Jonah and the whale. He undertook it, he says, because, as a surgeon, he knew something other tellers of the story, including the first one, did not know. He knew anatomy and could describe in detail the inside of the whale. It was not his assumption that earlier writers had not demonstrated that they knew enough anatomy to undertake a detailed description that is important but that he felt empowered to do so. In "The Prodigal" Bishop felt empowered on two accounts, I think; she had been around pigsties long enough to offer an inflected description of such places, and she had already become enough of a drinker to empathize, up to a point, with the "prodigal" moving before her in Nova Scotia. To broaden the appeal of her poem to a modernist readership, she withholds the information that the portrait is that of her aunt's stepson. As she reveals privately, it was a biographical experience that "suggested" the poem. She universalized her poem in still another way. She began by calling it "The Prodigal Son," which placed the prodigal of her poem well within the scriptural tradition of the familiar parable. But then she turned it up a notch by dropping the "Son" from her title to further the suggestion that her prodigal exemplifies prodigals of other sorts, beyond the wastrel who has spent his living in disreputable ways and will return home chastened, to include the drunkard. Removing the word "son" from the title also diminishes the idea of a family — of the existence of a mother or father who might be disappointed in a "prodigal" son. In short, the poet suppresses the biographical source and deflects in part, but only in part, the scriptural source, the knowledge of which enabled her to conceive the poem to begin with, in order to make her poem more universal. And of course she does not give the prodigal's habitation a name by locating it in Nova Scotia. This prodigal could be taking his morning drink anytime and anywhere pigs are kept and tended, for all that the poem makes explicit.

When Bishop first sent Robert Lowell "Prodigal Son," as she was calling the poem in 1948, she preceded her mention of the poem with a criticism of W. H. Auden's familiar poem "Musée des Beaux Arts." "It's just plain inaccurate in the last part," she writes. "The ploughman & the people on the boat will rush to see the falling boy any minute, they always do, though maybe not to help." One infers, of course, that that is what she would do: "rush to see... though maybe not to help." Certainly, this is suggestive of how she, a poet, sees herself. "Oh well," she follows up with this thought — "I want to see what you'll think of my 'Prodigal Son'" — and immediately goes on to share something she thinks extraordinary. "I like this story from *The N.Y. Times* — a composition by a child in the third grade: 'I told my little brother that when you die you cannot breathe and he did not say a word. He just kept on playing.'"[4] This anecdote is related, I think, not only to the poet's stance vis-à-vis the prodigal of her poem but to the ploughman and the people on the boat of Auden's poem. Faced with the image and knowledge of death, they — Bishop, ploughman and people — keep on playing. Before the death-in-life that alcoholism has turned into the alcoholic's home, the poet fiddles her tune. If Bishop's personal nonpoetic sense of the alcoholic's depravity is reflected in this poem, the poetic Bishop presents us with a poem that exploits that depravity. On November 23, 1955, she explained to Lowell that "'The Prodigal' shared the method of 'that spiritual exercise of the Jesuits — when they try to think in detail how the thing must have happened.'"[5] The quotation comes from Bishop's biographer, who continues: "She had read the Ignatian spiritual exercises, but the poem sprang first, she said, from her thoughts when 'one of my aunt's stepsons offered me a drink of rum, in the pig styes at about 9 in the morning,' on her trip to Nova Scotia in 1946." But, of course, "the poem also speaks painfully and eloquently to her own experience with alcoholism in 1950."[6] She has not limited herself to describing expertly the pigsties of her experience but she has used that description to tell something of the inside story of her prodigal's naturally unnatural character.

The coining of the term "scapegoat" is credited to 16th-century translator William Tyndale, who first rendered the New Testament into English in 1526. It occurs in Leviticus 16:10: "The goat, on which the lot fell to be scapegoat, shall be presented alone before the Lord, to make an atonement with him and to let him go for a scapegoat into the wilderness." Several verses later the story of Aaron is told: "And Aaron shall lay his hands upon the head of the live goat, and confess over him all the iniquities of the children of Israel, and all their transgressions in all their sins, putting them upon the head of the goat and shall send him away into the wilderness by the hand of a man who is in readiness. The goat shall bear all their iniquities upon him to a solitary land; and he shall let the goat go into the wilderness" (21–22).

Because the link between defiled being and alcoholism already inheres in Bishop's incident with her aunt's stepson, it is not surprising that the experience should have marked Bishop significantly.[7] Brett C. Millier, the poet's biographer, fills out the personal context.

Bishop's "life by 1939 was dominated by her need for alcohol and by the effects of heavy drinking on her body, mind, and relationships, the guilt and shame attached to her abuse of alcohol made it impossible for her to live comfortably, and alcoholism fed her homelessness," writes Millier. In fact, when Bishop wrote in 1948 that she "'left Wiscasset under a cloud,' the cloud was alcoholic," she adds. As for "The Prodigal," which dates from the same period, it "describes a young man self-exiled in the family pigsty—'(he hid the pints behind a two-by-four).' At times, he is at home among the pigs and their excrescence; at other times, he is horrified."[8]

When we recall that the incident that precipitated the poem involved a relative (an aunt's stepson) but that the figure in "The Prodigal" is not so identified, that should alert us to the fact that Bishop has decided to "displace" her "prodigal" from the family, thereby obscuring her own family connection to her chosen scapegoat. Nor, notably, is her scapegoat employed within or for the family; he works for a farmer somewhere else, and does his work away from his family's home. He is not, therefore, her family's scapegoat (a patient or sick person); that is a role, inferring from Millier's description above, that she reserves for herself—in her everyday life, one is quick to clarify, not in the transaction which is the poem "The Prodigal." The poet is far more authoritarian, projecting her "own weaknesses and faults onto others ... the essential aspect of the mechanism of scape-goating."[9] Her "Prodigal," of course, is a version of the "one who is sacrificed as a purification for others, a scapegoat: then since worthless fellows were reserved for this fate, an arrant rascal, polluted wretch"—the Pharmakos.[10] Inherent in the impulse to give the incident with her aunt's stepson poetic form, this sacrificial, scapegoating act is symbolically enacted in the writing of the poem itself.

As a secret (and thus problematic) drinker herself, Bishop, it is only natural to think, should empathize (if not sympathize) with her aunt's unnamed stepson. Indeed, she might well see in the stepson in the pigsties a disturbing example of someone mired in alcoholism, fittingly working and, in a sense, living in the pigsties. What finally bothers her, as the poem seems to indicate, is that the "prodigal" has found a home away from home, not in the pigsties as such, but in his alcoholism.

The prodigal will concern himself about returning to his home (read family) but he will not (or cannot) do it immediately; he will stay away another year, perhaps, before returning. In Eugene O'Neill's play, *The Iceman Cometh*, the phrase spoken time and again by Jimmie Tomorrow, "first thing tomorrow morning," expresses an alcoholic's illusion that if he puts his mind to it, he can leave the home he has found in a bottle. The actor Brian Dennehy remarks that the first time the line is uttered in a Dublin production, the audience laughs, getting the point that the speaker is going nowhere, not tomorrow, not any other day. This is Bishop's earned perception at the end of "The Prodigal." Remember that making up "his mind to go home" does not mean that he will act upon that determination. It is possible, of course, that this ambivalence expresses the scapegrace-poet's own worst fears for herself.

It has also been argued that "The Prodigal" invites consideration as a parody of the parable of the Prodigal Son as told in the Gospel According to St. Luke (15:11–32). If so, it can be questioned, how closely does it come to striking its target? Studying Bishop's poem along those lines, Frank J. Kearful writes: "If we insist on stylistic mimicry as a *sine qua non* of parody, Elizabeth Bishop's 'The Prodigal' will hardly qualify, nor can it readily be said to ridicule, or make simply innocent fun of, the biblical parable. Bishop's rewriting of a religious text for secular purposes may be read, however, as a secular parody on analogy to sacred parody, which transforms a secular text for quite different religious purposes." Kearful then decides that Bishop has written a "secular parody," one that "might be classified perhaps more tellingly as a sympathetic parody in two closely related senses. Bishop's text is not an adversarial countertext and thus might be said to be 'sympathetic' toward its source text, the suspension of whose theological aegis in turn engenders an emotional responsiveness to the prodigal in all his abject fecklessness."[11] My reluctance to give unstinted assent to this view of the matter stems from the questionable assertion that Bishop's poem is "a secular parody or analogy to sacred parody." The idea here, of course, is that secular and profane forms (of poetry, song, etc.) were at times adapted by church authorities to fit sacred requirements and meet liturgical purposes. Popular airs would be divested of their profane lyrics and reinvested with religious messages. In such cases the medium, it might be said, was adopted for the sake of transmitting a new meaning. It is the same process that is at work when a secular adoption of the form of a traditional prayer or a hymn turns into a vehicle for ridicule or satire. For example, in England from the 11th to 15th centuries, writes George Kitchin, we have the first great age of religious drollery in English: "The complete service of the Mass was applied to the worship of Bacchus and Venus, and of gaming. We have an excommunication pronounced by order of Venus, and the hymns to the Virgin are turned into mock hymns in honour of wine." The "Church catechism and Paternoster, and even the school grammar-book were regularly parodied, the victims being monks, peasants, and potentates. Erotic stories were told in the language of the Bible. Saints' lives were parodied." The fact is that "there was no language too sacred for the monkish parodist to defile, no ritual too solemn. Every experience of the cleric from the Latin grammar to the Office for the Dead and his Testament was made to contribute to the fool's game."[12]

Yet, as Kearful acknowledges, Bishop's poem does not mimic the style of Scripture, nor does it ridicule, satirize or merely "make innocent fun of" the Prodigal Son parable — hence he finds it "sympathetic" to the original story — so how useful is it to call it a parody at all? Indeed, I would suggest that the poem is less an act of parody than one of "raising" a text, as the Puritans used to say, or, better still, a telling of a different story — that the prodigal's life wherever he is constitutes his life at that time and where he is living at any given time is his home. By implication the poem questions not only the prodigal's willingness to give up his prodigality but his desire to return to whatever home it was that he left in the first place.

There may be a hint here in this talk about returning home, of Robert Frost's poem "The Death of the Hired Man," which can also be seen as drawing on the parable of the Prodigal Son. Frost's poem offers two definitions of "home" — "the place where, when you have to go there, they have to take you in" and "something you somehow haven't to deserve"[13] — but Bishop's poem does not expatiate on what "home" implies when the matter is introduced in the last line of the poem. Does it refer to a place belonging to other beings as well? Is it that home equals sobriety? From the point of view of "the prodigal," the big question is what will be his reception when he arrives at home. And if the poet is presenting her own story as that of the prodigal hired man, the question has genuine biographical relevance. Nor is it emphasized that the prodigal is a son — to a mother, to a father; he is merely the orphan prodigal that Bishop seems to think of herself as being, having suffered as a child the death of her father and the disappearance of her mother (permanent, it turned out) behind the walls of a mental hospital. That this omission was intentional is suggested by the fact that in the early stages of its composition, the poet took to referring to the poem as "my 'Prodigal Son.'" Seeing "The Prodigal" as a parody of the parable recounted in St. Luke should not keep the reader from noticing that the elements of parody are overshadowed by the poet's act of imaginative filling in of the details not present in Luke's account, details that take the poem well away from the story and obscure the point of the parable. If the title sets the reader, right off, on the road to seeing that the poem is related to the New Testament for the poet's intentions, it is useful for the poet's intentions, if not absolutely essential, to persuade the reader to connect the "life" described in the poem with one of the lives in the parable against which Bishop has chosen to play off autobiographical material. Yet, if not for the explicit allusion to the parable of the Prodigal Son, it is certain that fewer of the poem's readers would see in the details and incidents of Bishop's poem that the poet has expanded on bits of information provided by Luke to create a fuller (and different) story from the one that he actually tells.[14] In Scripture the details of the son's prodigality when he is away from home are suggestive but sketchy. It is only suggestively inferential, moreover, that his return to home will mark an end to his prodigality.

Luke's parable provides Bishop with three elements: the prodigal has lived riotously, has worked as a swineherd, and has returned home. Portrayed by Bishop, however, is a prodigal still at his drinking (the extent of his riotous living insofar as we know) with no real indication, despite his thinking so, that he will ever go home. Indeed, steeped in alcohol, as well as sharing a pigsty bound by walls streaked with mud and dung, he seems to have made of his situation his home. (I am reminded of a friend, who, sipping his first martini of the day, would always sigh, before saying, "It's good to be home.")

If Bishop will (perhaps) excuse Auden his lapses in "Musée des Beaux Arts" because he is "describing a painting," she cannot employ the same rationalization to excuse herself in "The Prodigal," which derives, not from a painting, it will be recalled, but from a personal experience. Taking the poem in its entirety, and ignoring for the moment its vivid details and its formal parts — for one thing, it is a double sonnet — one can legitimately ask if Bishop has found in the prodigal and his situation an objective correlative, to zero in on the matter, for how she wants to present herself. Or if not about herself alone about all prodigal alcoholics? If so, I would submit that the prodigal of her poem (and her aunt's stepson, too) is the poet's scapegoat — a sacrificial substitute for the self she will not write about directly. She will not resort, as she so famously said, to writing poetry that is confessional. Poetical scapegoating, one infers, is preferable and perhaps more decorous or genteel. Symbolically transferring her sins to a human being whose life is animal-like is a way out of facing those sins directly in a personal lyric. The hog's hand is the scapegoat's; never, in this case, the poet's. Bishop's "cousin" does not offer her his hand, but he does invite her to partake of his rum — to share — in a sort of identification, a communion — the indiscretion, the guilt of drink. Did she accept his offer? None of this finds its way into her poem. Forgive her, one might say, for she generalizes, she universalizes, she asks for unanimity of judgment of the Prodigal, all the while deflecting attention away from the fact that, characteristically, she needs (sometimes desperately) to find a personally appropriate surrogate victim (this Prodigal will not be the last such surrogate in her poetry).[15] It's a standard modernist device. T. S. Eliot does it in "The Love Song of J. Alfred Prufrock," or, by revising away specifics that might lead to biographical speculation, as he does in "Sweeney Among the Nightingales," for instance, or "Preludes," the specificity of locale, dropping the names of places in the areas surrounding Boston and Cambridge, which belong to the memories which are transformed into poems. Certainly Bishop was aware of the devices employed by those poets to help establish their claim that poetry is not an expression of personality but an escape from personality (as Eliot put it), tricks that throw the inquisitive reader off the biographical track. Time has been a deceitful partner in her determined attempt to keep private what other lyric poets of her time — Sylvia Plath, W. D. Snodgrass, Anne Sexton — too readily displayed in poems that became almost immediately known as the effusions of the so-called "confessional" poets, a term that Bishop abhorred, along with the poetry it (inadequately) described. "I *hate* confessional poetry," she said, "and so many people are writing it these days.... Mostly they write about a lot of things which I should think were best left unsaid."[16] The sad fact, however, is that, more and more, her poems have been discovered to be even more profoundly autobiographical than even she suspected, perhaps.

In offering his cousin (the speaker of the poem) a drink, this pig-man seems to be signaling that he recognizes another of his own kind — a secret drinker (but an effectively secret one). If the poet sees this as well then the writing of the poem (and the exact content of the poem as well) serves her as a tool by which she can distance herself from "the drunk" (the addict, the sinner) and her problem. It took a long time, but at the last she managed to face her own alcoholism in a self-directed poem.

In 1960, in the course of asking Robert Lowell to send her his poem "The Drinker," Bishop mentions an (unpublished) sonnet of her own, "The Drunkard."[17] Bishop published no such poem during her lifetime. In 1992, however, a Bishop poem called "A Drunkard" was published by Thomas Travisano in the *Georgia Review*.[18] He dates it "from the 1970s," a date supported by Alice Quinn, who in her notes to the poem in her edition of Bishop's uncollected poems, drafts, and fragments points to the survival of the first nine lines of a draft on Kirkland House stationery: as Quinn notes, Bishop moved into Kirkland House, the home of Harvard University's English Department, on October 3, 1970.[19]

"A Drunkard" is not a sonnet, however; it runs to 47 lines. Assuming that the sonnet and the poem as we now have it derived from the same material (that is, memories of the Salem fire and the presence of her mother during the aftermath, etc.), the slight change in title parallels (somewhat) the change Bishop made in the titles assigned to the poem about the boy working among the pigs, which carried the working title of "The Prodigal Son" but became, later, "The Prodigal." Whereas dropping the word "Son" from the title helps Bishop distance the poem a bit from the scriptural story she obviously alludes to, the change from "The" to "A" tends to diminish the archetypal or generic possibilities in the situation. This reduces a potentially larger claim, perhaps, to a smaller, more personal one thus making this poem, as Travisano concludes, "among the most personally revealing that Bishop ever produced."

Bishop's memory of "the Salem fire," which occurred when she was three, is entangled for her with memories of her mother and of her (unattended to) thirst at the time. The association of fire and water, thirst and drink, come together in her poem as a sort of explanatory cause of her adulthood-long alcoholism. Unlike "The Prodigal," in which she was able to employ the boy as her scapegoat and thereby avoid talking about herself as an alcoholic, she now speaks in her own confessional voice: "But since that night, that day, that reprimand / I have suffered from abnormal thirst," such that "by the age / of twenty or twenty-one I had begun / to drink, & drink." In fact, "I can't get enough / and, as you must have noticed," she admits, "I'm half-drunk now..."[20]

But these confessional lines do not bring the poem to conclusion. There is one more line, one that takes the poem in another direction. "And all I'm telling you may be a lie..." brings into doubt the authenticity of her account of the facts and the reliability of her "confession." Perhaps none of what she has just said actually happened and thus cannot be used to "explain" her drunkenness, in short, that it was the foundational moment for her thirst for alcohol. It is also, however, another kind of, and rather sly, bit of confession. Alcoholics lie, the truism runs, and at the end she holds out the possibility that the final statement itself may also be a lie. Just another explanation that does not explain the thing it is meant to explain. Beneath it all the poet may have qualms about scapegoating her personal past, especially her long-lost mother's role in those would-be primal events, the beginnings, perhaps, of taking personal responsibility. In this sense, "A Drunkard" stands in stark contrast to "The Prodigal." But, it must be noted, even though there may be some question as to whether or not the poem is "finished" as we have it, she did choose to finish it or, if the poem is complete (it seems finished to me) to send it off to the *New Yorker*. It is a well-known fact that Bishop deprecated the "confessional" bent of poets in her day — of course, what she usually meant was the Beats and their followers — but she was not averse to writing personal poems about her own family life — just, it seems — to making them public. Nor did she criticize Robert Lowell for his ever-greater dependence after the late 1950s on personal and family material for poems that have been long characterized — rightly or wrongly — as "confessional."

19

Burning Bridges

Surely one of the most popular poems of 19th- and early 20th-century England was Mrs. Felicia Hemans's "Casabianca," a poem extolling the old verities of filial love, unwavering loyalty, and unswerving obedience.

> The boy stood on the burning deck,
> Whence all but he had fled;
> The flame that lit the battle's wreck
> Shone round him o'er the dead.
>
> Yet beautiful and bright he stood,
> As born to rule the storm —
> A creature of heroic blood,
> A proud, though childlike form.
>
> The flames rolled on — he would not go
> Without his father's word;
> That father, faint in death below,
> His voice no longer heard.
>
> He called aloud: — "Say, father! say
> If yet my task is done!"
> He knew not that the chieftain lay
> Unconscious of his son.
>
> "Speak, father!" once again he cried,
> "If I may yet be gone!"
> And but the booming shots replied,
> And fast the flames rolled on.
>
> Upon his brow he felt their breath,
> And in his waving hair,
> And looked from that lone post of death
> In still yet brave despair;
>
> And shouted but once more aloud,
> "My father! must I stay?"
> While o'er him fast, through sail and shroud,
> The wreathing fires made way.

They wrapped the ship in splendor wild,
They caught the flag on high,
And streamed above the gallant child
Like banners in the sky.

There came a burst of thunder sound —
The boy — O, where was he?
Ask of the winds that far around
With fragments strewed the sea!

With mast, and helm, and pennon fair,
That well had borne their part;
But the noblest thing which perished there
Was that young faithful heart.[1]

As the starting point for this romantic poem, published in 1826, Mrs. Hemans took her hint from Robert Southey's brief notation of the well-established historical incident. In the *Life of Horatio, Lord Nelson* (1813), the poet-historian had referred to the naval battle of the Nile that provided English literature and popular culture with the figure of "the boy who stood upon the burning deck" (to use the catchphrase coined by Mrs. Hemans). Southey tells the story of the young Giacomo Jocante Casabianca's death simply and without highlights: "About half of the *Orient's* crew were saved by the English boats. Among the many hundreds who perished were the Commodore, Casa-Bianca, and his son, a brave boy, only ten years old. They were seen floating on a shattered mast when the ship blew up."[2]

This was germ enough for Felicia Hemans, who felt free to embroider the incident into a moral tale of filial loyalty and steadfast courage. She changes the boy's age from ten to thirteen, thereby making him more conscious of what his conscience owes to his parent. As she explains in a footnote to the poem, "Young Casabianca, a boy about thirteen years old, son to the Admiral of the Orient, remained at his post (in the Battle of the Nile) after the ship had taken fire, and all the guns had been abandoned; and perished in the explosion of the vessel, when the flames had reached the power."[3]

Stressing the boy's moral virtue, especially the lesson to be learned from his loyal obedience to his father, Mrs. Hemans's poem became wildly popular. At mid-century, for instance, a writer in the *Child's Friend and Family Magazine* prefaced a retelling of the story with this paragraph: "Did you ever hear the story of that noble little French boy, Casabianca, who died because he would not disobey his father? Perhaps you have, and perhaps not. I will tell it to you, because, even if you have, I am sure you will not be sorry to hear so beautiful a story again. We cannot hear of good and noble actions too often."[4] A prominent New York politician — Roscoe Conkling — named Mrs. Hemans's "Casabianca" his "model poem," and Mrs. Hemans's version of the Casabianca story was told over and over in newspapers and journals throughout the century, often in detailed prose.[5]

Late in the century, however, there were those who demurred. The poem, it was said, had a "false ring" about it.[6] Indeed, according to the London *Saturday Review* in 1874, behavior that was in accord with something it called "Casabianca-ism" had become less than salubrious.

> By Casabianca-ism ... is to be understood a blind adherence to the letter of an order, or of an engagement, or to a state of things, when all the conditions under which the order was promulgated, or the engagement entered into, or the state of things came into existence, have essentially altered. Of course, it was an act of sublime obedience in Casabianca to remain where his father had told him, to perish in the flames, and in a child such an action was not only magnificent, but perfectly intelligible. But, had he possessed the mental flexibility which comes with maturer years, he would probably have perceived that the tremendous change in the state of things on board the Orient, since his father's order was given, virtually canceled that order, and restored to him his freedom of action.[7]

But none of that, of course, was what was reported as having occurred. When the ship caught fire, "all but he," as Mrs. Hemans tells us, had fled; the admiral had fallen in the conflict, and if he had "been as quick-witted as he was brave," he would have "reconsidered his situation and the duty which had been assigned to him, from the point of view of the exigency which had supervened, and of his father's wish, had he been alive, in the new crisis, to express it."[8] After all, "the last tiding his father would have desired was that he should stay to perish in the final explosion." He should have "flung himself into the waves, and endeavored to save a life so precious to his family and to France."[9]

But Mrs. Hemans's sentimental account would not give way. Even the satire of the redoubtable Samuel Butler could not do it in. In *The Way of All Flesh* (1903), the adult Ernest Pontifax looks back on his youth:

> He thought of Casabianca. He had been examined in that poem by his father not long before. 'When only would he leave his position? To whom did he call? Did he get an answer? Why? How many times did he call upon his father? What happened to him? What was the noblest life that perished there? Do you think so? Why do you think so?' And all the rest of it. Of course he thought Casabianca's was the noblest life that perished there; there could be no two opinions about that; it never occurred to him that the moral of the poem was that young people cannot begin too soon to exercise discretion in the obedience they pay to their papa and mamma. Oh, no! the only thought in his mind was that he should never, never have been like Casabianca, and that Casabianca would have despised him so much, if he could have known him, that he would not

have condescended to speak to him. There was nobody else in the ship worth reckoning at all: it did not matter how much they were blown up. Mrs. Hemans knew them all and they were a very indifferent lot. Besides, Casabianca was so good-looking and came of such a good family.[10]

A century after Felicia Hemans's death, however, the Victorian infatuation was pretty much over. In a commemorative piece, the London *Times* voiced the lament that unfortunately "the boy who stood on the burning deck has cast a faint aura of ridicule" around Mrs. Hemans.[11] And by 2000, even Mrs. Hemans's latest editor writes that this "anthology standard, its ballad form making it easy to memorize for public recitals," had attracted "numerous, often scurrilous parodies."[12] Singled out from those many parodies, Elizabeth Bishop's "Casabianca" (published in 1936, along with two other poems by Bishop, in *New Democracy* on the "New Directions" literary page edited by James Laughlin IV, and collected a decade later in *North & South*, Bishop's first book), is viewed by Mrs. Hemans's editor as "an exception to the legion of [scurrilous] parodies," for it takes seriously the "blending of filial affection and patriotic martyrdom" celebrated in "Casabianca."[13] But Bishop's poem is a parody with a wrinkle; not only is it a literary parody of a popular poem but a parody of a parody as well — the latter too scurrilous in any of its many versions to be set down here.

Surely it misrepresents Bishop's "Casabianca" to say that it, like Mrs. Hemans's poem, is about "filial affection" or "patriotic martyrdom." First of all, its title notwithstanding, Bishop's poem takes no stand on the steadfast, stiff-upper-lip heroism of the young boy who populates Mrs. Hemans's lines, one way or the other. But neither does Bishop's poem limit itself by being about lust and sex, as are the many scurrilous parodies of Mrs. Hemans's poem, or the 19th-century poem's exposition of undying if unexamined filial loyalty or love. Rather it plays extravagantly on the notion that the conviction that the wages of a fiery romantic, sentimental love are unremittingly harsh and destructive. What Bishop's "Casabianca" does, actually, is define love through the appropriated terms of Mrs. Hemans's poem, redefined, radically and operatically, into a series of metaphors serving her single, overarching conceit: "Love's the obstinate boy," love is the "ship," love is the "swimming sailors," love is the "burning boy."[14] To define Love, then, Bishop writes a poem in which she imagines the boy standing on the deck of the ship trying to recite the poem that praises him — the boy — for his putative last stand. Thus Love becomes, finally, the son who stands stammering elocution while the (poor) ship goes down in flames. Then Love is the "obstinate" boy and the ship and the swimming sailors who (fantastically) would also like a school-room platform (presumably to recite their version of the events) or, perhaps, an excuse to have enabled them to have stayed on deck. Finally, Love is the burning boy. If it is the element, the essence of "performance" in the standard version of the boy Casabianca's exploit that nails down her definition-of-love poem, it takes the whole historical catastrophe and the poem that reenacts, as it modifies, that morsel of history — poor ship, swimming sailors, obstinate burning boy — to define Love, that in its moods and phases is a poor, burning, swimming, stammering, and obstinate thing. Needless to say, the poem owes much of its aura of unsentimental objectivity to the fact that it successfully parodies Mrs. Hemans's exceedingly popular exploitation of the historical incident as well as the well-known crude parodies of adolescence that have accrued to the original "Casabianca." Notice, too, Bishop's playful nod in the direction of the long history of Hemans's poem as a favorite recital or elocutionary piece in her decision to theatricalize the boy and his "stammering elocution" as he tries to recite the original "Casabianca."

But there is something else, I think. There is more than a hint in "Casabianca" that besides taking on Mrs. Hemans's romanticism, Bishop was also drawing a bead on the great love poetry of the American 1920s and 1930s: specifically, perhaps, the poems of Edna St. Vincent Millay, her predecessor at Vassar. It is true that as early as 1928, the 17-year-old high school student reviewed Millay's volume *The Buck in the Snow*, praising it knowingly if somewhat mystically for its "almost touchable reality of beauty."[15] But by 1931, the celebrated Millay was on her sixth book of poems, publishing *Fatal Interview*, a sonnet sequence of 52 poems detailing and memorializing a fervent but doomed-to-fail love affair. Amidst much praise for this volume of poems, there were also dissenting voices that questioned the poet's poetic sincerity. If Bishop recorded her opinion on the matter, I have not found the evidence, but like Millay's Sonnet XXX, Bishop's later "Casabianca" offers a definition of "love" in terms, partly, of what "love" is not, including the human flotsam and jetsam of a shipwreck: "Love is not all; it is not meat nor drink / Nor slumber nor a roof against the rain," the poem begins, continuing with an image faintly reminiscent of Mrs. Hemans's "Casabianca," perhaps, "Nor yet a floating spar to men that sink / And rise and sink and rise and sink again...."[16]

Millay was also notoriously famous for what her biographer has called a "cheeky quatrain" that, with its publication in June 1918, just when the United States was entering the Great War, "ignited the imagination of a generation of American women," giving them their "rallying cry." It, too, involves burning and fire: "My candle burns at both ends; / It will not last the night; / But ah, my foes, and oh, my friends —/ It gives a lovely light!"[17] If nothing else, Bishop's burning-deck poem can serve as a reality check to Millay's warmly self-congratulatory but very memorable message.

20

The Misprint and the Mouse

Among Elizabeth Bishop's earliest publications after graduating from college were poems and stories in the British periodical *Life and Letters To-Day*: "The Man-Moth" (Spring 1936), "The Baptism" (Spring 1937), "The Hanging of the Mouse" (Autumn 1937), "The Sea and Its Shore" (Winter 1937), "Sleeping on the Ceiling" (October 1938), and "Sleeping Standing Up" (November 1938). I shall focus on two of those contributions, the poem "The Man-Moth" and the story "The Hanging of the Mouse," partly, but not entirely so, because each of them has an affinity with the fiction of Franz Kafka.

When Bishop included "The Hanging of the Mouse" in *Complete Poems* (1969), she fudged its generic status. In this book of poems the story appears under the rubric "New and Uncollected Works." Did she consider "The Hanging of the Mouse" a prose-poem, albeit an example of that rare thing, a narrative prose-poem? Or did she just put it in, along with "Rainy Season; Sub-Tropics," comprised of other prose pieces "Giant Toad," "Strayed Crab," and "Giant Snail" (all three of them interior dramatic monologues, linked in time since they take place over the same duration of time) to stretch out a volume she insisted on calling *Complete Poems*?

In any case, "The Hanging of the Mouse," which stands second in this section of *Complete Poems*, is best approached, I think — story or prose poem — by viewing it in the tradition of the animal fable, stretching back to Aesop, of course, and through La Fontaine (a favorite with her friend Marianne Moore, who later translated his work to great acclaim), the movie cartoons of Bishop's day, and the fiction of Franz Kafka — "The Burrow," for example, and "Metamorphosis," the latter first published in English translation in the mid–1930s.

The Kafka story published in *Life and Letters To-Day* in the issue immediately preceding the one that published Bishop's "The Hanging of the Mouse" (the autumn issue for 1937) was "The Trapeze Artist." Not a beast fable this time, Kafka's story about the trapeze artist whose obsession with his artistry takes over his waking and sleeping life to the extent that he spends his days and nights on the trapeze platform and swing (an absurdist, surreal situation) relies for its texture on realistic details. "The Hanging of the Mouse," though the connection is mostly a matter of affinity, is structured on the absurdist situation that insects and animals can desire, engineer and execute a hanging. Accepting the situation as a given, the reader is then treated to the morality of the state's ritual killing of a criminal (as the mouse is characterized once and one time only, though its crime is never revealed). Every bit of the "ceremony" is carried out according to the best authorities (as Tom Sawyer might say when setting up Jim's incarceration and escape at the Phelps farm). The beetles (beadles?) escort the criminal and, when necessary, prop him up (though the mouse's gender is never specified) and keep him on the direct path to the gallows. The religious portion is provided by a praying mantis, one that seems to have no stomach for the proceedings and clearly looks down on the executioner, guards, and criminal alike. The raccoon executioner wears his mask, of course, and wears kid gloves — but only after he has ritually washed the rope that will be used in the hanging. Echoing the final scene of a contemporary crime movie, *The Public Enemy*, in which the criminal (played by James Cagney) is dragged screaming for surcease to the electric chair (he feigns cowardice so that he will not serve as a model to young would-be criminals — a sop, undoubtedly, to the Hays Office), Bishop's mouse, after the rope has been "tied exquisitely behind one of his little round ears," raised "a hand and wiped his nose with it"— a gesture that the admiring crowd misinterprets as, perhaps bravely, a "farewell wave," spoken of by the crowd for weeks after. As if in a cartoon, when the trap is sprung (by the hangman's son, no less), the criminal's "whiskers rowed hopelessly round and round in the air a few times and his feet flew up and curled into little balls like young fernplants." The effect of all this on the crowd is particularized in sentences centering on the tears of a cat, "who had brought her child in her mouth," and now "shed several large tears," which "roll[ing] down on to the child's back," cause the child to "squirm and shriek." This behavior on the part of the child the mother cat — a mouse's natural enemy, under ordinary circumstances — decides is evidence "that the sight of the hanging had perhaps been too much" for the child. But she thinks it "an excellent moral lesson, nevertheless."

That "The Hanging of the Mouse" is an absurdist story seems to be the point in not specifying what the mouse has done to brand him as a criminal deserving of a public execution. One possible inference — and it would be entirely warranted were "The Hanging of the Mouse" a story by Kafka — the author of, say, *The Trial*—is that the mouse's crime is simply that he exists.

Perhaps it can be said that the mouse is a scapegoat — the best or worst epitome of its society (no matter which) — in a society that requires its scapegoats. Early in the year in which "The Hanging of the Mouse' was first published, Bishop wrote to Marianne Moore. "I once hung Minnow's [her cat's] artificial mouse on a string to a chairback, without thinking what I was doing — it looked very sad."[1] The execution of Minnow's artificial mouse, done "without thinking," is an absurdist image, one worthy of an absurdist animal fable.[2] It is also a ritual of the execution — one step removed — of an anthropomorphized mouse. It is no coincidence that Walt Disney's Mickey Mouse, by the 1930s, was already a near-constant presence in movie-house cartoons and the comic pages of newspapers across the land and beyond. It has been said that Mickey Mouse had that "crucial trait" in the midst of the Great Depression, "indefatigable, cheerful pluck in the face of adversity."[3] This was not a trait that would have endeared him to the depressive Bishop. But even Disney was no longer entirely happy with Mickey. In an interview published in *Life and Letters To-Day* in September 1935 — two years before the same journal published Bishop's "The Hanging of the Mouse" — Disney is himself reported as having become "rather tired of that mouse," for good reason. "Disney says sadly, that Mickey now has to behave." "In the old days (which some of us still remember), Mickey was as metaphysical as that felicitous cat he finally chased out of films," comments the interviewer. "Not so now. His logic is literal. He is matter-of-fact. Disney foresaw this ... Mickey now is not poetry, but verse. That is because the women's clubs of America have taken hold of him. They welcomed certain aspects of that mouse, refused others. Mickey, therefore, has become limited in personality."[4]

In "The Man-Moth" Bishop gives us a Kafkaesque antihero, not unlike his trapeze artist. Robert Lowell saw a connection. "I gave my class your 'Man-Moth,' unidentified, last week, as an illustration of good description that also builds a new world like Kafka. How breathlessly real, the little creature, — itself, us, you, — is! I had been talking to you, all veils off, and was very much surprised."[5] Thus Lowell made the connection — with "Metamorphosis" on his mind if not his tongue — that must occur to many readers. In 1974, thanking Lowell for sending on a clipping of a piece by Irvin Ehrenpreis, Bishop writes: "I don't think it makes too much sense — logically speaking (? right? — sounds funny) but it is nice to have someone like me that much. But" — she goes on — "did you notice the weird misprint? — 'the little of our earthly *crust*' instead of *trust*? Misprints are so much worse when they seem to make sense" — or better, depending on the reader.[6] "The Man-Moth," of course, is a case in point, especially when the poet is Bishop and if she is to be believed.

For *Poet's Choice*, Paul Engle and Joseph Langland's 1962 anthology of poems selected by their authors, along with an authorial comment or explanation, Elizabeth Bishop chose "The Man-Moth." Bishop explained that the poem, written in 1935 (and first published in 1936, in *Life and Letters To-Day*) shortly after she arrived in New York City, had been inspired by a misprint she had noticed in a daily newspaper. "I've forgotten what it was that was supposed to be 'mammoth,'" she wrote, "but the misprint seemed meant for me. An oracle spoke from the page of the *New York Times*, kindly explaining New York City to me, at least for a moment."[7] This appears to have been the first time that she identified the *New York Times* as the newspaper source for the (for her) so fruitful misprint. It should be noted, however, that when the poem was first published, the note explaining Bishop's title read simply, as it has in all subsequent printings of the poem, "newspaper misprint for 'mammoth.'"[8]

Through the search engine ProQuest I have gone through the *New York Times* searching (unsuccessfully) for the term "man-moth" during the 1930s. Perhaps Bishop's memory failed her in this instance, and it was some other newspaper that carried the misprint. What I did find in my search was the curious coincidence that on December 1, 1900, the *New York Times* reported Oscar Wilde's death in Paris: "Oscar Wilde died at 3 o'clock this afternoon in the Maison du Perier, Rue des Beaux Arts, in the Latin Quarter. It is a small, obscure hotel, at which Wilde had been living for several months under the name of Manmoth."[9] This appearance of "Manmoth" is readily explained; it is a misprint for the "Melmoth" portion of Wilde's well-known alias, "Sebastian Melmoth." One would like to imagine this misprint as being the thing that stirred Bishop's imagination — consider the drab, brownish color of the ordinary moth in contrast with the purple coats and cravats of Oscar Wilde in his heyday, preening before the delighted miners in Leadville, Colorado. But that Wilde was a source for Bishop's poem is at best improbable.[10]

If the ProQuest search turned up no other instances of the misprint "Manmoth" in the *New York Times*, it did provide two other instances of the term — in *The American Farmer* in 1839 and in *Life* in 1923. The former reported on a case of "Manmoth" chicken eggs — a clear case of a misprint.[11] In the latter, however, the word is not a misprint. It appears in "Necessities," a poem by F. M., who remains unidentified, and it refers to a lumberjack with a saw seen from the point of view of a 60-year-old tree that is about to be cut down.[12] He is "the Man-moth, / With the saw-tooth blight." As the tree laments, "The Moth says I'm worth / Nothing as I am," but "a great deal to Grand Rapids." What is interesting here is that a dozen years before Bishop wrote her poem, the author of "Necessities," this otherwise rather pedestrian poem, had hit on the fanciful notion of presenting the woodcutter or sawyer of forests as a destructive insect bringing about "the saw-tooth blight" that "consumes" forests. It, too, like the common garden-variety moth comes out of darkness to do its part for furniture-making factories. Now it is not impossible that, as she claimed, Bishop's idea of the "Man-Moth" derived from a "mis*print*" — possibly, even, from "Necessities," the poem in *Life* in 1923. On the other hand, it may be conjectured, the fanciful conceit of a "Man-Moth" existing underground in New York City, coming out only at night to be attracted by the light of the moon, might have been independently conceived. In which case her assertion of its appearance on the first page of the *New York Times* would give it, strangely enough, the kind of actuality that she preferred as a basis for much of her poetry. She saw it somewhere. She didn't make it up out of whole cloth. And she saw it — keen observer that she is — in the *New York Times*, the newspaper that prides itself on printing "all the news that's fit to print."

At first glance, moreover, it seems odd that Bishop's "Moth-Man" (to bring him more in line with superheroes about to emerge) should make his appearance when he does. The second half of the decade of the 1930s, in the area of the American comic-book, is a period of beginnings. Those years saw the first comic book gestures toward the invention of the first modern superheroes. "Superman" appeared on the scene in 1938 and "Batman" (a nocturnal creature who lives in a cave) in 1939, two and three years, respectively, after the publication of Bishop's "The Man-Moth" appeared in London in 1936 (well before the appearance of "Spiderman" in the American comics[13]). But her "Man-moth" is the anti-superhero, *avant la lettre*, the answer to a superhero some others might have called "Mothman." Moreover, Bishop's super-anti-superhero, "The Moth-Man," is the superhero artist, in some ways reflecting, as has been noted above, Kafka's trapeze artist, who moves in the air, high above ground, in a tale that is told in English in the 1937 issue of *Life and Letters To-Day*, in which appears, fortuitously, Bishop's "The Hanging of the Mouse."

It is not incidental either that Bishop's "Man-moth" appears in a decade that saw the widespread growth of fascism and the consolidation of dictatorships in many countries, notably Germany, Spain, Portugal and, preeminently, Italy, in the persons of Hitler, Franco, Salazar and Mussolini. The politicization of Nietzsche's notion of the *übermensch*, insinuated so successfully in practical politics, also insinuated itself into the notion of the comic-book superhero. I would also argue that it worked its way into Elizabeth Bishop's poetry in the form, curiously, not of the *übermensch* but his opposite, the nocturnal man-moth (a Kafka-like insect-man) who is the reticent, timid, diffident antihero of the underworld — a silent version of Dostoyevsky's underground man.

But Bishop's superhero is also a comic figure. The "man-moth is a tortured figure in his Chaplinesque way."[14] He is "Charlito"—Chaplin's famous alter ego—the small, low man, the schlemiel, the victim, always beset, distressed, under stress, but victorious in small ways. "Yet, as his agonies are expressed," it has been ventured, "they have been distilled into a rejuvenating substance, 'cool as from underground springs and pure enough to drink.'"[15] Even the gesture in Bishop's poem (last lines) recalls Chaplin—"Slyly he palms it [the tear], and if you're not paying attention / he'll swallow it. However, if you watch, he'll hand it over, / cool as from underground springs and pure enough to drink." This piece of potential capitulation brings to mind in some small but meaningful way those familiar scenes from one of Chaplin's movies where he hands over to the pursuer, persecutor, policeman, soldier (what have you) whatever he has been hiding from him.[16]

Edmund Wilson's "Philoctetus: The Wound and the Bow," an essay published in the *New Republic* in 1941 and collected in Wilson's *Wound and the Bow* in the same year, appeared five years after Bishop published "The Man-Moth" in *Life and Letters To-Day*; otherwise one might entertain the idea that Bishop's central notion of the social function of the artist was derived from Wilson. As it stands, however, it is possible that Wilson's notion that society ostracizes the artist until there is a social crisis owes something to Bishop.

The fact that the "man-moth" is a nocturnal creature was important enough to Bishop to prompt her to offer a correction to Oswaldino Marques's translation of the "moth" part of "man-moth," that "*bruxa*" ("nocturnal") was preferable to "*traça*" ("clothes moth").[17] It is interesting that while Flora Süssekind follows Bishop's suggestion,[18] Paulo Henriques Britto, Bishop's Brazilian translator, opts for "Homem-Mariposa," that is, "butterfly" or "nocturnal moth."[19] He sacrifices the appropriately precise "*bruxa*" for the connotation of "*mariposa*," which in colloquial Brazilian speech denotes "a call-girl, a high-class prostitute,"[20] but in Spanish colloquial speech refers to a "fairy" or "queer."[21] One of the interpretive effects of choosing "*mariposa*" over Marques's "*traça*" and Bishop's "*bruxa*" is to call attention to what may be one of the more secreted (even Wildean) intentions in "The Man-Moth."

Like Wilson's Philoctetes-like artist who stands and waits for the call of a society in distress, Bishop's Man-moth-artist can also be said to be "on call." But language is a wonderfully funny thing: Marques's "*traça*" has its own appropriateness. If it foregoes the greater precision of "*bruxa*," it does evoke the word "*traçada*," meaning "swallow," "gulp," and "swig,"[22] which, in turn, recalls the tear that Bishop's Man-moth will swallow, if not caught as he is about to do so.

21

Building a Rhyme for Ezra

It was thus — the "Ezra Pound Song" — that Bishop described "Visits to St. Elizabeths," a poem first published, strangely enough, in Italian and in an Italian journal.[1] This episode started out simply enough. An insert in *Nuova Corriente di letteratura*, published in Genoa, announcing an upcoming "Ezra Pound" issue, advertises, as a feature, "Elizabeth Bishop: Intervista con Ezra Pound."[2] Unfortunately, Bishop's proposed interview with Pound did not materialize, not then, not later. But the American poet did send a contribution: a poem about Pound. It was offered in lieu of the "interview," as explained in an editorial footnote when in 1956 *Nuova Corriente* published "Visits to St. Elizabeths" (in English) and "Visite all'Ospedale di Santa Elisabetta" (in an Italian translation by Alfredo Rizzardi) on facing pages.[3] Since this poem's existence, in some version or other, dates from no later than November 1951,[4] the fact that she held "this bitter jingle"[5] from publication until 1955 and then chose to offer it for first publication in an Italian journal suggests that she may have felt safer with an Italian readership, one that would be less hostile to a poem about Pound, than with an English-reading audience. After all, it could be said that in the 1930s and '40s the American poet, rightly or wrongly, had acted in good faith on behalf of the Italian nation. In any case, the Italian publication of the poem (in English and in Rizzardi's Italian translation) preceded its appearance in the *Partisan Review* in 1957, where it led off the issue. Below the title she added the date "1950," making it clear that her visits to Pound at St. Elizabeths took place during her period of service as Consultant in Poetry to the Library of Congress.[6] Perhaps, it was a case of lapse of memory, for she had visited Pound at St. Elizabeths before she went to Washington, for in a letter to Robert Lowell, dated May 18, 1948, she thanks him for taking her to see Pound, adding "I am really endlessly grateful for the experience."[7] It is important to note that Bishop's and Lowell's visit to St. Elizabeths preceded the great controversy, a year later, over the awarding of the first Bollingen Prize for *The Pisan Cantos* (1948) in 1949, an award made by the Library of Congress fellows, to Pound for his *Pisan Cantos*, poems written while he was imprisoned at the end of World War II in Italy by the U.S. military. Sample newspaper headlines give some sense of the furor provoked by the award to Pound: "Ezra Pound, Held as Traitor, Gets Poetry Award," *Los Angeles Times*, February 20, 1949, p. 1, and "Pound, in Mental Clinic, Wins Prize for Poetry Penned in Treason Cell," *New York Times*, February 20, 1949, pp. 1, 14 — the latter taken from the Associated Press.[8] In literary circles at large the brouhaha over giving the Bollingen award to Pound would persist for years, if not decades. Its effect on politics in Washington did not last nearly as long, but it was still very much in the air in D.C. in September 1949, when Bishop assumed the position of Consultant in Poetry. The matter did not quiet down in Washington until Congress took away the Library of Congress's role in administering the Bollingen Prize or, for that matter, the ability to award any prize whatsoever. That Bishop continued to visit Pound at St. Elizabeths throughout her stay in Washington attests to her continued curiosity about the poet as well as her courage.

Yet the recollections of Bishop's San Francisco friend, Marjorie Brush, should be taken into account as evidence of how Bishop recalled those visits of 1949–50 nearly two decades later, in 1968. Elizabeth told her that the visits were a "duty" but "awful" and "how she suffered visiting Pound because he lived in a room with no doors.... People would go in and out, guards and other patients, and Pound was cross and kind of mean.... She wasn't sympathetic to Pound personally."[9] Testimony as to Bishop's actions and feelings at the time when she was making those visits to Pound at St. Elizabeths in March 1950 is provided by the poet Weldon Kees in a letter to a friend: "I looked up Elizabeth Bishop, a very nice person, and she asked me if I'd like to see Pound. She had to go over to the hospital the next afternoon to take him some books from the Library of Congress." Noting that Pound was allowed to receive "visitors from 2 to 4 every afternoon," he recorded that "Mrs. Pound, who lives in Washington, goes to see him daily." But Kees found his own visit dispiriting though valuable. "I found the experience somewhat inhuman, rather like visiting a museum, but certainly not an experience to have missed. He 'receives' at the end of a corridor in the hospital, which is a pretty gloomy affair, with catatonics and dementia praecox cases slithering about; but he certainly keeps up a spirit." Pound was "very lively and brisk," his eyes going "through you like knives." He notes, too, that Pound called Bishop "'Liz Bish,' which she doesn't care for; nor does she care much for Pound, regarding him as a pretty dangerous character, through his influence — particularly the anti–Semitism — on the young. ... But he's far from crazy, I'd say, though an egomaniac of the first water."[10]

Bishop's published letters tell something of the story of her interest in

Pound, a preoccupation that began in college. Her published letters provide ample evidence. While still at Vassar, she wrote to her friend, Donald E. Stanford, on January 21, 1934: "I've just been reading the article on Pound he [R. P. Blackmur] has in the last *Hound & Horn*. I think he is very good."[11] In a letter to her friend, Frani Blough, on January 30, 1935, she quoted Pound: "Then, as Ezra Pound says somewhere, 'The further poetry departs from music, the more decadent it gets,' etc., and I want to learn whatever I can about the periods when it hadn't yet departed — which is approximately up to the end of the clavichord days..."[12] To Marianne Moore, on April 2, 1935, Bishop wrote: "I didn't know until Mr. Wilson told me last night that Ezra Pound plays some early instruments himself, and has written about Arnold Dolmetsch."[13] Sometime later, on September 21, 1938, Bishop writes to Moore: "My friend Frani Blough brought me a whole collection of little books of Provençal poetry. I had never read any except the quotations in Pound's essay, and I have been reading it a great deal, and also 'Mother Goose,' which I brought along too [to Key West]. Between Peire Vidal and 'The House That Jack Built,' I have enclosed some rhyme schemes that I hope will impress you — or *amaze*, anyway."[14] Here, interestingly enough, Bishop loosely associates Pound with the "Mother Goose" and "The House That Jack Built" rhymes, nearly a decade before his internment in St. Elizabeth's Hospital. We shall come back to this. By 1949, while serving as Consultant in Poetry, Bishop took it upon herself to visit Pound. To Robert Lowell, on December 22, 1949, she wrote: "I'm about to go to see Pound and take him some eau de cologne. So far my presents have not met with much success but maybe this will. He's reading Mirabeau's memoirs at a great rate. Mrs. [Pound] now has a telephone and calls me up. I think she holds out very well."[15] The visits were not without their problems, of course. For instance, to Robert Lowell, on June 27, 1950, she wrote: "Pound is mad at me because I put off getting something microfilmed for him. He thought there wasn't a moment to waste because once Luther [Evans] (who'll be hung, anyway) finds out what inflammable material it is, etc. etc."[16] Something of the unpleasant curmudgeon that Bishop knew Pound to be is revealed in an August 17, 1950, letter to Lowell: "I took your ex-pupil, John Edwards, out there [to St. Elizabeths] Friday afternoon. We had quite a pleasant visit, I thought, & Pound is very forgiving about my not coming oftener, although he sees right through me — tells everyone how I always 'have to bring someone else along.'"[17] On August 23, 1950, she reported to Lowell: "Yesterday I had lunch with John Edwards'[s] wife, & 9-month old baby — they were taking *him* to spend the afternoon with Pound & I'm sorry I couldn't see that interview."[18] Writing to Pearl Kazin, on November 16, 1953, Bishop speculated about poets, their longevity, and what they managed to get away with: "*Why* do some poets manage to get by and live to be malicious old bores like Frost or — probably — pompous old ones like Yeats, or crazy old ones like Pound — and some just don't!"[19]

By 1956 Bishop had written and published her Pound poem, "Visits to St. Elizabeths," in which she avoids identifying Pound by name. To Robert Lowell, on September 24, 1956, she wrote, somewhat misleadingly, about the date of the poem's composition (she later set the date as November 1951). "I wrote a kind of poem, not much, for Mr. Rizzardi's number on Pound."[20] "Mr. Rizzardi translated it — and sounded rather well in Italian, I thought," she wrote on "May Day" 1957 to Isabella Gardner, who had told Bishop that she liked "the Pound poem." "I really couldn't tell much myself whether it conveyed my rather mixed emotions or not," she confessed.[21] Some of those "mixed emotions" persisted over the years, affecting even her behavior where Pound was concerned. To Robert Lowell, on October 30, 1958, she wrote: "Frost — the Bad Gray Poet. I read some remarks of his about Pound — just what the public wants to hear, I'm afraid."[22] But when Pound died she did not participate in the "Requiem" program. As she wrote to James Merrill, on January 8, 1973: "Cal Lowell is here, or en route — I'm having dinner with him. He came over for the Pound 'Requiem' affair Friday night in N.Y. I refused to participate."[23] She could not have been pleased with Lowell's decision, when he received the National Book Award on Bishop's behalf for her *Complete Poems* in 1970, to read her "Visits to St. Elizabeths" and to remarking that Pound's *Drafts & Fragments of Cantos CX-XXVII* should have been nominated as well. What could Lowell have been thinking? Obviously, he wished to make a point about poetry, prizes, and politics. In a letter to Bishop, dated March 11, 1970, Lowell offered a description of the incident, as well as an explanation for what he had done on the occasion — using Bishop's rhyme about Pound to buttress his complaint about the jury's having left Pound's name off its list of writers to be considered for the Award. "No one even noticed the omission, but there was great clamor about [Vladimir Nabokov's] *Ada* and [Philip Roth's] *Portnoy* not being listed." With this brief account of the background for his bold actions, he plunged into an account of what happened next. When it came his turn to speak, he started out by apologizing that he felt "very shy receiving the award" for Bishop, that she had always been his "favorite poet and favorite friend." "I spoke of your enormous powers of realistic observation and of something seldom found with observation, luminism (meaning radiance and compression etc.)," he wrote. "Then I said I was going to say something perhaps ungracious, but that I cared not, because I would consider myself dishonored if I didn't say it." He would talk about Pound, an important author "who had published a little book in June, one of his good books and quite possibly his last," but who not been mentioned by any one at the awards. He noted that his remarks had been preceded by the reading of "a long communication from the author of the prize-winning Huey Long biography" and that "not a word of criticism" had been spoken. It was, he said, "like Humphrey speaking of Johnson five years ago." And before that, "Lillian Hellman had made a 'courageous' attack on [the then U.S. vice president, Spiro T.] Agnew." "You've just heard about two great statesmen," Lowell persevered ironically. "Pound was a very small statesman and a very great poet." It was then that he read Bishop's "Visits to St. Elizabeths," "a clear poem whose meaning was hard to determine," its tone "reverential mockery or mocking reverence." When he returned to his seat on the stage he received "decent applause," but behind him heard a voice saying, "I announce that I sever myself from this anti-semitic fascist performance." The words, as he later learned, were spoken by Kenneth Rexroth, one of the judges. But the master of ceremonies, Lowell acknowledged, "saved my life by instantly saying, I want to announce that I disassociate myself from anyone who could say what you've just heard was anti-semitic or Fascist. There was faint applause for Rexroth and more for the master of ceremonies."[24]

Perhaps it was due to its form that Lowell was enticed into thinking that at least on balance "Visits to St. Elizabeths" did not convey, finally, any disapproval of the incarcerated Pound. Employing a structure of accumulative rhyme, most notably exemplified by the folk poem "The House That Jack Built," Bishop's poem offers less a portrait of the man doomed to spend his days in this "house of Bedlam" than a protectively coded presentation of Bishop's "mixed emotions" about him.[25] Thus, availing herself of the seeming objectivity of the folk rhyme, she is able to express her conflicted take on Ezra Pound. It licenses her to express her feelings — mainly pity and censure — about the vexed and vexing poet by pointing to the traits and habits of the other habitués of this house of Bedlam without dropping into sentimentality. Consider, too, the words Bishop uses to describe Pound, in the order in which they appear in the poem: "tragic," "talkative," "honored," "old, brave," "cranky," "cruel," "busy," "tedious," "poet," and "wretched." (Note that the designation "poet" appears next to last in this sequence, not last, where another, more sympathetic poet might have placed it.) And since, in a sense, Ezra had "earned" his stay in the madhouse — 12 years, it turned out, in a secure ward for the criminally insane — by his traitorous, anti–American and anti–Semitic radio broadcasts in Italy in the 1930s and 1940s, Bishop feels free to bring in the Semite ("Jew in a newspaper hat / that dances weeping down the ward") and the patriot (the "batty," "silent," "staring," "crazy" sailor). The ironic point, of course, as Bishop knew, was that the "Jew" and the "sailor" were legitimate inmates of St. Elizabeths Hospital, while the poet's bona fides as a patient amounted to his having been declared unfit to stand trial, a somewhat engineered decision that saved him from being executed for the treason that he had unmistakably committed. Indeed, the facts behind Pound's confinement has led Bishop's Brazilian translator to a still contentious question: "madmen, like children, are beyond judgments of good and evil; but how mad *is* Pound?"[26]

This question of Pound's madness leads to another matter: the possibility that Bishop's anxiety and confusion over how to understand Pound's situation and character may also be related to the question of Bishop's own failure to accept the facts (as presented to her, a child) of her own mother's madness and internment in the "house of Bedlam" where she would die. The connection is fortuitously buttressed (if ironically) in Bishop's decision to risk the identity that readers might make between her given name and the name of the institution housing Pound and to do so in a "parody" of a bona fide *children's* folk rhyme. Then there is the teasing possibility — not to be gone into at this time — that there are below-the-surface connections to be made among the terms "Saint," "The Pope" (a Pound sobriquet) and "The Bishop" (when a student at Vassar).

Given the complexity of her feelings about Pound, it is not surprising, thus, that she was less than pleased at the news that upon his release from St. Elizabeths Ezra Pound would make his home not in Italy, but, surprisingly, in Brazil. Anxious, apprehensive, sure that an Ezra Pound living in Brazil could bring no good, she wrote to Lowell about the rumor on May 8, 1958: "There is an enormous Italian colony in São Paulo, and he might well have fascist friends there, and he *did* translate some of Camões, and the exchange *is* extremely high now (but so are prices here) ... so I suppose there are reasons why it may be true. It depresses me terribly, though, to think of him spreading more anti–Americanism here, where there is already a lot of it."[27] Of course, if he did come, she continued, she would call on him in Rio, and help Mrs. Pound, even have him up to Samambaia — "maybe." As a final thought, she decided that Pound would probably be settled in São Paulo, and if he ever saw that poem of hers, he might not want to see her anyway. As it happened and to what must have been Bishop's great relief, Pound did not retire to Brazil but to Italy.

If at some point the old poet in exile did read her "Ezra Pound Song," as Bishop feared he might, or had it sung to him,[28] or had even just learned of its existence, there is no mention in the records consulted. It would be nice to think that the old poet might have found something to agree with in Randall Jarrell's assessment. "I like the Pound poem," he told Bishop, "it gets all the ways one feels about him and the poor contradictory awful and nice ways he is, and it's more varied and specifically live, than I'd have thought it possible for a House-that-Jack-built poem to be."[29] Not a good bet, though.

22

Send in a Toy

The 20th-century Portuguese poet Jorge de Sena once offered the paradox that the act of giving a poem a title creates a second poem. Changing the title of a poem does something different. It may modify the original poem such that it becomes a new poem. A case in point is Bishop's "Cirque d'Hiver," which the poet originally called "Spleen," the title it carried when she first submitted it to *The New Yorker* for editorial consideration. To Marianne Moore, on November 20, 1939, Elizabeth Bishop reported: "*The New Yorker* took the little poem about the toy horse — only I changed the title to 'Cirque d'Hiver.'"[1] The poem's new title referred to the famous building in Paris, where since 1852 it has been the venue for concerts, wrestling matches, fashion shows, and, of course, grand circuses. Pleased with her success at having broken into *The New Yorker*, she nevertheless underplayed the feat by describing her poem, somewhat disingenuously, in a letter to her friend Frani Blough (Muser), as "very minor"—and (no longer burdened with the title of "Spleen") to Marianne Moore, as the little poem "about the toy horse."[2] But minor or not, "Cirque d'Hiver" initiated her long career as a writer for *The New Yorker*, for, as she told Marianne Moore at the time, they asked to see more of her work.

By originally calling her poem "Spleen," Bishop rather directly gave it (boldly if not brazenly) an explicitly French literary context. The title recalled Charles Baudelaire's depressive poems about ennui, acedia or vapory malaise, a reference that would serve as background to her poem's last, brave response: "Well, we have come this far." But *The New Yorker* would not have it. "There's only one change we much insist upon," insisted her editor. "The title *Spleen* doesn't seem to us to suit the poem at all and I'm sure you will be able to find one that is more appropriate."[3] Calling the poem "Cirque d'Hiver" maintained an overall French context, though not a remarkably literary one. And the new title "created" a different poem. Rather than sharing something of the depressive tone and sentiments of Baudelaire's "Spleen," Bishop's poem now offered its readers an opportunity to partake of the sense of play and reap the rewards of amusement that is the institution of the Parisian Cirque d'Hiver, though, to be precise, it is not even Paris's Cirque d'Hiver itself that is present in the poem. It's there symbolically, or more precisely, metonymically in a simulacrum of the circus's flesh-and-blood horse and rider. Standing in for the real thing in the flesh, the mechanical wind-up toy represents only a piece of the live performance at the Cirque d'Hiver, as it moves through its moves. Twice it canters a few steps and bows before winding to a stop. It has not moved much but it cannot be denied that it has moved, modestly, "this far." Notably the sentence, placed within quotation marks, is spoken — but by whom? Has the poet merely given voice (and an attitude) to the voiceless mechanical toy, and if so, to what part of the toy? The rider? The horse? To the two of them, taken together as they are pinned one to the other, as well as to the large key that must be wound up to give them movement? And "this far" — does it refer merely to the movement in space effected by the toy's few short "steps" or to the distance in time it has taken to take these few steps? Perhaps, the words quoted are attributable to the toy, words that remind the poet of where she has been and where she is now. Or does the toy remind the poet of what she has accomplished in writing the poem, and, more important, that the poem is itself something of a mechanical toy (meter, rhyme, etc.)? And to boot, in the dancer's attachment to the horse we have, perhaps, an allegory of the poet's relationship to her horse — Pegasus, the muse of poetry. If the poet anthropomorphizes the toy, endowing figure and animal with sensation (and more than a touch, perhaps, of sensuality — the horse "bears" the dancer and "feels her pink toes dangle toward his back / along the little pole / that pierces both her body and her soul") — recall that the "little pole" that "pierces both her body and her soul" goes through his body, reappearing "under his belly, as a big tin key." Oddly, this key to the toy's movement is also the sign of an irrevocable joining of dancer to horse, poet to muse, as well as the means used by an outside, determinant agent of whatever movement (or action) will or can possibly take place. And how depressive is this recognition of the limits of what a poet can do with the words of her poem? In these descriptive lines of performance replace "he" with "the poem": "The poem canters three steps, then the poem makes a bow, / canters again, bows on one knee, / canters, then clicks and stops, and looks at me." The poet has looked at the poem and now the poem looks back. She will not flinch. It was not for nothing that Bishop kept a picture of Baudelaire on the wall of her studio in Samambaia (along with pictures of Marianne Moore and Robert Lowell) or that "Le Cygne," that allegory of the dispirited poet in a dry season in a desiccated world, was among her favorite poems.[4]

If we go back to Bishop's original title for her poem, moreover, we may discover one of the salubrious effects of the poet's experience with the mechanical toy — rider-and-horse — and, perhaps, by extension with the Cirque d'Hiver in the flesh. It has taken her splenetic self out of its melancholic, depressive state, at least for the time being. The experience — the seeing or the imagining — has done for her what the single crow in winter has casually done for Frost. The way it has shaken down on him the "dust of snow" from "a hemlock tree" has given his heart "a change of mood" and saved "some part" of a day he had "rued."[5] For this momentary stay against confusion — the experience and the poem that records it, itself becoming a transformative force — is but a local, circumscribed instance of the far-reaching repercussions, as they say, attributed to the proverbial single flutter of a butterfly's wing in Brazil.

In changing her title from "Spleen" to "Cirque d'Hiver," Bishop did manage to sharpen the point on what, arguably, could have been seen as already a modestly buoyant poem. By elevating this emblematic toy to her regard, Bishop is able to meditate on the salubrious effect of experiencing the living performances at the Cirque d'Hiver itself, not to mention its according her an opportunity to draw a concluding moral. And as for that rather desperate face-off at the end of "Cirque d'Hiver" — "his eye is like a star —/ we stare and say, 'Well, we have come this far,'" — it is not far-fetched, I think, to see in those lines a trace of Frost's wisdom that when worldly considerations are too much with us, "We may choose something like a star / To stay our minds on and be staid."[6]

23

Down to the Sea

While still in college, in her essay on timing in the poetry of Gerard Manley Hopkins, Elizabeth Bishop came down in favor of a certain kind of poetry that characterized his work and that critics of Bishop have subsequently applied to her poetry. In 1944, in the February issue of the *Vassar Review*, she wrote astutely and admiringly of the writing of the English metaphysical poets: "The[ir] manner of timing so as to catch and preserve the movement of an idea, the point being to crystallize it early enough so that it still has movement — it is essentially the baroque manner of approach." She then quotes from Morris W. Croll's scholarly article, "The Baroque Style in Prose": "Their purpose was to portray, not a thought, but a mind thinking.... They knew that an idea separated from the act of experiencing it is not the same idea that we experienced," for the "ardor of its conception in the mind is a necessary part of its truth; and unless it can be conveyed to another mind in something of the form of its occurrence, either it has changed into some other idea or it has ceased to be an idea, to have any evidence whatever except a verbal one."[1]

Bishop is not usually associated with the idea of what can be called, for lack of a better term, the concept poem — to be distinguished from what she called the "composite" poem (made up of various elements and having various sources, one surmises, or the poem that purports to set down experience directly as it actually happened).[2] Rather by concept poem I mean the poem that is worked out in ex post facto fashion. It is a poem in which a preexisting poetic idea is fleshed out and nailed down. To put it another way, when a Bishop poem offers an insight, an aperçu, a bit of wisdom — summary or not — the poet wants the reader to feel that it has grown out of, or emerged from details selected from direct experience and couched in the dramatized turns of thought that have gone into the making of the poem.

In the case of "At the Fishhouses," published in *The New Yorker* on August 9, 1947, the matter of the concept poem versus the poem that earns its wisdom in the course of its dramatic unfolding is not so clear-cut as one usually finds it to be in Bishop's poetry. As for myself, with no prejudice whatsoever against the achieved quality of the poem, I plump down for concept poem in the case of "At the Fishhouses"; it is, admittedly, a close call. In the summer of 1946, while at Lockeport Beach on the Atlantic Ocean, she set down in her notebook a concept that may have been the germ for her poem. "Description of the dark, icy, clear water — clear dark glass — slightly bitter (hard to define). My idea of knowledge. this cold stream, half drawn, half flowing from a great rocky breast."[3] Recording her impressions on the experience, the note nevertheless expatiates on the wisdom of an old English proverb, "As true as the sea burns," the employment of which among sailors was "extremely sarcastic."[4] Though unexpressed as such, the proverb is at the heart of Bishop's greatly admired poem. For the putative wisdom of the proverb employed sarcastically is beautifully subverted in Bishop's poem. In fact, it is the poet's insight that something like its exact opposite obtains. In her musings upon the sea "icily free above the stones," she posits facts. Should you dip your hand in, for instance, your wrist would ache, your bones would ache, and your hand would burn. And were you to taste this water from the sea, it would taste bitter and briny, burning your tongue. From this emerges the telling insight: "It is like what we imagine knowledge to be: / dark, salt, clear, moving, utterly free, / drawn from the cold hard mouth / of the world."

If the experience of meditating on what sensations and feelings would occur if the poet dipped her hand into the seawater she finds before her leads her to contemplating its poetic or even metaphysical semblance to gaining "knowledge," it is a quasi-metaphysical "truth" that emerges as the poem comes to conclusion. And the truth is luminous, as foreshadowed (or foreordained) by the poem's telling details (whether from the first moments of composition or in revision is of no matter in this context): "All is silver" — the "surface of the sea," benches, lobster pots and masts, old tree trunks — "an apparent translucence," "emerald moss," "creamy iridescent coats of mail" and "small iridescent flies," "beautiful herring scales" and "sequins" (on the fisherman's vest and thumb) that are the scrapings of "scales." In this last instance, it seems to me, Bishop may have borrowed from a poem available to her several years before writing "At the Fishhouses" in *New Road 1944*, the London annual that included her poem "Jeronymo's House" (retitled "Jeronymo's House, Key West"). Long before his "strange metamorphosis," as Bishop called it, from a poet into a writer of "pornography,"[5] Alex Comfort published "Sixth Elegy," a seascape-poem with human figures, which opens with an image of oarless boats by an "invisible sea," boats with "salt" dropping "from their thwarts" and "light scales fall[ing] from the nets in the darkness." One fisherman walks among the "blackened tubs" in which "living fishes twitch," beating "like fists" in the dark. These fish have passed "between the stone and the coral," taking "interminable journeys." "Long after midnight the unquiet fishes beat / and the boats settle and move, and the salt dries and falls."[6]

Notably, this still but curiously still moving seascape is anchored and personalized by the figure of the solitary man, an updated avatar, perhaps, of those solitary men epitomized by Wordsworth's leech-gatherer in "Resolution and Independence."[7] In Bishop, the solitary figure also becomes a person of interest, one the poet would engage in talk. But this "ancient mariner" (a friend of her grandfather's, a fact that has the effect of distancing Bishop's poem from its poetic predecessors in Wordsworth and Comfort) is a man of little or no talk. The all but wordless exchange between the poet and this mender of nets — hardly Gorton's familiar Gloucester fisherman at the helm — amounts to the poet's modest gift of a cigarette. Yet that is enough. If the old man "netting, / his net" benefits from the poet's offer of "a Lucky Strike," so does the poet. Having treated herself to one of those Luckies as well, she is now able to offer the reader the results of a smoker's meditation — the drawing in of smoke mimicking the taking in by the poet of the whole of her spatial and temporal surroundings as she stands before the fish houses and the sea.

24

Free to Be Free

Disappointed and annoyed, Camille Paglia finds herself compelled to admit that when looking for poems for her 2006 book, *Break, Blow, Burn: Camille Paglia Reads Forty-three of the World's Best Poems*, she could not find a single poem by Elizabeth Bishop worth including. "With my eye on the general reader, I was keenly anticipating a cascade of sensuous tropical imagery drawn from Bishop's life in Brazil," she writes, "but when I returned to her collected poems, the observed details to my surprise seemed oppressively clouded with sentimental self-projection." For proof, she points to "The Fish," having found it to be "nearly unbearable" due to Bishop's "obtrusively simmering self-pity." "The Fish," in short, exemplifies those "wounded animal poems, typifying the anthropomorphic fallacy," that have become "an exasperating cliché over the past sixty years." Unfortunately, "even splendid, monumental Brazil evidently couldn't break into Bishop's weary bubble, which travelled with her wherever she went," Paglia writes. No wonder that she turns to the critics and advises, "It may be time to jettison depressiveness as a fashionable badge of creativity."[1]

If Bishop's "depressiveness" determined her decision to exclude Bishop from her book, Paglia might have singled out as evidence Bishop's poem "The Bight," a birthday greeting to the poet herself. In form it can be described as a meditation employing a landscape that seems to reflect, for all of the poet's vaunted capacity for objective description, her feelings that not all is right with the world as she sees it or, perhaps more accurately, as she imagines it to be. The poem ends with the witticism that, later, was chiseled on her gravestone: "Awful but cheerful." After all, not everyone shares, as she acknowledged to Robert Lowell, "my taste for the awful, I'm afraid."[2]

The story begins with a visit to a flea market in Putnam, Connecticut, just south of Worcester, Massachusetts, Bishop's place of birth and sometime home in childhood, where I came upon a dust-covered box of greeting cards. The box was not full, but there were still cards enough — seven of the original

18 cards: congratulatory cards for weddings, anniversaries, childbirth, get well greetings and (one) birthday card — to give one the flavor of what was available by way of greeting cards 60 and 70 years ago. The verse of the one remaining birthday card reads "There aren't many wishes / As warm, sincere, and true. / And there aren't / many people / So nice to *wish* it to!" Rather unremarkable verse, even for greeting-cards. What had first caught my attention, however, was the writing on the small square box the cards came in: "18 Smart 'n Cheerful Cards." On the basis of that rubric alone, I decided to pay $12.50 for this "All Occasion Assortment" of cards and envelopes.

It was a serendipitous moment for me. Here, possibly, I thought to myself, is the source for the famous last line of Elizabeth Bishop's poem "The Bight" — "awful but cheerful" — a closing in a poem written, as the poet says, "on my birthday." In effect, the poem is the verse on a greeting card she composes for and sends to herself. "The Bight" appeared in the *New Yorker* on February 19, 1949, eleven days after Bishop's 38th birthday.

That the last line of "The Bight" — "awful but cheerful" — should have been chosen to adorn her gravestone is intriguing with its possibilities of meaning, especially since below its title she wrote the words "on my birthday." The brevity of the phrase and its quasi-epigrammatic quality turn it, I think, into a sort of heraldic motto on the roughly coat-of-arms-like gravestone itself.

The "activity" is "untidy" but it "continues" — much like lives in the midst of being lived, even if all the probing and the digging result in no more than "a dripping jawful of marl" — which predicts rather straightforwardly the "awful" of the poem's last phrase. Indeed, I see in this "awful" in a birthday poem an anticipation of the "awful" Robert Lowell employs in a poem, not about a birthday but about a death-day (and we should have such a word; after all, death anniversaries for the famous, particularly, are regularly celebrated in the media and elsewhere). In the last line of "Terminal Days at Beverly Farms" (*Life Studies*), a poem about his father's death, the poet reports that his father's last words to the poet's mother were "I feel awful."[3]

I made a second acquisition, at a somewhat later date (this time from a bookseller listed on the Web) in consonance with my interest in Elizabeth Bishop's poetry. I purchased a copy of the limited-editions run of James Merrill's poem, "Overdue Pilgrimage to Nova Scotia," first published in the *New Yorker* in 1990. Merrill's poem opens, as it happens, with these lines: "We're off — Excuse our dust! With warm regards, — / Gathering phrases for tomorrow's cards." The copy of "Overdue Pilgrimage to Nova Scotia" that I purchased once belonged to the Scots poet Edwin Morgan, whose signature appears on a front fly-leaf. Merrill's signature appears at the end and the copy is not inscribed. The question remains open as to whether the copy was a gift from Merrill or the publisher or whether Morgan acquired it in some other way. A further question: was Morgan interested primarily in Merrill or Bishop? As evidence in favor of one possible answer, I offer Morgan's poem "The Poet in the City" (collected in Morgan's *Sonnets from Scotland* in 1984). In "rain stockaded Glasgow" we "paused, changed gears," and "found him *solitary but cheerful.*" We watched him follow the gulls intently, "see them beat and hear them scream / about the invisible sea they smelt / and fish-white boats they raked from stern to stem."[4] In a setting resembling Bishop's — white boats, seabirds flying about — Morgan describes his subject in Bishop-like terms: "solitary but cheerful," echoing her "awful but cheerful." As is Bishop in her first-person poem, moreover, Morgan's poet is an avatar himself, talked about in the third person. The "we" is the "collective" narrator of the poem talking about "him," the subject of the poem as he is in his writer's (and writing's) brown study. That Bishop chose this phrase to be engraved on her headstone tells us that that the whole of what she described in "The Bight" is a systemic metaphor for the poet herself and the nature of her poetically industrious mind — digging and moving marl, etc.

Bishop, the dominatrix of depressive art, saw sorrow and pain in a birthday, if no one else's, certainly her own. She saw above all else the bite in the customary celebratory occasion of a birthday. That it was awesome in the original sense of the word (not the modern sense) makes it amenable to the way she interprets the landscape on that gray day of a birthday. It is not a serene, calming landscape that she sees but one of machinery, chewing up, excavating. This is a perfectly good metaphor for the poet who will see her birthday as a day of reckoning for the memories of the past. "Awful but cheerful," yes. It's too bad that the final note of resigned cheerfulness, surprise that it is at the end of a poem of just barely held back complaint, does not convince if we are looking for consolation and consilience. The words do tell us something about the poet who wrote them down, especially when we consider that they are imposed on experience of a day that may well have been one marked by pain and rue. Say it's so, Elizabeth, and so you have. We just don't believe it.

In the Bishop canon, "The Bight," her poem for her own birthday — a day for rue — has a late companion. If the concluding view of "The Bight" is metaphorically of the "dredge" that "brings up a dripping jawful of marl" and thematically of "all the untidy activity" that "continues, / awful but cheerful," we are told early in "Santarém" that, in the scene before her, all she sees is "bright, cheerful, casual." Even the final clause in the line — "or so it looked" — is merely a faint (and unimportant) tic of the younger, more depressive Bishop. All's right with this world, even the lightning-struck cathedral and the priest's brass bed that lightning has "galvanized black" cannot deter those who would be thankful to God for good fortune, as the poet enhances the casual irony in the "Thank God!" of her native tongue by rendering it in the Portuguese of "*Graças a deus.*"

Perhaps to no avail, but Bishop tried her best to head off at least one critic. To Jerome Mazzaro she wrote just over two months after her poem "Santarém" appeared in the *New Yorker* in 1978: "You say you are 'reading about wasps'—in reference to my poem 'Santarém.' Now if I'd written 'bee-hive'!—I *have* read about bees, but know nothing of wasps except for being stung once. 'Santarém' *happened*, just like that, a real evening & a real place, and a real Mr. Swan who said that—it is not a composite at all."[5] So Santarém is a mise en scène, the wasps' nest is a thing seen, and Mr. Swan on the spot fulfills the Portuguese proverb that says: "An ass that goes to Santarém comes back an ass" ("Burro que vai a Santarém burro vem"). So much for Mr. Swan, who though he does not value the wasp's efforts, is nevertheless not entirely in disagreement with the Victorian critic of art, literature, and culture John Ruskin, who in *Flors Clavigera* (III, Letter L) wrote that "one reverences the fervid labours of a wasp's nest, though the end of all is only a noxious lump of clay."[6]

In "Santarém" the pharmacist has appropriated the wasps' nest for his shop and Bishop will emulate the pharmacist by asking for and taking it with her. In both instances it can be said that they have "aproveitado" the nest that Mr. Swan finds so ugly. In both instances—the pharmacist's and the poet's— the wasps' nest is a found object made art by placing it in a new context, first in the shop and then, of course, Bishop's poem. Bishop's love for the word "aproveitar" and the act it denotes allies her with Joseph Cornell, that other lover of what to others might be merely "junk." In "Trouvée" Bishop "aproveita" the chicken flattened (like a cartoon character) in the middle of the street. It becomes the source of her meditation, remains at the center of her concern, and sticks there as a symbol, radiating out and gathering back to itself to no final result—no "resultado"—the word used by Mrs. Brant to show her disappointment at the meager royalties resulting from *The Diary of "Helena Morley,"* Bishop's translation of her book, *Minha Vida de Menina.*

"Santarém" is announced as what might be called a "memory" poem— that is, a memorial poem to an earlier episode in the poet's life. "Of course I may be remembering it all wrong," she begins her poem, "after, after—how many years?" (But, as Silviano Santiago reminds us, "All is remembered in memory in a correct—most correct—manner, as two plus two equals five."[7]) That it is a memory poem releases her from any temptation or need to dram-atize the "vision" she might have experienced those unnumbered years earlier.

She is free to mix memory with the perspective gained over the years as well as desire. She tells us how she felt then on a ship "in the conflux of two great rivers, Tapajós, Amazon": "That golden evening I really wanted to go no farther; / more than anything else I wanted to stay awhile." The two great rivers remind her of the Garden of Eden and its four rivers — something of a false start — before she settles in to hold up for our consideration that her two rivers might lead to literary thoughts of bipolarity such as "life / death, right / wrong, male / female." But "such notions," she is quick to point out, "would have resolved, dissolved, straight off / in that watery, dazzling dialectic." Of course, she sweeps aside the opposites, for this is a poem about unity, color, beauty in things — houses, "buttercup yellow," "faced with *azulejos*" —figured porcelain tiles in blue and white. Her recovered vision, moreover, is lasting — even in the face of the Dutch Mr. Swan of the modern world of Philips Electric. Ignoring the Emersonian imprecation about removing beautiful things from their natural setting so as not to diminish their beauty, "Santarém" concludes with the pharmacist's gift to the poet of the "empty wasps' nest" he has had hanging from a shelf—"small, exquisite, clean matte white, / and hard as stucco." The artifact is as lovely to her as it is ugly to Mr. Swan, "the retiring head of Philips Electric," the Dutch Company, who wanted to see the Amazon "before he died," and who is given the final if not the last word on the matter: "'What's that ugly thing?'" One wonders what Mr. Swan made of the Dutch painters. As for Bishop herself, she had written to Dr. Anny Baumann in 1949, obviously about "The Bight": "I still think if I can just keep the last line in mind, everything may still turn out all right."[8]

That all or much of it turned out all right is suggested by "Sonnet," the poem not yet published when Bishop died, unexpectedly, on October 6, 1979. This poem (the *New Yorker* always seemed to have an unpublished poem by its regulars on hand to be published immediately within a week or two of a poet's death) can be called a sonnet only if the only requirement for a poem in that form is that it be divided into fourteen lines. Otherwise, Bishop's poem — with no end rhymes, and its irregular metrics (it is not in pentameter, not divided into quatrains, tercets or couplets) — is entirely of her own devising. It does, however, evoke the practices of earlier poets — Emily Dickinson, the Metaphysical poets, and the English Neo-Classical writers — and contains an oblique reference to herself. In "Sonnet" she offers two metaphors for the "caught" self: the bubble in the spirit level ("creature divided"), and the wobbling and wavering compass needle ("undecided"). The poem turns away from "entrapment," then, and offers two metaphors for "freedom": a broken thermometer's mercury runs off, and a narcissistic rainbow-bird that, flying away from an empty mirror, "feels like, gay!"[9]

Like one of Dickinson's definition poems ("Pain has an element of blank"
or "Hope is the thing with feathers," for example), Bishop's poem has defined
two terms (or states of being): "caught" and "free." The definition of the former, again like Dickinson, has recourse to metaphors that are close to "metaphysical" conceits: the spirit level (division) and the compass needle
(indecision), while the definition of the latter calls for metaphors of broken
thermometer and rainbow-bird and mirror. The neo classic precept that the
artist's task is to hold a mirror up to nature is spurned by the bird that flies
away from a mirror. Three of these metaphors — level, compass, and thermometer — smack of Dickinson's poetry: the short line, breathless phrasing,
hyphens, bird imagery ("A route of evanescence"), nautical imagery ("Wild
Nights"—"Done with the compass"). And these metaphors are employed just
as Dickinson would employ them, that is, stacking them up as reinforcements
for one another as the poet builds her definition. Bishop also domesticates
Dickinson's New England small birds, for her rainbow bird is assuredly Brazilian. As such, it appears almost serendipitously in the poem (echoing visually
the rainbows that are featured in earlier poems). Freed of the compulsion to
brook or broker divisions or to decide things (the needle of the compass as
well as the artist's imprecation to mirror nature), the released mercury hurries
off and the rainbow bird flies wherever it likes and, by implication, becomes
whatever it wishes to be. "Sonnet" is Bishop's celebration of her life in her
70th year — whatever the day of the poem's composition or whatever specific
moment it was meant to commemorate. "[C]oming in and out of your room,
are little humming-birds the size of a large bee, looking like an emerald or a
ruby flitting about," Isabel Burton had written, " and if you have the sense
not to offer to touch them, and put a little wet sugar in a saucer, they will
stay there for days; but if you try to catch them, they break their hearts and
die."[10] The enticements and entrapments of a Brazil made attractive by Lota
and Samambaia and Ouro Prêto are now in the past and she has emerged
uncaught. At the last, the poet is free, free from her fretful narcissism, it
seems, free to feel free, free to be joyful, to be as free — well — free as the
proverbial bird.[11]

Epilogue: The Last Book

Elizabeth Bishop is known to have fussed a great deal about what poems to include in any given collection and, of course, the order in which they were presented. She fussed over dates. Of the contents of her first book, *North & South*, published in 1946, she seems to have believed that it was important, as a curious note on the copyright page indicates, to state that "Most of these poems were written, or partly written, before 1942." Was this intended to ward off any possible criticism that her poetry did not much reflect the years that America had been at war?

Later, feeling the pressure to bring out a second book of poems, she permitted Houghton Mifflin to reprint the contents of *North & South* as part of a new book, one awkwardly titled *Poems: North & South—A Cold Spring* (1955). (Whether the change in the title of the poem "The Gentleman of Shalott" to "The Gentlemen of Shalott" was deliberate or simply an error that was not caught by the proofreader is not known. What is known is that "Gentleman" is the restored reading in all subsequent printings of the poem.) The poem "Arrival at Santos" is the penultimate poem in the book, followed by another of her so-called "Brazil" poems.

She had no compunctions about co-opting "Arrival at Santos" ten years later for her next book, *Questions of Travel*, where it appears as the first poem in the first section of a book in which the poems are presented in two parts, the first one labeled "Brazil" and the second one "Elsewhere." In fairness to Bishop, it should be noted that in the small print of the copyright page she does acknowledge that "'Arrival at Santos' appeared in *Poems: North & South—A Cold Spring*." Interestingly, she chose not to include the second Brazilian poem, "The Shampoo," though it would seem to be a good fit. The omission was noticed by a friend, the poet May Swenson, who, in a note to herself wrote on the back of the gift card the publisher included with the book: "Where's the poem abt washing L's hair in a basin?"[1] Perhaps Swenson was especially attuned to noticing that "The Shampoo" was missing in *Questions*

179

of Travel. She had seen the poem a couple of years before it was published, after *The New Yorker* had passed on it, in the *New Republic* in 1955. In 1953 she had written to Bishop: "THE SHAMPOO I like *very* much... but I would have a deuce of a time saying why... that is, it feels like something has been left out — but this makes it better, in a way... a mysteriousness, although the expression is perfectly straightforward."[2] Curious, as well, is the fact that *Selected Poems*, published by Chatto & Windus in London in 1967 — there was no equivalent American edition — does contain "The Shampoo."

There was also one more prominent oddity about the contents of *Questions of Travel*. Bishop had decided to include "In the Village," a piece of prose dutifully identified as "a story" in the table of contents but not at the point within the body of the book when the story appears. But she omitted this piece of Nova Scotia memorial writing from the section marked "Questions of Travel" in *The Complete Poems* (1969), even though, under the rubric "New and Uncollected Work," she reprinted such prose pieces as "Rainy Season; Sub-Tropics" and "The Hanging of the Mouse."

Published less than three years before her death, *Geography III* (1976) is Elizabeth Bishop's shortest book by far. It contains merely ten poems, though several, most readers agree, are among her very best. The table of contents lists them: "In the Waiting Room", "Crusoe in England", "Night City", "The Moose", "12 O'Clock News", "Poem", "One Art", "The End of March", "Objects & Apparitions", and "Five Flights Up." But the fact is that one of ten poems listed — "Objects & Apparitions" — is not by her at all. Its author is Octavio Paz, and this poem about Joseph Cornell is identified as a translation only by a phrase, "from the Spanish of Octavio Paz," following the text. Otherwise, both in its listing as the book's ninth poem and in its presentation on pages 46–48, the title is given in the same italicized type as are the nine Bishop poems.

A second oddity about *Geography III* is that between the page labeled "Contents" and the first poem "In the Waiting Room" there appears a piece entitled "From 'First Lessons in Geography,' Monteith's Geographical Series, A. S. Barnes & Co., 1884" on unnumbered pages x–xi. Excerpted from a textbook, it starts on the verso side of the contents page and runs over to the facing page. It can function as an epigraph, but even here there's a break with convention, since the source caption of the material quoted is presented at the beginning, as if it were a title, and not, as customary, following the quoted material. Actually the excerpt has the markings of a poem; its title is given in italics (linking it typographically to the nine poems — and one translation — that follow). In fact, if he so wishes, the reader may take this textbook excerpt to be a "found" poem, rather than an epigraph, even if it is not listed on the book's contents page. When Bishop's editor, Robert Giroux, reprinted *Geography III* as part of the *Complete Poems* in 1983, he not only removed Bishop's translation of Paz's poem from the section devoted to poems from *Geography III* but placed it in the section on translations, as well as reducing the size of the type of the title Bishop gave to her excerpt from the 1884 textbook. He also placed the title within brackets, pushing it further in the direction of taking it as an epigraph. Now here is a further oddity. In a late interview, conducted by the poet Susan Howe and Charles Ruas on April 19, 1979, at her apartment in Wharf Harbor, Boston, Bishop starts the session by reading from her published work. The oddity is that the very first thing she reads is "From 'First Lessons in Geography,' Monteith's Geographical Series, A. S. Barnes & Co., 1884: Lesson VI [and] Lesson X" — from *Geography III*. She does not identify it as either epigraph or poem. That, one presumes, is for the listener to decide.[3]

Finally, there is the matter of the order in which Bishop's poems appear in *Geography III*. Apparently, the final order was not what Bishop had at first planned. Originally, she wanted "One Art" (about "losing") presented as the last poem in the book.[4] Moreover, if I am right about the excerpt from "First Lessons in Geography" as a "found" poem, then to have placed "One Art" as the end would have encapsulated the entire book in a way — one beginning with a found poem — a geography catechetic — and ending with a poem about losing "things," among them, two rivers and a continent.

Chapter Notes

Preface

1. *The Notebooks of Robert Frost*, ed. Robert Faggen (Cambridge: Harvard University Press, 2006), p. 487.

2. "The Manipulation of Mirrors" (1956), in Elizabeth Bishop, *Prose*, ed. Lloyd Schwartz (New York: Farrar, Straus and Giroux, 2011), p. 270.

3. J. C. "X-rated," *Times Literary Supplement* no. 5623 (January 7, 2011): 32.

4. "A Conversation with Elizabeth Bishop," *Ploughshares* 3, nos. 3–4 (1977): 11–29; reprinted in *Conversations with Elizabeth Bishop*, ed. George Monteiro (Jackson: University Press of Mississippi, 1996), pp. 82–97. (Quotation is from page 88 of the latter.) On Bishop's sense of the mystery of just what goes into the making of a poem, see also her letter to Jerome Mazzaro, April 27, 1978 (*One Art: Letters*, ed. Robert Giroux [New York: Farrar, Straus and Giroux, 1994], p. 621).

5. Wallace Stevens to José Rodríguez Feo, December 19, 1946, *Letters of Wallace Stevens*, ed. Holly Stevens (New York: Knopf, 1972), p. 544.

6. Robert Lowell to Elizabeth Bishop, February 22, 1974, in *Words in Air: The Complete Correspondence Between Elizabeth Bishop and Robert Lowell*, ed. Thomas Travisano with Saskia Hamilton (New York: Farrar, Straus and Giroux, 2008), p. 760.

7. *One Art: Letters*, 246.

8. *Words in Air*, 315.

9. C. K. Doreski, *Elizabeth Bishop: The Restraints of Language* (New York: Oxford University Press, 1993), p. xii.

10. Anne Stevenson, *Five Looks at Elizabeth Bishop* (London: Bellew, 1998), pp. 109–10.

Introduction

1. According to Brett C. Millier, Bishop first met Lota de Macedo Soares in New York City in 1942, at Loren MacIver's studio on Perry Street in Greenwich Village. Lota had accompanied Mary Stearns Morse to New York. The two of them invited Bishop to visit them in Rio de Janeiro if and when she traveled to South America (*Elizabeth Bishop: Life and the Memory of It* [Berkeley and Los Angeles: University of California Press, 1993], p. 170).

2. Anna Cristina César, *A Teus Pés* [1982], 8th ed. (São Paulo: Brasiliense, 1992), p. 44. My translation.

3. Monteiro, *Conversations*, 79.

4. Millier, *Life and the Memory*, 538.

5. In "On the Railroad Named Delight" (1965), Bishop celebrates Lota's public work. Reaching from the "commercial section of the city southwest along Guanabara Bay," she writes, Flamengo Park "now looks like a green tropical atoll just risen from the water, but it is really the result of three year's hard work on an unpromising, hideous stretch of mud, dust, pipes and highways long known as the 'the fill'" (*New York Times*, May 7, 1965; Elizabeth Bishop, *Poems, Prose, and Letters*, ed. Robert Giroux and Lloyd Schwartz [New York: Library of America, 2008], p. 441).

6. Elizabeth Bishop to Dr. Anny Baumann, March 29, 1966, *One Art: Letters*, 445.

7. *Elizabeth Bishop: Poemas*, trans. Horácio Costa (São Paulo: Companhia das Letras, 1990); Flora Sussekind, "A Geléia & o Engenho: Em Torno de Uma Carta-poema de Elizabeth Bishop a Manuel Bandeira," *Revista USP*, no. 7 (September/October/November 1990). Collected in her *Papéis Colados* (Rio de Janeiro: Editora UFRJ, 1993), pp. 332–365.

8. *An Anthology of Twentieth-Century Brazilian Poetry*, eds. Elizabeth Bishop and Emanuel Brasil (Middletown, CT: Wesleyan University Press, 1972); reissued by Wesleyan University Press / University Press of New England in 1997 on the 25th anniversary of its publication.

9. Marianne Moore, *Poemas*, ed. João Moura, Jr., trans. José Antonio Arantes (São Paulo: Companhia das Letras, 1991).

Prologue: The Map

1. Jorge Luis Borges brought attention to Royce's formulation in his famous essay, "Partial Magic in the *Quixote*" (*Labyrinths: Selected Stories & Other Writings*, ed. Donald A. Yates and James E. Irby [New York: New Directions, 1964], pp. 195–6).

2. Alberto Manguel, *The Library at Night* (New Haven & London: Yale University Press, 2006), p. 38.

3. Implied here is a concern for "people," something not every reader has granted her. "Cool-eyed, she described human beings, in Florida and in Brazil," as if "they were herons or some rare sort of mango," runs one complaint (Joseph Epstein, "Elizabeth Bishop: Never a Bridesmaid," [Spring 1995], 48: 45).

Chapter 1

1. Elizabeth Bishop, "Love from Emily," *New Republic* 125 (August 27, 1951): 20–21; "Unseemly Deductions," *New Republic* 127 (August 18, 1952): 21.

2. Millier, *Life and the Memory*, 237–41.

3. Elizabeth Bishop to Pauline Hanson, November 12, 1951, Elizabeth Bishop Papers, Vassar College Libraries, Vassar College, Poughkeepsie, New York (hereafter cited as Elizabeth Bishop Papers).

4. Elizabeth Bishop Papers.

5. Bishop, "Unseemly Deductions," 21.

6. Quoted in David Kalstone, *Becoming a Poet: Elizabeth Bishop with Marianne Moore and Robert Lowell*, ed. Robert Hemenway, afterword by James Merrill (New York: Farrar, Straus and Giroux, 1989), p. 194.

7. "I can read Camões, etc., pretty well now, and he — his sonnets — are superb — as good as any in English, certainly," she wrote to Lowell on July 28, 1953, and, on December 5, 1953, "Camões is very much like what Ezra Pound says, but have you ever seen any of his holy sonnets? They are superb, 'Jacob & Rachel' etc." (*Words in Air*, 142, 149). In *The Spirit of Romance* (1919) Pound trashes Camões's epic poem *Os Lusíadas*, drawing not on a reading of the poem in Portuguese but on Voltaire's strictures on the poem. See Norwood Andrews, Jr., *The Case Against Camões: A Seldom Considered Chapter from Ezra Pound's Campaign to Discredit Rhetorical Poetry*, Utah Studies in Literature and Linguistics 27 (New York: Peter Lang, 1988).

8. The sonnet was first attributed to Camões in the surviving index to the so-called *Cancioneiro do Padre Pedro Ribeiro* (1577), the manuscript of which was used by Barbosa Machado (*Bibliotheca Lusitana*) but which was, it is said, destroyed in the 1755 Lisbon earthquake (see Hernani Cidade, preface to Luis de Camoens,

Obras Completas, vol. 1, *Redondilhas e Sonetos*, 4th ed. [Lisbon: Sá da Costa, 1861], pp. xxxii–xxxiii). The sonnet appeared 15 years after Camões's death in the first edition of his lyrics, *Rhythmas*, published in 1595 in Lisbon by Manoel de Lyra for Estêvuão Lopez, as well as *Rimas*, published in 1598 in Lisbon by Pedro Crasbeeck for Estêvuão Lopez. Leodegário A. de Azevedo Filho contests Camões's authorship but does not reject the sonnet outright; see *Lírica de Camões*, vol. 1, *História, Metodologia, Corpus* (Vila da Maia: Imprensa Nacional-Casa da Moeda, 1985), p. 285. Most students of Camões have found no reason to question his authorship; see, for example, Jorge de Sena, *Os Sonetos de Camões e o Soneto Quinhentista Peninsular*, 2nd ed. (Lisbon: Edições 70, 1980), p. 88, note 4.

9. My translation. The original reads:
Quem vê, Senhora, claro e manifesto
o lindo ser de vossos olhos belos,
se não perder a vista só em vê-los,
ja não paga o que deve a vosso gesto.
Este me parecia preço honesto;
mas eu, por de vantagem merecê-los,
dei mais a vida e alma por querê-los,
donde ja me não me fica mais de resto.
Assi que a vida e alma e esperança
e tudo quanto tenho, tudo é vosso,
e o proveito disso eu só o levo.
Porque e tamanha mas-aventurança
o dar-vos quanto tenho e quanto posso,
que, quanto mais vos pago, mais vos devo.
(Luis de Camões, *Lírica Completa*, vol. 2, *Sonetos*, preface and notes by Maria de Lurdes Saraiva [Vila da Maia: Imprensa Nacional-Casa da Moeda, 1980], p. 21.)

10. Elizabeth Bishop, *Questions of Travel* (New York: Farrar, Straus and Giroux, 1965), p. viii. My translation.

11. For Bishop's translations of poems by Manuel Bandeira, Joaquim Cardozo, Carlos Drummond de Andrade, Vinicius de Moraes, and João Cabral de Melo Neto, see *An Anthology of Twentieth-Century Brazilian Poetry* and for her translation of *Minha Vida de Menina*, see *The Diary of "Helena Morley"* (New York: Farrar, Straus and Cudahy, 1957).

12. Elizabeth Bishop to Loren and Lloyd Frankenberg, November 17, 1965, Elizabeth Bishop Papers.

13. Frank J. Warnke, "The Voyages of Elizabeth Bishop," *New Republic* 154 (April 9, 1966): 19.

14. Elizabeth Bishop Papers.

15. Lorrie Goldensohn, *Elizabeth Bishop: The Biography of a Poetry* (New York: Columbia University Press, 1992), p. 193.

16. Quoted in Kalstone, *Becoming a Poet*, 150.

17. Elizabeth Bishop to Loren and Lloyd Frankenberg, November 17, 1965, Elizabeth Bishop Papers.

18. The Penteado drawing also appears on the dust jacket for Anne Stevenson's *Elizabeth Bishop*, Twayne's United States Authors Series (New York: Twayne, 1966).

19. Elizabeth Bishop to Loren and Lloyd Frankenberg, November 17, 1965, Elizabeth Bishop Papers.

20. *Poesias Escolhidas de Emily Dickinson*, trans. Olívia Krähenbühl (São Paulo: Saraiva, 1956).

21. Quoted in Kalstone, *Becoming a Poet*, 132.

22. Goldensohn, *Biography of a Poetry*, 69.

23. Millier, *Life and the Memory*, 384.

24. Lloyd Schwartz, "Annals of Poetry: Elizabeth Bishop and Brazil," *New Yorker* 67 (September 30, 1991): 85–97.

25. Elizabeth Bishop, untitled poem, in Schwartz, "Annals of Poetry," 86; *Poems* (New York: Farrar, Straus and Giroux, 2011), p. 313.

26. Quoted in Millier, *Life and the Memory*, 378.

27. Elizabeth Bishop, "Under the Window: Ouro Preto," in *The Complete Poems 1927–1979* (New York: Farrar, Straus and Giroux, 1983), pp. 208–10.

28. Millier, *Life and the Memory*, 384.

29. Ibid., 368.

30. Schwartz, "Annals of Poetry," 86.

31. Ibid.

32. Ibid.

33. Ibid.

34. J. D. McClatchy writes of "One Art" (as well as some other poems): "It *shares* its subject with the person who reads and not just with the person written about" ("'One Art': Some Notes," in *Elizabeth Bishop*, Modern Critical Views Series, ed. Harold Bloom [New York: Chelsea House, 1985], p. 154).

35. In 1977 Bishop identified the lost houses in "One Art": "one in Key West, one in Petrópolis, just west of Rio Bay, and one in Ouro Prêto, also in Brazil" (interview with David W. McCullough, *Book-of-the-Month Club News* [May 1977]; reprinted in *Elizabeth Bishop and Her Art*, eds. Lloyd Schwartz and Sybil P. Estess [Ann Arbor: University of Michigan Press, 1983], pp. 309–10). Lota de Macedo Soares was of course the key association with the two Brazilian houses.

36. Quoted in Millier, *Life and the Memory*, 523. In a late letter to Katherine White, Bishop described "One Art" as "very SAD — it makes everyone weep, so I think it must be rather good, in its awful way" (Elizabeth Bishop to Katherine White, January 16, 1976, *Elizabeth Bishop and The New Yorker: The Complete Correspondence*, ed. Joelle Biele [New York: Farrar, Straus and Giroux, 2011], p. 378).

37. Millier asserts that "One Art" apparently grew out of the poet's "desperate fear of losing Alice [Methfessel]" but that "the poem is also Elizabeth's elegy for her whole life" (*Life and the Memory*, 506, 513).

38. Bishop, "One Art," in *Geography III* (New York: Farrar, Straus and Giroux, 1976), p. 41.

39. Goldensohn, *Biography of a Poetry*, 31.

40. For accounts of the evolution of "One Art" through "the seventeen available drafts" of the poem, see Millier, *Life and the Memory*, 506–14, and "Elusive Mastery: The Drafts of Elizabeth Bishop's 'One Art,'" *New England Review* 13 (Winter 1990): 121–29.

41. *Selected Writings of Edgar Allan Poe*, ed. Edward Davidson (Boston: Houghton Mifflin, 1956), p. 38.

42. Roy Campbell, *Portugal* (Chicago: Henry Regnery, 1958), p. 143. Campbell had published the poem in one of his autobiographical volumes, *Talking Bronco* (London: Faber & Faber, 1946), where the opening lines read: "Camões, alone, of all the lyric race, / Born in the black aurora of disaster" (11). It is possible that Bishop was influenced as well by Jay Macpherson's poetry in his *Welcoming Disaster* (Toronto: n.p., 1974), which includes poems entitled "Lost Books & Dead Letters" (10) and "Masters and Servants" (26). Bishop's copy of Macpherson's book is at the Houghton Library, Harvard University, Cambridge, Massachusetts.

43. Goldensohn, *Biography of a Poetry*, 125.

44. The same rhyme is employed by John Rees Moore in his poem "Elizabeth Bishop," which concludes: "Sometimes the loss is a disaster. / It's an art, she tartly says, easy to master" (*Sewanee Review* 117 [Fall 2009]: 556).

45. Written on a copy of "One Art" on a single page from the *New Yorker* (Elizabeth Bishop Papers). In Horácio Costa's translation of "One Art" into Brazilian Portuguese, "disaster" is readily rendered as "desastre" but "master" becomes "aprender" — to learn ("Uma Arte," in *Poemas*, 207). Interestingly, when Jorge de Sena translated Campbell's sonnet on Camões, he employed the cognate words — "desastre" and "mestre" — in slant rhyme ("Luís de Camões," *Diario de Lisboa* [June 9, 1952]: 3; reprinted in *Poesia do Seculo XX*, ed. and trans. Jorge de Sena [Porto: Inova, 1978], p. 402). The reader who brings a knowledge of Camões to "One Art" might well see in the "master-disaster" rhyme a sliding pun on Adamastor, the "Spirit of the Cape," whereas Emily Dickinson's readers will recall that she addressed several "letters" of love and loss to an otherwise unidentified (or probably fictitious) "Master."

46. *The Complete Prose of Marianne Moore*, ed. Patricia C. Willis (New York: Viking, 1986), p. 328.

47. Lloyd Schwartz, "One Art: The Poetry of Elizabeth Bishop, 1971–1976," in Schwartz and Estess, *Bishop and Her Art*, 150.

48. J. D. McClatchy, "Elizabeth Bishop: Some Notes on 'One Art,'" in *White Paper: On Contemporary American Poetry* (New York: Colum-

bia University Press, 1989), p. 145; Helen Vendler, *Last Looks, Last Books: Stevens, Plath, Lowell, Bishop, Merrill* (Princeton and Oxford: Princeton University Press, 2010), p. 111. See also David Kalstone, *Five Temperaments: Elizabeth Bishop, Robert Lowell, James Merrill, Adrienne Rich, John Ashbery* (New York: Oxford University Press, 1977), p. 40: "The last stubborn heartbreaking hesitation — 'though it may look like (*Write* it!) like disaster' — carries the full burden, and finally confidence, of her work, the resolve which just barely masters emptiness and succeeds in filling out, tight-lipped, the form"; Thomas J. Travisano, *Elizabeth Bishop: Her Artistic Development* (Charlottesville: University Press of Virginia, 1988), p. 178: "Her desperate '*Write* it!' implies that she must *force* herself to use the word *disaster* in a personal context, even though it is hedged by transparent disclaimers and demanded by the villanelle's form"; Joanne Feit Diehl, *Women Poets and the American Sublime* (Bloomington: Indiana University Press, 1990), p. 97: "The poem itself has made, through its formal demands, an inevitable resolution"; Elizabeth Dodd, *The Veiled Mirror and the Woman Poet: H.D., Louise Bogan, Elizabeth Bishop, and Louise Glück* (Columbia: University of Missouri Press, 1992), p. 143: "In the final line the speaker must even exhort herself to complete the rhyme" — '(*Write* it!)' — since disaster looms very large indeed"; and C. K. Doreski, *Restraints of Language*, 15: "That parenthetical cure for the only true disaster ... this rare command — ('Write it!')"

49. James Joyce, *Giacomo Joyce*, ed. Richard Ellmann (New York: Viking, 1968), p. 16. Italics added.

50. Goldensohn, *Biography of a Poetry*, 261.

51. Millier, *Life and the Memory*, 538.

52. James Merrill, "Elizabeth Bishop (1911–1979)," in *Recitative: Prose by James Merrill*, ed. J. D. McClatchy (San Francisco: North Point Press, 1986), pp. 122–23.

53. See *Remembering Elizabeth Bishop: An Oral Biography*, eds. Gary Fountain and Peter Brazeau (Amherst: University of Massachusetts Press, 1994), pp. 266–67.

Chapter 2

1. Gilberto Freyre, *The Masters and the Slaves: A Study in the Development of Brazilian Civilization*, 2nd English-Language ed., trans. Samuel Putnam (New York: Knopf, 1956), p. 85.

2. Elizabeth Bishop and The Editors of *Life*, *Brazil* (New York: Time Incorporated, 1962), p. 116.

3. This reprinting of "Jeronymo's House" is not listed in Candace W. MacMahon's *Elizabeth Bishop: A Bibliography 1927–1979* (Charlottesville: Bibliographical Society of the University of Virginia / University Press of Virginia, 1980).

4. Everaldo Dayrell de Lima, "Brazilian Poetry," in *New Road 1944: New Directions in European Art and Letters*, ed. Alex Comfort and John Bayliss (London: Grey Walls Press, 1944), pp. 247–69.

5. Ibid., 253.

6. Olavo Bilac, "Brazilian Land," in *New Road 1944*, 256. See also Bilac's "Língua Portuguesa" where he sees the same erotic qualities in the language itself: "I love your rank wildness and scent / Of virgin forests and open seas!" (my translation).

7. As Gilberto Freyre states, "The brown-skinned woman was preferred by the Portuguese for purposes of love, at least for purposes of physical love." With specific application to Brazil, an old saying has it, he continues, "'White woman for marriage, mulatto woman for f— —, Negro woman for work,' a saying in which, alongside the social convention of the superiority of the white woman and the inferiority of the black, is to be discerned a sexual preference for the mulatto" (*Masters*, 13–14). In *New World in the Tropics*, published in 1945, Freyre offers a historical explanation for Portuguese attitudes toward "darker" peoples: "To the Portuguese, the Moors had been not only the efficient agricultural workers who knew how to transform arid lands into gardens as if by a miracle, but also a dark race who had not always been the serfs, but sometimes had been the masters of a large part of the Iberian peninsula," he writes. "Portuguese of the purest Nordic blood had found in brown Moorish women, some of them princesses, the supreme revelation of feminine beauty." It was this "idealization, by the Portuguese people of the brown woman, or the Moorish girl or woman, as the supreme type of human beauty" that had probably "a very important effect on the direction taken by their relations with Indian (Amerindian) women in Brazil" (*New World in the Tropics* [New York: Vintage Books, 1963], pp. 54–55).

8. Thomas E. Skidmore, *Brazil: Five Centuries of Change* (New York and Oxford: Oxford University Press, 1999), p. 23.

9. *The Letter of Amerigo Vespucci Describing his Four Voyages to the New World 1497–1504*, intr. Oscar Lewis (San Francisco: Book Club of California, 1926), p. 7.

10. Freyre, *Masters*, 85. The English-language edition of *The Masters and the Slaves* was first published in 1946.

11. Hélio Vianna, *História do Brasil*, vol. 1, *Período Colonial*, 3rd ed. (São Paulo: Melhoramentos, 1965), p. 50.

12. Bishop may also have noticed that Pêro Vaz de Caminha links the painted bodies of natives to a famous tapestry: "[They] had those

colours in quarters, others in halves, and others in such colours as in the tapestry of Arras..." ("uns andavam quartejados daquelas tinturas, outros de metades, outros de tanta feição [*de cores*] como em pano de ras...") ("Letter of Pedro Vaz de Caminha to King Manuel," in *The Voyages of Pedro Álvares Cabral to Brazil and India*, Hakluyt Society Publications, 2nd Ser., no. 81, trans. William Brooks Greenlee [London: Hakluyt Society, 1938], p. 24); Leonardo Arroyo, *A Carta de Pêro Vaz da Caminha* [São Paulo: Melhoramentos / Rio de Janeiro: Instituto Nacional do Livro, 1971], p. 56). Greenlee explains that "the tapestries of Arras, France, were the most celebrated in Europe during the fourteenth and fifteenth centuries" ("Letter," 24, note).

13. Luis de Camões, *Os Lusíadas*, ed. Frank Pierce (Oxford: Clarendon Press, 1973), IX: 60, 1–4, p. 213.

14. *The Lusiads of Luiz de Camões*, trans. Leonard Bacon (New York: The Hispanic Society of America, 1950), p. 330.

15. Ibid., 332.

16. Emily Dickinson employs the word "luxury" in exactly this sense: "Wild Nights — Wild Nights! / Were I with thee / Wild Nights should be / Our luxury!" (*The Poems of Emily Dickinson*, ed. R. W. Franklin [Cambridge, MA and London: Belknap Press of Harvard University Press, 1999], p. 120).

17. Elizabeth Bishop, "Brazil, January 1, 1502," in *Complete Poems*, 91–92.

18. Lorrie Goldensohn has noticed that Bishop anticipates the poem's last three lines in her review of W. H. Hudson's *Green Mansions*, a piece written when she was 17 years old: "I wished that the book had been twice as long when I put it down, and I was filled with longing to leave for South America immediately and search for those forgotten bird-people," she writes. "It seemed still unfinished, even more than that delightful region in my mind I told about, and I felt sure that if I could only find the right spot, the right sun-lighted arches of the trees, and wait patiently, *I would see a bright-haired figure slipping away among the moving shadows, and hear the sweet, light music of Rima's voice*" (quoted in *Biography of a Poetry*, 203–04).

19. The quoted phrases come from Sir Richard Fanshawe's *Lusiad; or, Portugals Historical Poem* (1665); reprinted in Luis de Camões, *The Lusiads*, ed. Geoffrey Bullough (Carbondale: Southern Illinois University Press, 1963). See page 291 of the latter.

20. Bacon, *Lusiads*, 333.

21. Brett C. Millier writes: "'Brazil, January 1, 1502,' another of these second-wave poems, is the only one of her Brazil poems without an obvious personal angle; it draws instead from the years of reading she had been doing on the history of the country" (*Life and the Memory*, 301).

22. However, in "Elizabeth Bishop's 'Brazil, January 1, 1502' and Max Jacob's 'Etablissement d'une communauté au Brésil': A Study of Transformative Interpretation and Influence," Sylvia Henneberg argues for affinities with a French poem (*Texas Studies in Literature and Language* 45 [Winter 2003]: 337–51).

23. See Jeffrey Gray, "Bishop's 'Brazil, January 1, 1502,'" *Explicator* 54 (September 1995): 36–39.

24. William Blake's presence in Bishop's poetry is even more evident in her poem "Sandpiper," first published in the *New Yorker* 38 (July 21, 1962): 30.

25. Elizabeth Bishop, "The Shampoo," in *Complete Poems*, 84.

26. Quoted in Millier, *Life and the Memory*, 302.

27. Greenlee, "Letter," 15.

28. Ibid., 8.

29. Ibid., 10–11.

30. Ibid., 13.

31. Ibid., 14.

32. Ibid.

33. Ibid., 16.

34. Ibid., 20–21. Curiously — to turn to the 19th century for a moment — Caminha's description of the Indian women is strangely replicated in 1870, with greater Victorian circumspection, naturally, though the women are not racially identified. "Today we are at Cametá" where "we have *romantic* maidens with raven hairs and complexions varying from that of a swan to that of the robin redbreast or the raven," writes an American scientist. "The ladies are very affectionate and kind! No introductions are necessary; all is taken for granted. You are supposed to be an old acquaintance of every one you meet. They don't have that 'airy-stock crazy' like sort of a way, nor that shyness so noticeable among our tamer ladies of the north" (W. S. Barnard, "News from the Brazilian Expedition," in Albert Hazen Wright, *Letters to C. F. Hartt*, Studies in History, no. 16, Pre-Cornell and Early Cornell II Ser. [Ithaca, New York: Privately printed, 1953], p. 39).

35. Freyre, *Masters*, 332. Bishop refers to Gilberto Freyre's *The Masters and the Slaves* in a letter to U. T. and Joseph Summers, July 18, 1955 (*One Art: Letters*, 307).

36. Freyre, *Masters*, 185.

37. Arroyo, *Carta*, 27. My translation.

38. Vespucci describes the frustration of trying to communicate with one group: "We were not able, neither by force nor for love, to obtain any conversation whatsoever ... they fled through the forests and did not await us" (*Letter*, 17).

39. L'Homme Armé Masses, http://music.olivet.edu/nwoodruff/1%27homme.htm.

40. Waldo Frank, *South American Journey* (New York: Duell, Sloan and Pearce, 1943), pp. 289–90.

41. This connection was suggested by Myriam Ávila, I believe, at "The Art of Elizabeth Bishop, An International Conference & Celebração in Brazil," Ouro Prêto, Minas Gerais, May 19–21, 1999.

42. Pedro Luiz Correia de Araújo (1874–1955) was born in Paris of Pernambucan parents and educated in Recife. In 1917 he returned to France to broaden and deepen his knowledge of art. His work was included in collective exhibitions in Rio de Janeiro (1931, 1947, and 1952). His work was exhibited posthumously in Rio (1961, 1982, and 1984), Belo Horizonte (1963), São Paulo (1981 and 1984), and Olinda (1983). http://www.itaucultural.org.br/AplicExternas/Enciclopedia/artesvi.

43. The "green frond," symbolizing Brazil's ability to regenerate or resurrect gives theme and title to the Parnassian poet Alberto de Oliveira's poem "Green Frond." In Diogenes B. Monteiro's translation, it begins: "Let thyself be shaken by the violent storm / Green frond! a torture and a blessing is the wind, / It makes thee moan, but takes away the dust that dares" (Dayrell de Lima, "Brazilian Poetry," 257).

44. *Conquistadores e Conquista* is reproduced in Jacob Klintowitz, *Pedro Luiz Correia de Araújo* (n. p.: André Galeria de Arte, 1981), p. 51. I am thankful to the student in my weeklong seminar, "Robert Frost and Elizabeth Bishop," given at the Universidade Federal de Minas Gerais, in May 1999, who generously gave me a copy of Klintowitz's book.

45. Greenlee, "Letter," 32.

46. Elizabeth Bishop to Marianne Moore, September 21, 1969, *One Art: Letters*, 508.

47. A different view of the "conquest" of the women is offered by James McCorkle: "Rendering the women 'maddening'— with the implicit connotations of hysteria and its history of incarceration of women — as well as transforming them into a flight of birds, elides the history of conquest as well as our ongoing complicity in it" ("'Flowing, and Flown' Reveries of Childhood in Elizabeth Bishop's Poetry," in *Jarrell, Bishop, Lowell, & Co.*, ed. Suzanne Ferguson [Knoxville: University of Tennessee Press, 2003], p. 183, note). I would say only that it seems fanciful to torque "maddening" into "mad" in order to talk, in the context of Bishop's poem, about hysteria in women.

48. Mário de Andrade, *Macunaíma*, trans. E. A. Goodland (New York: Random House, 1984), p. 108. ("A civilização européia de-certo esculhamba a inteireza do nosso caráter"— Mário de Andrade, *Macunaíma: O herói sem nunhum caráter*, ed. Telê Porto Ancona Lopez, UNESCO Coleção Arquivos 6 [Forianópolis, SC, Brasil: Editora da Universidade Federal de Santa Catarina, 1988], pp. 114–15).

49. Roger Gilbert, "Framing Water: Histor-ical Knowledge in Elizabeth Bishop and Adrienne Rich," *Twentieth Century Literature* 43 Summer 1997: 156.

50. I am grateful to Anna Klobucka and Susan Geary for pointing out that there are echoes here of T. S. Eliot's "The Love Song of J. Alfred Prufrock," a poem that closes with references to "mermaids singing, each to each."

51. Justin Reed makes the following conceptual categorization of Bishop's "Brazil, January 1, 1502": "This is not just the natural landscape, but a painted portrait of the natural landscape; and in turn, this is not just a painted portrait of the natural landscape, but an English-language poem about a painted portrait of the natural landscape" ("Manners of Mistranslation: The *Anthrofagismo* of Elizabeth Bishop's Prose and Poetry," *CR: The New Centennial Review* 3 [Spring 2003]: 322). Significantly, however, Reed identifies no painting that Bishop may have seen, an omission that might suggest, to some perhaps, that Bishop's poem was based on her conception of an imaginary painting. Not incidentally, perhaps, literary scholars have had similar notions about the urn of Keats's poem, i.e., that it, too, is an artifact conceived out of the whole cloth of the imaginary.

Chapter 3

1. Elizabeth Bishop, "Cape Breton," *New Yorker*, June 8, 1949, 24.

2. Bishop, *Brazil*, 32.

3. Elizabeth Bishop to May Swenson, February 18, 1956, *One Art: Letters*, 316.

4. Elizabeth Bishop to Robert Lowell, April 22, 1960, *Words in Air*, 317.

5. Elizabeth Bishop to May Swenson, July 3, 1958, *One Art: Letters*, 361.

6. Elizabeth Bishop to Alfred Kazin, December 10, 11 or 12, 1951, *One Art: Letters*, 226.

7. Elizabeth Bishop to Dr. Anny Baumann, December 28, 1952, *One Art: Letters*, 252.

8. Bishop's full statement reads: "The only recognized organ to most Brazilians seems to be the liver; one gets awfully tired of the endless discussions of the state of everyone's *fígado*" (Elizabeth Bishop to Dr. Anny Baumann, July 28, 1952, *One Art: Letters*, 243). To Pearl Kazin she wrote: "I was relieved to hear you had received the ms. [*The Diary of "Helena Morley"*] safely and that you seem to go on liking it. No, *thank you* for telling me there are too many *coitados* ['poor dears']. Take out every other one, if you want to" (January 26, 1956, *One Art: Letters*, 313). She also came to see the bite with which the Brazilian could use words like "coitado," "coitadinho," and "pobrezinho." Former President Juscelino Kubitschek's enemies called the movement of his supporters to bring him back

to power "'Operation *Coitadinho,*' a splendid example of the diminutive of *coitado,* 'poor little one,' one of the most frequent exclamations on the lips of the soft-hearted, but ironical, Brazilians" ("On the Railroad Named Delight," 446).

9. Elizabeth Bishop to Ilse and Kit Barker, February 9, 1952, *One Art: Letters*, 234.

10. Elizabeth Bishop to U. T. and Joseph Summers, November 26, 1957, *One Art: Letters*, 342. In an earlier letter, to the poet James Merrill, Bishop refers to "a small generator that everyone says wouldn't give good results with a record-player" (March 1, 1955, *One Art: Letters*, 303).

11. Quoted in Millier, *Life and the Memory*, 372.

12. In *Viva Belo Horizonte* (no publisher, no date), a publication left for guests in hotel rooms, "Crime perfeito" by André Carvalho opens: "Bebe uisque em pé, a beira da piscina," which is translated: "He's standing, drinking scotch, close to the swimming pool" (p. 59).

13. September 17, 1952, *One Art: Letters*, 248.

14. Freyre, *New World in the Tropics*, 24.

15. Elizabeth Bishop to Joseph and U. T. Summers, November 26, 1957, *One Art: Letters*, 342. In "Dona Elizabetchy: A Memoir of Elizabeth Bishop," Pearl K. Bell describes the practices of "the Brazilian *alfandega*, or customs, a peculiar and capricious institution": "Packages were routinely held at the customs house for months, and when they ran out of space they either returned them to the sender or exacted outrageous amounts of duty" (*Partisan Review* 58, no. 1 [1991]: 31–42).

16. May 24, 1953, *One Art: Letters*, 265.

17. March 3, 1952, *One Art: Letters*, 236–37.

18. In *Heart of Darkness*, published in 1902, it is at the first mention of Kurtz that Conrad uses the word "interior": "'One day he [the accountant] remarked, without lifting his head, "In the interior you will no doubt meet Mr. Kurtz"'" (Harmondsworth: Penguin Books, 1983; p. 46). Marlow "had started for the interior with a light heart, and no more idea of what would happen to him than a baby" (91). The author of "The Map" would have been particularly taken with the young Marlow's passion for maps: "'I would look for hours at South America, or Africa, or Australia, and lose myself in all the glories of exploration. At that time there were many blank spaces on the earth, and when I saw one that looked particularly inviting on a map (but they all look that) I would put my finger on it and say, When I grow up I will go there'" (33).

Coincidentally in 1951, the Southern African writer Laurens Van Der Post (1906–96) published his autobiographical volume *Venture to the Interior* (New York: Viking, 1961). On page 51, he writes: "For a voyage to a destination, wherever it may be, is also a voyage inside one-self; even as a cyclone carries along with it the centre in which it must ultimately come to rest." Rimbaud, too, was seen as having gone into the heart of Africa. "He became a merchant of coffee, perfumes, ivory, and gold, in the interior of Africa; then an explorer" (Arthur Symons, "Arthur Rimbaud," in *Studies in Two Literatures* [London: Martin Secker, 1924], p. 140). On the other hand, in *The Country of the Pointed Firs* (1896), the American writer Sarah Orne Jewett refers, typically, not to "interior" but to "inland": "Strangers began to arrive from the inland country" (10); others were "islanders or from the inland country" (45); and "we were in the heart of the inland country" (74) (*The Country of the Pointed Firs and Other Stories* [London and New York: Penguin Books, 1995]). It is equally interesting that Elizabeth Bishop herself, when accepting the *Books Abroad*/Neustadt Prize in Norman, Oklahoma, mentioned the irony that after hanging around seaports her whole life she was being honored so far "inland."

19. Millier, *Life and the Memory*, 246.

20. Elizabeth Bishop Papers.

21. Anne Stevenson, "Letters from Elizabeth Bishop," *Times Literary Supplement*, March 7, 1980, 261.

22. An unnamed reviewer in the London *Times Weekly Review* (October 4, 1956, p. 14) writes of *Brazilian Interior*, a travel book: "Mr. [Kenneth] Matthews's title is not altogether apt: there is a ring of Fleming or Fawcett about it, a suggestion of serious exploration and arduous travel." If my reading of Bishop's "Arrival at Santos" is not amiss, I would venture that Bishop's last line pokes gentle fun at the seriousness and potentially arduous nature of her vaunted drive to the interior.

23. Randall Jarrell to Elizabeth Bishop, December 1951, *Randall Jarrell's Letters: An Autobiographical and Literary Selection*, ed. Mary Jarrell (Boston: Houghton Mifflin, 1985), p. 297.

24. Ronald de Carvalho, "Interior," trans. Dudley Poore, in *New Road 1944*, 260.

25. E. E. Cummings, *XAIPE: Seventy-one Poems* (New York: Liveright, 1930), poems 6, 18, and 41.

26. Elizabeth Bishop to U. T. and Joseph Summers, October 19, 1967, in *One Art: Letters*, 479. In a note informing Bishop that the *New Yorker* was buying "Manuelzinho," Howard Moss calls it "*the* best poem I've read in ages": "The tone is handled marvelously — one of those absolutely right poems where the sense of someone's life is all there, and, as you know, it's very funny in that special way you have, without ever going against the grain of what it's doing" (December 28, 1955, *Bishop and* The New Yorker, 166), p. 161.

27. Thomas Lask, "Modern Verse," *New York Times*, March 10, 1957, p. X16.

28. An older, more patriotic Monteiro Lo-

bato would reinvent Jeca Tatu as an exemplary hero in Brazil's vigorous effort to promote its public health policies. This later Jeca Tatu has nothing to do with Bishop's poem.

29. Elizabeth Bishop to Pearl Kazin, April 23, 1961, *One Art: Letters*, 397.

30. June 7, 1956, *One Art: Letters*, 320.

31. July 5, 1956, *One Art: Letters*, 321.

32. Elizabeth Bishop to May Swenson, January 27, 1956, *One Art: Letters*, 315.

33. Millier, *Life and the Memory*, 271.

34. Elizabeth Bishop to Robert Lowell, August 26, 1963, *Words in Air*, 497.

35. "Manuelzinho" does not appear in *Poemas*, Horácio Costa's collection of Elizabeth Bishop's poetry in translation.

36. Regina M. Przybycien, "Tainted Paradise: Elizabeth Bishop's Vision of Brazil," paper presented at the XXIV SENAPULLI meetings, João Pessoa, PB, on January 27, 1992, p. 18. In chapter 2, "Caminhos Poéticos," pp. 37–38, of "Feijão Preto e Diamantes: O Brasil na Obra de Elizabeth Bishop," (Ph.D. diss., Faculdade de Letras da Universidade Federal de Minas Gerais, Belo Horizonte, Brasil, 1993), she writes: "Dando voz à Lota no poema, Bishop distancia-se tanto do personagem quanto daquela que os descreve.... No discurso de sua patroa, ele é o outro, encerrado na diferença de sua classe social. Para a poeta, ele é duplamente outro pois, além da classe, também a cultura local o separa dela."

37. Nineteenth-century Americans, particularly in the South, understood this relationship readily enough. "Toward my tract of land and the things that were on it — the creeks, the swamps, the hills, the meadows, the stones, the trees —," writes Charles Chesnutt, "he maintained a peculiar personal attitude, what might be called predial rather than proprietary" ("Mars Jeems's Nightmare"). I wonder, too, if Randall Jarrell, a Southerner, felt particularly close to the characters and "plantation" situations given in "Manuelzinho" and that that was the reason he chose to read the poem, at the time still unpublished in book form, at the Academy of Arts and Sciences.

38. Elizabeth Bishop to Loren MacIver, January 25, 1964, *One Art: Letters*, 424.

39. November 19 (?), 1956, *One Art: Letters*, 329.

40. Elizabeth Bishop to Dr. Anny Baumann, May 22, 1958, *One Art: Letters*, 359. For an amusing description of the hurly-burly turmoil in the household, see Elizabeth Bishop to May Swenson, November 25, 1956, *One Art: Letters*, 331.

41. December 3, 1947, *Words in Air*, 18.

42. Elizabeth Bishop, "Gerard Manley Hopkins: Notes on Timing in His Poetry," *Vassar Review*, 1934, pp. 5–7; reprinted in *Bishop and Her Art*, 273–75. I quote from the latter, p. 273.

43. Elizabeth Bishop's unpublished journal, quoted in Goldensohn, *Biography of a Poetry*, 93.

44. William Carlos Williams, "Comedy Entombed: 1930," in *Make Light of It* (New York: Random House, 1950), p. 327.

45. "Gregorio Valdes, 1879–1939," *Partisan Review* 6 (Summer 1939): 91–97, and "Jeronymo's House," *Partisan Review* 8 (September/October 1941): 382.

Chapter 4

1. Michael Greenberg, "Freelance," *Times Literary Supplement*, July 29, 2005, p. 14. Kate Monteiro reports that today there is a gas station across the street from the old Bishop house in Great Village, put there (I would like to think) in homage to the poet who once lived in that house.

2. October 6, 1949, *One Art: Letters*, 638.

3. Elizabeth Bishop to Howard Moss, November 2, 1955, *Bishop and* The New Yorker, 158–59.

4. Elizabeth Bishop to Howard Moss, November 2, 1955, *Bishop and* The New Yorker, 159.

5. Elizabeth Bishop to Katherine White, January 15, 1963, *Bishop and* The New Yorker, 255–56.

6. At this point Bishop's poem calls to mind Robert Frost's poem "Blue-Butterfly Day," in which butterflies, "having ridden out desire," now "lie closed over in the wind and cling / Where wheels have freshly sliced the April mire." (*Collected Poems, Prose, & Plays*, ed. Mark Richardson and Richard Poirier [New York: Library of America, 1995], p. 208.)

7. *The Collected Poems of W. B. Yeats*, 2nd ed., ed. Richard J. Finneran (New York: Simon & Schuster, 1996), p. 58.

8. Elizabeth Bishop to Robert Lowell, February 27, 1970, *Words in Air*, 663.

9. February 5, 1940, *One Art: Letters*, 87.

10. January 31, 1949, *One Art: Letters*, 182.

11. Margaret Atwood, *Survival: A Thematic Guide to Canadian Literature* (Toronto: Anansi, 1972), p. 74.

12. Ibid., 80.

13. "Edwin A. Robinson, Poet, is Dead at 66," *New York Times*, April 6, 1935, p. 15.

14. João Cabral Neto, "On Elizabeth Bishop," trans. Celso de Oliveira, *Verse* 4 (November 1987): 58.

Chapter 5

1. Elizabeth Bishop to Howard Moss, August 15, 1956, *Elizabeth Bishop and* The New Yorker, 180.

2. Elizabeth Bishop Papers.

3. Bishop, "On the Railroad Named Delight," 448.

4. The *New Yorker* altered Bishop's title for

"Manuelzinho" in similar fashion, inserting the word "Brazil" into her original title — "Manuelzinho (Brazil. A Friend of the Writer is Speaking)."

5. Robert Lowell to Elizabeth Bishop, September 11, 1957, *Words in Air*, 230.

6. Robert Lowell to Elizabeth Bishop, April 20, 1958, *Words in Air*, 258. See also Lowell's letter to Randal Jarrell, October 24, 1957: "It was good to talk to you again and terribly refreshing to know that you and Mary like my *Skunks*. I've been working like a skunk, doggedly and happily since mid–August and have seven or eight poems finished (?) some quite long and all very direct and personal" (*The Letters of Robert Lowell*, ed. Saskia Hamilton [New York: Farrar, Straus and Giroux, 2005], p. 297).

7. Robert Lowell to Elizabeth Bishop, June 10, 1957, *Words in Air*, 204.

8. Robert Lowell to Elizabeth Bishop, December 1957 — "I'm dedicating 'Skunk Hour' to you. A skunk isn't much of a present for a Lady Poet, but I'm a skunk in the poem" — *Words in Air*, 239.

9. Elizabeth Bishop to Loren MacIver, December 19, 1950, *One Art: Letters*, 215. A slightly different version of "The Owl's Journey" is included in Elizabeth Bishop, *Edgar Allan Poe & The Juke-Box: Uncollected Poems, Drafts, and Fragments*, ed. Alice Quinn (New York: Farrar, Straus and Giroux, 2006), p. 91.

10. *Poe & The Juke-Box*, 91; *One Art: Letters*, 215. Quinn goes into the possible sources for Bishop's dream of rabbit and owl, along with Bishop's own explanations (297–99).

11. Elizabeth Bishop to Marianne Moore, October 25, 1943, *One Art: Letters*, 117–18.

12. *Poe & the Juke-Box*, 298.

13. Elizabeth Bishop to U. T. and Joseph Summers, October 19, 1967, *One Art: Letters*, 479.

14. Elizabeth Bishop, "A Flight of Fancy," *The Blue Pencil*, December 1929; reprinted in the *Gettysburg Review* 5 (Winter 1992): 21–25. I quote from page 25. Thomas Travisano anticipates me in suggesting the connection between the fire-balloons of "A Flight of Fancy" and those of "The Armadillo" ("Emerging Genius: Elizabeth Bishop and *The Blue Pencil*, 1927–1930," *Gettysburg Review* 5 [Winter 1992]: 45.

15. Bishop also wrote a quite different poem about the St. John's Day celebrations in June but it appears to have little to do with "The Armidillo"; see "St. John's Day," *Poe and the Juke-Box*, 109.

16. Elizabeth Bishop to Mary Eliot Summers, June 24, 1959, Elizabeth Bishop Papers.

17. Matthew Arnold, "Dover Beach," in *Masters of British Literature*, vol. B, eds. David Damrosch and Kevin J. H. Dettmar (New York: Pearson Longman, 2008), pp. 863–64.

18. Freyre, *Masters*, 254–55. In the original the two lines of folk poetry Freyre quotes read: "Dai-me noivo, S. Jôao, dai-me noivo, / dai-me noivo, que me quero casar."

19. Elizabeth Bishop to Donald E. Stanford, November 20, 1933, *One Art: Letters*, 12. She quotes from Morris W. Croll, "The Baroque Style in Prose," *Studies in English Philology: A Miscellany in Honor of Frederick Klaeber*, eds. Kemp Malone and Martin B. Rudd (Minneapolis: University of Minnesota Press, 1929), pp. 427–56.

Chapter 6

1. Note, "Squatter's Children," *Anhembi* 6 (April 1956): 288–89.

2. Victoria Harrison, *Elizabeth Bishop's Poetics of Intimacy* (Cambridge: Cambridge University Press, 1993), pp. 150–51.

3. Susan McCabe, *Elizabeth Bishop: Her Poetics of Loss* (University Park: Pennsylvania State University Press, 1994), p. 184.

4. Elizabeth Bishop to Howard Moss, February 23, 1969, *Bishop and* The New Yorker, 305.

5. Elizabeth Bishop to May Swenson, November 10, 1959, *One Art: Letters*, 377.

6. As Bishop notes, a lot of the film *Black Orpheus* was "taken on the hill of Babilônia" (Elizabeth Bishop to Howard Moss, January 29, 1964, *Bishop and* The New Yorker, 258.

7. Elizabeth Bishop to Randall Jarrell, February 25, 1965, *One Art: Letters*, 431.

8. TS letter, Elizabeth Bishop to James Merrill, February 27, 1969, San Francisco, CA, Elizabeth Bishop Papers.

9. Her marvelous treatment of loss, "One Art," would not appear until 1976.

10. Elizabeth Bishop, *The Ballad of the Burglar of Babylon* (New York: Farrar, Straus and Giroux, 1968), p. [5].

11. "Cordel poetry is the Brazilian equivalent of the popular ballad" ("Um equivalente brasileiro da balada popular é a poesia de cordel"), writes Regina Maria Przybycien ("Feijão Preto e Dimantes," 234).

12. João Cabral de Melo Neto, "On Elizabeth Bishop," 58.

13. Bishop's choice of trimeter over tetrameter in "The Burglar of Babylon" is explained by Regina Maria Przybycien as resulting from the influence of João Cabral de Melo Neto, who in his "nordestino" poem *Morte e Vida Severina* (part of which Bishop translated) employs trimeter lines throughout ("Feijão Preto e Dimantes," 218).

14. To Regina Przybycien's explanation that it was "Bishop's concern for the disappearance of local folk art [that] made her collect booklets of the northeastern *literatura de cordel* (the oral

poetry sung by the *repentistas* who improvised their verses as they went along)," I would add that such works contributed to her poetic choices as to subject matter and, to a lesser extent, form in the case of "The Burglar of Babylon" ("Elizabeth Bishop in Brazil: Traveler, Ethnographer, and Castaway," in *The Art of Elizabeth Bishop*, eds. Sandra Regina Goulart Almeida, Gláucia Renate Gonçalves and Eliana Lourenço de Lima Reis [Belo Horizonte: Editora UFMG, 2002], p. 68). In her Time-Life book, *Brazil*, Bishop writes: "There is a group of folk songs devoted to lacemaking; some of them relate the saga of a notorious bandit of the northeast, Lampião, who was shot in 1938. Strange to say, the riding song of Lampião's followers was 'The Lacemaker': 'Oh, lacemaker! / Teach me to make lace / And I'll teach you how to love...'" (Bishop, *Brazil*, p. 85).

15. April 22, 1960, *Words in Air*, 315.

16. José Cordeiro, "Visita de Lampião a Juazeiro," in *Literatura de Cordel: Antologia*, 3rd ed., ed. Edison de Souza Leão Santos (Fortaleza, CE: Banco do Nordeste do Brasil, S.A., 1994), p. 395.

17. Elizabeth Bishop to Howard Moss, December 6, 1964, *Bishop and* The New Yorker, 267.

18. Elizabeth Bishop to Howard Moss, January 29, 1964, *Bishop and* The New Yorker, 257.

Chapter 7

1. Quoted in Bonnie Costello, *Elizabeth Bishop: Questions of Mastery* (Cambridge: Harvard University Press, 1991), p. 90.

2. Henry David Thoreau, *Cape Cod* (New York: Penguin, 1987), p. 215. What Thoreau says about the sea and the shore in *Cape Cod* warrants closer consideration as an overall influence on Bishop's poetic imagination as well as on specific poems.

3. Elizabeth Bishop to Katherine White, January 15, 1963, *Bishop and* The New Yorker, 254–55.

4. Millier, *Life and the Memory*, 298.

5. Bishop worried that others might consider her poems to be merely "tourist poem[s]," as even her friend Robert Lowell was wont to see them at times (Lowell to Bishop, June 18, 1956, *Words in Air*, 181). The *New Yorker*, in particular, seemed to be deliberately encouraging the notion of Bishop as a rare species of travel writer by expanding the titles of poems such as "Manuelzinho (Brazil. A Friend of the Writer Is Speaking)" and "The Armadillo — Brazil" to suggest that they might be taken as a form of report from an exotic Brazil. Bishop's sensitivity to this accounts for the fact, perhaps, that while "Twelfth Morning; or What You Will" was published in

the *New York Review of Books* without the Cabo Frio place-line, when she collected it in *Questions of Travel* (1965) she felt safe, in the protection afforded her in an ample collection of varied poems, to restore the identifying words "Cabo Frio" following the poem. Similar is the change in "Sandpiper," where the word "ocean" in the *New Yorker* version becomes, more specifically (and more grandly), the "Atlantic" in *Questions of Travel*.

6. Elizabeth Bishop, "Laureate's Words of Acceptance," in *Poems, Prose, and Letters*, 731–32.

7. Elizabeth Bishop to Robert Lowell, October 1960, *Words in Air*, 345.

8. Elizabeth Bishop, "Sandpiper," *New Yorker*, July 21, 1962, 30; *Complete Poems*, 131.

9. Elizabeth Bishop, "Twelfth Morning; or What You Will," *Complete Poems*, 110–11.

10. Elizabeth Bishop to U. T. and Joseph Summers, July 18, 1955, *One Art: Letters*, 307.

11. Freyre, *Masters*, 472.

12. Bishop, *Brazil*, 87.

13. Elizabeth Bishop to Jean Stafford, January 4, 1965, George Monteiro Collection. Since there is no sign of a postal cancellation or affixed stamp, it is possible that the card was not mailed, unless, that is, it was mailed in an addressed envelope. There was no envelope with the card when I acquired it. A similar picture of the "Kings" enacting the *Bumba-meu-boi* appears in Bishop, *Brazil*, 92.

14. January 22, 1964, *Words in Air*, 516.

15. Ibid., 517.

16. In some ways Bishop's performing Balthazár is also reminiscent (as in the case of "Filling Station") of Robert Browning's exuberant Pippa and her joyful ditty, sung on the first of January, her one holiday a year: "The year's at the spring / And day's at the morn; / Morning's at seven; / The hill-side dew-pearled; / The lark's on the wing; / The snail's on the thorn: / God's in his heaven — / All's right with the world!" Notice, incidentally, how Browning's "dew-pearled" hillside becomes, in Bishop, "the world's a pearl."

17. Cassiani Ricardo, *Martim Cererê*, 11th ed. (São Paulo: Saraiva, 1962), pp. 107–08. My translation.

18. This was not the only issue she had with Cassiano Ricardo's poetry, whose work she seems to have enjoyed, on the whole. In her copy of *Martim Cererê*, for instance, along with the numerous markings signifying interest and approval, there is the notable instance when she crosses out boldly the jingoistic quatrain that concludes the poem "zozé, columí e joiô," which can be translated: "What, after all, is Hope? / in a country that is still a child, / it is a very Brazilian thing, / it is a form of marching" (179). My translation. That Cassiano Ricardo's poem "Festa no Morro" (*Montanha Russa e Mais*, 1960) has an affinity with Bishop's "Squatter's Children" (1956) is suggested by Luiza Franco Moreira in *Cassiani*

Ricardo, ed. Luiza Franco Moreira (São Paulo: Global, 2003), p. 11. It is noteworthy that "Squatter's Children" was first published in Brazil, appearing in *Anhembi* a year before its publication in the *New Yorker*.

Chapter 8

1. Elizabeth Bishop to Randall Jarrell, Feb. 25, 1965, *One Art: Letters*, 432.

2. Elizabeth Bishop to Marianne Moore, July 15, 1943, *One Art: Letters*, 114. While a student at Vassar, Bishop interviewed T. S. Eliot.

3. Quoted in *Selected Letters of Marianne Moore*, eds. Bonnie Costello, Celeste Goodridge, and Cristanne Miller (New York: Knopf, 1997), p. 420.

4. T. S. Eliot, "East Coker," Four Quartets, in *The Complete Poems and Plays* (New York: Harcourt, Brace, 1952), p. 128.

5. This comparison parallels T. S. Eliot's in "The Love Song of J. Alfred Prufrock," which begins: "Let us go then, you and I, / When the evening is spread out against the sky / Like a patient etherised upon a table" (*Collected Poems*, 3). But consider, too, the fact that three of the key terms in Bishop's description of the bakery's display of wares — "red," "white," and "glazed" — appear in William Carlos Williams's best known poem, "The Red Wheelbarrow": "so much depends / upon / a red wheel / barrow / glazed with rain / water / beside the white / chickens." See, too, Bishop's New York poem, "Trouvée."

6. Quotations from "Going to the Bakery" are taken from Bishop's *Complete Poems*, 151–52.

7. This is reminiscent of T. S. Eliot, who says of the Crucifixion and the taking of Communion: "The dripping blood our only drink, / The bloody flesh our only food: / In spite of which we like to think / That we are sound, substantial flesh and blood —/ Again, in spite of that, we call this Friday good" ("East Coker," *Four Quartets, Collected Poems*, 182).

8. Bishop, "On the Railroad Named Delight," *Poems, Prose, and Letters*, 443.

9. William Blake, "London," in *Songs of Experience*, in *Blake: The Complete Poems*, 2nd ed., ed. W. H. Stevenson (London and New York: Longman, 1989), pp. 213–14.

Chapter 9

1. Pryzbycien, "Elizabeth Bishop in Brazil," 71.

2. Elizabeth Bishop to Ashley Brown, January 8, 1979, *One Art: Letters*, 629.

3. Howard Moss to Elizabeth Bishop, January 3, 1979, *Bishop and* The New Yorker, 392.

4. March 1, 1979, *One Art: Letters*, 632.

5. See also the lyrics to the traditional samba

"Rio de Janeiro" as translated by Bishop: "Rio de Janeiro, / My joy and delight! / By day, there's no water. / By night, there's no light!" (Bishop, *Prose*, 346).

6. Enhancing its traditional lyric possibilities, the voice in this poem recalls the narrative voice of the bossa nova song. "It is not just that the lyrics [of the song] are about intimate relationships between men and women," writes Stephen Brown. "[T]he action of the lyrics is taking place *inside* the narrator's head. He isn't actually talking to the girl, he's thinking about her. He's not telling the story of their lives, and he's not telling it to her; he's telling *himself* what he's thinking, and, only incidentally, what he's feeling. Inward thoughts, inward music" ("Chopin came from Ipanema," *Times Literary Supplement*, June 30, 2003, p. 21).

7. In "Going to the Bakery" the poet refers to "loaves of bread" that "lie like yellow-fever victims / laid out in a crowded ward" and a "sickly" baker who suggests the "'milk rolls,'" which feel "like a baby on the arm."

8. In *New Road 1944*, which reprinted Bishop's poem "Jeronymo's House, Key West" (237–38), in a section called "South American Section: Brazilian Poetry" (247–69), there appear two poems in Dudley Poore's translation that may have caught Bishop's attention: Carlos Drummond de Andrade's "Fantasia" (263) and Manuel Bandeira's "The Highway" (264). Bandeira notes that "country dogs" always "have the air of business men: / They are always preoccupied."

9. Freyre, *Masters*, 472.

10. Ibid., note.

11. "When the Red Robin Comes Bob Bob Bobbin' Along," words and music by Harry Woods, was part of the repertoire of singers such as Ruth Etting, Bing Crosby, and Dean Martin.

12. James Merrill, "Elizabeth Bishop, 1911–1979," 121.

13. Ashley Brown, "An Interview with Elizabeth Bishop," *Shenandoah* 17 (Winter 1966): 3–19; reprinted in Monteiro, *Conversations*, 26.

14. Bishop, *Brazil*, 88.

15. Comparing "Pink Dog" to "Exchanging Hats," James McCorkle notes that "Bishop uses costuming as a transgressive mode to critique the deep class divisions in Brazil as 'Exchanging Hats' offers a critique of gender restriction" ("'Flowing, and Flown' Reveries of Childhood in Elizabeth Bishop's Poetry," in *Jarrell, Bishop, Lowell, & Co.*, 184 note).

16. "Merchants and residents hire off-duty policemen to exterminate the street children ... [they] are kidnapped and then shot." (*Los Angeles Times*, July 28, 1993; and, on the current situation, see Jon Lee Anderson, "Gangland," *New Yorker*, October 5, 2009, 53.

17. Elizabeth Bishop, Review of *XAIPE: Seventy-one Poems* by E. E. Cummings, *The United*

States Quarterly Book Review 6 (June 1950), 160–61.

18. *XAIPE* (1950), 49.

19. The English lyrics of "The Girl from Ipanema" are far different from those of Vinícius. See Vinícius de Moraes, "Garota de Ipanema," in *O Operário em Construção e Outros Poemas*, ed. Sérgio Buarque de Holanda (Rio de Janeiro: Nova Fronteira, 1979), p. 108. The English-language version, "The Girl from Ipanema" — credited to "Jobim — Gimbel — de Moraes" — is readily available online.

20. Dante Alighieri, *The New Life*, trans. Dante Gabriel Rossetti (London: George G. Harrap / New York: Brentanos, 1916), p. 110.

21. Ibid., 111.

Chapter 10

1. Elizabeth Bishop's translation of Carlos Drummond de Andrade's poem "No Meio do Caminho" in *Anthology of Twentieth-Century Brazilian Poetry*, 89.

2. Bishop, Review of *XAIPE*, 160; reprinted in *Bishop and Her Art*, 280.

3. James Merrill, afterword to David Kalstone, *Becoming a Poet*, 258.

4. Fountain and Brazeau, *Remembering*, 228.

5. Elizabeth Bishop to Harold Leeds and Wheaton Galentine, December 5, 1967, *One Art: Letters*, 483–84.

6. Millier, *Life and the Memory*, 170.

7. Bishop, *Brazil*, 85.

8. Bishop's translation of Lispector's "Uma Galinha" appeared as "A Hen" in the *Kenyon Review* 26 (Summer 1964): 507–09.

9. Elizabeth Bishop to Rachel MacKenzie, July 16, 1967, *Bishop and* The New Yorker, 295.

10. "Chronicle," Channel 5, Boston, February 6, 2001.

11. In the poem "Jerónimo's House" Bishop refers to the house as a "perishable ... wasps' nest." That the Brazilian Indian might keep something for its own sake was noted by Bishop on her visit to the Amazonas. "Hanging in the rafters over our heads was an enormous polished black calabash and someone asked the Cambridge man what it was doing there. 'Oh, they just happened to like it,' he informed us, and added once. 'They're human beings too, you know.'" (Bishop, "A New Capital, Aldous Huxley, and Some Indians" [1958], in *Poems, Prose, and Letters*, 395–96).

12. See Gary Fountain, "Elizabeth Bishop's 'Idea of the Place': Collecting, Culture, and the Aesthetics of National Identity," in *The Art of Elizabeth Bishop*, 260, and Fountain and Brazeau, *Remembering*, 321–22.

13. James Clifford, *The Predicament of Culture: Twentieth-Century Ethnography, Literature, and Art* (Cambridge: Harvard University Press,

1988), p. 231; quoted in Fountain, "'Idea of Place,'" 261. (Emphasis added.) I am reminded, too, of Wallace Stevens's "Connoisseur of Chaos" (from *Parts of a World*): "A great disorder is an order. Now A / And B are not like statuary, posed / For a vista in the Louvre. They are things chalked / On the sidewalk so that the pensive man may see." (*Collected Poems of Wallace Stevens* [New York: Knopf, 1955], p. 216.)

14. For an account of the Bishop-Clarice relationship, marked by friendship, praise for her stories, and exasperation over the Brazilian writer's behavior, see Benjamin Moser, *Why This World: A Biography of Clarice Lispector* (New York: Oxford University Press, 2009), pp. 227, 256–57, and 259–60.

15. *One Art: Letters*, 141.

16. Elizabeth Bishop to Aunt Grace, December 2, 1956, *One Art: Letters*, 334.

17. Elizabeth Bishop to Mrs. V. L. Chittick [Edna], Oct. 28, 1958, Elizabeth Bishop Papers.

18. *Go Down, Moses* (New York: Vintage, 1973), p. 163.

19. Atwood, *Survival*, 80.

Chapter 11

1. T. S. Eliot, *The Waste Land: A Facsimile and Transcript of the Original Drafts*, ed. Valerie Eliot (New York: Harcourt Brace Jovanovich, 1971), p. 4.

2. Greenlee, "Letter of Pedro Vaz de Caminha to King Manuel," 7

3. Carlos Drummond de Andrade, "Infância," trans. Elizabeth Bishop, in *Anthology of Twentieth-Century Brazilian Poetry*, 86–87.

4. Elizabeth Bishop, "Crusoe in England," *Geography III*, 16.

5. Elizabeth Bishop, "A New Capital, Aldous Huxley, and Some Indians," *Poems, Prose, and Letters*, 396.

6. Ibid., 392.

7. Elizabeth Bishop, "On the Railroad Named Delight," *Poems, Prose, and Letters*, 444.

Chapter 12

1. Elizabeth Bishop to Robert Lowell, July 28, 1953, *Words in Air*, 142.

2. Elizabeth Bishop to E. E. Cummings, December 5, 1956, Houghton Library, Harvard University, Cambridge, Massachusetts.

3. "Sonêto," *Estrêla da Vida Inteira* (Rio de Janeiro: José Olympio, 1966), p. 395.

4. See *Estrêla da Vida Inteira*, 406.

5. Manuel Bandeira to Elizabeth Bishop, September 1, 1953, Houghton Library, Harvard University. My translation.

6. Manuel Bandeira to Elizabeth Bishop, October 25, 1953, Houghton Library, Harvard University.

7. Ms., Houghton Library, Harvard University. In signing his poem "Xaire, Elizabeth" Bandeira alludes to Cummings' title — a Greek salutation translatable as "rejoice" or "greetings."

8. Bishop, *One Art: Letters*, 280–81.

9. Ibid., 269.

10. Ibid., 289.

11. *Words in Air*. 154.

12. Ibid., 161.

13. *One Art: Letters*, 289.

14. Ibid., 281. In the introduction to *An Anthology of Twentieth-Century Brazilian Poetry*, Bishop and Emanuel Brasil tell the following anecdote to make their point that "poets and poetry are highly thought of in Brazil," that "among men, the name of 'poet' is sometimes used as a compliment or term of affection, even if the person referred to is a businessman or politician, not a poet at all." Special favors were accorded "one of the most famous twentieth-century Brazilian poets, Manuel Bandeira," who was presented with "a permanent parking space in front of his apartment house in Rio de Janeiro, with an enameled sign POETA — although he never owned a car and didn't know how to drive." And when he came up short of the number of years of service required for a pension, "the Chamber of Deputies, to great applause, unanimously voted to grant him a full pension" (xiii).

15. *One Art: Letters*, 318.

16. "Poetry Born Out of Suffering," *Jornal do Brasil*, May 8, 1977, pp. 22–23; Monteiro, *Conversations*, 79.

17. The poem appears in several places, including Süsskind, "A Geléia & O Engenho," 349–50.

18. *Words in Air*, 409. Elsewhere Bishop warns her Brazilian audience against Bandeira's translations: "Much as I admire Bandeira — I must tell you now are very bad translations — don't judge [American poetry] by them" ("Three American Poets," [dated "'68–'69?"], Elizabeth Bishop Papers).

19. *Words in Air*, 411. There seems to have been a falling-out between Bishop and Bandeira, as Bishop implies in a letter to Robert Lowell in January 1963: "I hear that Bandeira has *stopped* being cross with me — too bad it wasn't before you left — and today I have already received two gift books (not B's however) — one prose, one poetry. I can't keep up with this flow — they keep coming & coming. Part of the general over-volubility —" (*Words in Air*, 440).

20. *One Art: Letters*, 363.

21. *Words in Air*, 273.

22. *One Art: Letters*, 579–80.

Chapter 13

1. Oswaldino Marques, *Teoria da Metáfora & Renascença da Poesia Americana* (Rio de Janeiro: Livraria São José, 1956), p. 104.

2. Oswaldino Marques, *O Laboratório Poético de Cassiano Ricardo*, 2nd ed. (Rio de Janeiro: Civilização Brasileira, 1976), p. ix.

3. Ricardo, *Martim Cererê*, 11th ed. (São Paulo: Saraiva, 1962). I purchased this copy a dozen or so years ago from Bibliolatry, a bookseller in East Hampton, Connecticut.

4. Bishop and Brasil, *Anthology of Twentieth-Century Brazilian Poetry*, 24–27.

5. Ibid., viii.

6. MacMahon, *Elizabeth Bishop: A Bibliography*, 165.

7. Oswaldino Marques tells the story of his relationship to Bishop in "O Realismo Alegórico de Elizabeth Bishop," in *Ensaios Escolhidos* (Rio de Janeiro: Civilização Brasileira, 1968), pp. 267–82.

8. Elizabeth Bishop to Howard Moss, March 23, 1964, *Bishop and* The New Yorker, 261.

Chapter 14

1. Elizabeth Bishop to Robert Lowell, June 25, 1961, *Words in Air*, 364–65.

2. Elizabeth Bishop to May Swenson, February 5, 1956, *One Art: Letters*, 316.

3. Millier, *Life and the Memory*, 367.

4. Elizabeth Bishop to Robert Lowell, April 4, 1962, *Words in Air*, 400.

5. Ibid., 399. For David Weimer's memory of his experience with Bishop and her book on Brazil in 1963, see Fountain and Brazeau, *Remembering*, 173. As she was wont to do in similar instances, Bishop made corrections in the copy of *Brazil* that Weimer asked her to sign.

6. It is notable, however, that she passed up at least one opportunity, perhaps because of the absurdly tight deadline, to revise her text for a second edition. "They [Time] wrote and asked me to do a small revision job on the *Brazil* book — not much work and a hunk of money, but in about ten days, of course — and it did me good to Tel-Ex back NO..." (Elizabeth Bishop to Robert Lowell, October 11, 1963, *Words in Air*, 507.

7. Quoted in MacMahon, *Elizabeth Bishop: A Bibliography*, 54.

8. Elizabeth Bishop to Robert Lowell, April 4, 1962, *Words in Air*, 397.

Chapter 15

1. Elizabeth Bishop to Ilse and Kit Barker, July 13, 1953, *One Art: Letters*, 266.

2. Richard F. Burton, *Explorations of the Highlands of Brazil*, 2 vols. (London: Tinsley Brothers, 1869), 1:333.

3. Elizabeth Bishop to Ilse and Kit Barker, February 7, 1952, *One Art: Letters*, 234. Emphasis added.

4. Elizabeth Bishop to Marianne Moore, Feb. 4, 1952, *One Art: Letters*, 236. Emphasis added.

5. Rudyard Kipling, *Brazilian Sketches* (New York: Doubleday, Doran, 1940), pp. 36, 51.

6. Ibid., 28.

7. Isabel Burton, *The Life of Captain Sir Richard F. Burton, K.CM.G., F.R.G.S.*, 2 vols. (New York: D. Appleton, 1893),1:423.

8. Elizabeth Bishop to Ilse and Kit Barker, July 15, 1953, *One Art: Letters*, 268.

9. *Life of Captain Sir Richard F. Burton*, 1:422, 430.

Chapter 16

1. Elizabeth Bishop to John Malcolm Brinnin, November 9, 1955, *One Art: Letters*, 309.

2. Vicki Feaver, "Hemingway's Hat," *New Yorker*, December 23, 1996, p. 108.

3. Vicki Feaver, "Elizabeth Bishop: The Reclamation of Female Space," in *Elizabeth Bishop: Poet of the Periphery*, New Castle/Bloodaxe Poetry Series 1, eds. Linda Anderson and Jo Shapcott (Northumberland, U.K.: University of Newcastle Upon Tyne / Bloodaxe Books, 2002), pp. 87–102.

4. Elizabeth Bishop to Pearl Kazin, July 19, 1952, *One Art: Letters*, 241.

5. Bill Bryson, *A Short History of Nearly Everything* (New York: Broadway Books, 2003), pp. 335–36.

6. That Bishop's "The Shampoo" and Marvell's "To His Coy Mistress" are somehow connected is hinted at but not pursued in Peter Robinson's description of Bishop's poem as "an after-the-fact poem by a coy mistress feeling pushed into something, yet glad to have been pushed" ("Pretended Acts: 'The Shampoo,'" *Poet of the Periphery*, 105).

Chapter 17

1. October 10, 1952, *Bishop and* The New Yorker, 85.

2. Elizabeth Bishop to Lloyd Frankenberg, March 22, 1960, *One Art: Letters*, 380.

3. Bishop, "In the Village," *Questions of Travel*, 57.

4. Millier, *Life and the Memory*, p. 14.

5. Robert Lowell to Elizabeth Bishop, October 18, 1965, *Words in Air*, 591. Lowell himself had already done something similar when he included his prose account, "91 Revere Street," among the poems of *Life Studies* in 1959.

6. Elizabeth Bishop to Kit and Ilse Barker, October 12, 1952, *One Art: Letters*, 249.

7. Elizabeth Bishop to U. T. and Joseph Summers, October 19, 1967, *One Art: Letters*, 477.

8. Elizabeth Bishop to Ilse and Kit Barker, February 25 or 26, 1954, *One Art: Letters*, 291.

9. Elizabeth Bishop to Emanuel Brasil, May 3, 1971, Elizabeth Bishop Papers.

10. James Joyce, *A Portrait of the Artist as a Young Man: Text, Criticism, and Notes*, ed. Chester G. Anderson (New York: Viking, 1968), pp. 7–8.

11. Dorothy Van Ghent, *The English Novel: Form and Function* (New York: Holt, Rinehart and Winston, 1953), p. 265.

12. Ibid., 265–66.

13. January 1, 1954, *Words in Air*, 151.

14. Elizabeth Bishop to Randall Jarrell, February 25, 1965, *One Art: Letters*, 431.

15. Joyce, *Portrait*, 485.

16. Bishop, Jacket blurb for *Life Studies*, in *Bishop and Her Art*, 285.

17. Robert Lowell, "The Scream," in *Collected Poems*, eds. Frank Bidart and David Gewanter (New York: Farrar, Straus and Giroux, 2003), p. 326.

18. Elizabeth Bishop, "In the Village," *Questions of Travel*, 48.

19. January 1, 1954, *Words in Air*, 151.

20. Lowell, "Scream," 326–27.

21. Elizabeth Bishop to Robert Lowell, April 5, 1962, *Words in Air*, 402.

22. David Kalstone, *Becoming a Poet*, 200–01. Emphasis added.

23. Elizabeth Bishop to Robert Lowell, April 5, 1962, *Words in Air*, 401–02. Lowell's surprising reaction to Bishop's comments was "Glad ... my tampering with 'In the Village' didn't annoy you. When 'The Scream' is published I'll explain, it's just a footnote to your marvelous story" (April 14, 1962, *Words in Air*, 405).

24. It is hardly surprising that later she would choose to translate "Viagem na Família" ("Travelling in the Family"), Carlos Drummond de Andrade's "family-memory" poem; see *Anthology of Twentieth-Century Brazilian Poetry*, 56–61.

25. "The Maple Leaf Forever," by Alexander Muir (1830–1906).

26. July 9, 1978, *One Art: Letters*, 624–25.

27. "At present I am very deep in the poems of— D. H. Lawrence! Oh dear, but they're very good, all the same," writes Bishop from Paris in an October 20, 1935, letter to Frani Blough (*One Art: Letters*, 37).

Chapter 18

1. Randall Jarrell to Robert Lowell, April 1951, *Randall Jarrell's Letters*, 248.

2. *New Yorker*, March 17, 1951, 31.

3. Ibid., 30.

4. Elizabeth Bishop to Robert Lowell, September 8, 1948, *One Art: Letters*, 170–71.

5. Millier, *Life and the Memory*, 230.

6. Ibid.

7. Elizabeth Bishop to U. T. and Joseph Summers, October 19, 1967, *One Art: Letters*, 479.

8. Millier, *Life and the Memory*, 149.

9. Theodor Adorno et al., *The Authoritarian Personality* (New York: Harper & Row, 1950), quoted in Tom Douglas, *Scapegoats: Transferring Blame* (London and New York: Routledge, 1995), p. 119.

10. H. G. Liddell and R. Scott, *Lexicon* (Oxford: Clarendon Press, 1896), quoted in Douglas, *Scapegoats*, 13.

11. Frank J. Kearful, "Elizabeth Bishop's 'The Prodigal' as a Sympathetic Parody," *Connotations* 12, no. 1 (2002/2003): 14–16.

12. George Kitchin, *A Survey of Burlesque and Parody in English* (London: Oliver and Boyd, 1931), pp. 2–3.

13. Robert Frost, "The Death of the Hired Man," in *Collected Poems, Prose, & Plays*, 43.

14. In "The Prodigal" the allusion to the story of Noah and the Ark (at night the animals are "safe and companionable as in the Ark"), beyond the indication of Noah's drunkenness when he receives his orders and the possible irony in the fact that Bishop's animals sleep tranquilly in a barn while those on the Ark ride the seas of a flood, yields considerably less than does the allusion to the parable of the Prodigal Son.

15. René Girard distinguishes between the enactments of communal and individual sacrifice: "If there were no surrogate victim to transform the sacrifice from an essentially private concern into one involving the whole community, we would be obliged to regard the victim as a substitute for particular individuals who have somehow provoked the sacrificer's anger." And if the transfer is "purely personal, as it is in psychoanalysis, then sacrifice cannot be a true social institution involving the entire community. But sacrifice, as we know, is essentially a communal institution. 'Individualization' marks a later, decadent stage in its evolution, a development contrary to its original spirit" (*Violence and the Sacred*, trans. Patrick Gregory [Baltimore and London: Johns Hopkins University Press, 1977], p. 101). One may speculate further that the poet's sacrifice of the Prodigal through the symbolism of poetry stands in for a ritual expiation of her own alcoholism.

16. Monteiro, *Conversations*, 45.

17. February 15, 1960, *Words in Air*, 386.

18. Elizabeth Bishop, "A Drunkard," *Georgia Review* 46 (Winter 1992): 608–09.

19. Elizabeth Bishop, *Edgar Allan Poe & The Juke-Box*, 344.

20. Ibid., 151.

Chapter 19

1. *The Poetical Works of Felicia Hemans* (Boston: Phillips, Sampson, 1858), p. 434.

2. *Robert Southey's Life of Nelson*, ed. Edwin L. Miller (New York: Longmans, Green, 1898), p. 135.

3. *Poetical Works of Felicia Hemans*, 434, note 1.

4. A., "Casabianca," *The Child's Friend and Family Magazine* 8 (April 1847): 17.

5. E. Benjamin Andrews, "A History of the Last Quarter Century in the United States," *Scribner's Magazine* 18 (September 1895): 283.

6. "Comment on New Books," *Atlantic Monthly* 69 (January 1892): 137.

7. Quoted in "Contemporary Sayings," *Appletons' Journal of Literature, Science and Art* 12 (September 19, 1874): 383.

8. Ibid.

9. Ibid.

10. Samuel Butler, *The Way of All Flesh* (New York: Modern Library, 1998), p. 135.

11. "Mrs. Hemans: A Gentle Poet,'" London *Times Weekly Edition*, May 23, 1935, p. 18.

12. Susan J. Wolfson, ed. *Felicia Hemans: Selected Poems, Letters, Reception Materials* (Princeton and Oxford: Princeton University Press, 2000), p. 428. An early "clean" parody, purportedly "translated from the original Chinese into 'pigeon English,'" appears in *The Galaxy* 11 (May 1871): 756 and is reprinted in *Forest and Stream* 1 (December 4, 1873): 260.

13. Wolfson, *Felicia Hemans*, 430, note 4.

14. Bishop, *Complete Poems*, 5.

15. Elizabeth Bishop, "The Buck in the Snow," *Gettysburg Review* 5 (Winter 1992): 19.

16. Edna St. Vincent Millay, *Fatal Interview* (New York and London: Harper & Brothers, 1931), p. 30.

17. Nancy Milford, *Savage Beauty: The Life of Edna St. Vincent Millay* (New York: Random House, 2001), p. xiii.

Chapter 20

1. Elizabeth Bishop to Marianne Moore, February 4, 1937, *One Art: Letters*, 59.

2. How far one can go in seeing in this hanging of Minnow's mouse an act of cruelty or symbolic revenge becomes problematic when one considers "Lullaby for the Cat," a poem addressed to Minnow, also dating from 1937.

3. Robert Gottlieb, "Nearly Anything Goes," *New York Review of Books* 56 (December 3, 2009): 33.

4. R. H., "Walt Disney and René Clair," *Life and Letters To-Day* 13, no. 1 (September 1935): 199. It is doubtful that Bishop would have much if anything to approve of in Disney's achievement, especially as it is described by the cultural historian Warren I. Sussman. "Walt Disney, one of the true geniuses of the age who often created its most important symbols (and used the science

and technology of the machine age to do it)," he writes, "seemed to know precisely how to take American fears and humiliations, and transform them in acceptable ways so Americans could live with them." In fact, "from The *Three Little Pigs* in 1933 to 'Night on Bald Mountain' (the terrors of the natural order) and 'The Sorcerer's Apprentice' (the errors of the technological order), both episodes of *Fantasia* (1940), Disney provided a way to transform our most grotesque nightmares into fairy tales and pleasant dreams" (*Culture as History* [New York: Pantheon, 1984], p. 196).

5. Robert Lowell to Elizabeth Bishop, ca. May 12, 1960, *Words in Air*, 325.

6. March 13, 1974, *Words in Air*, 761.

7. Elizabeth Bishop, "On 'The Man-Moth,'" in *Poet's Choice*, eds. Paul Engle and Joseph Langland (New York: Dial, 1962), p. 104.

8. There does not appear to be any "man-moth" misprint in the *New York Times*.

9. "Death of Oscar Wilde," *New York Times*, December 1, 1900, p. 1. The same information, including the reference to Wilde's alias as "Man-moth," appears in "Oscar Wilde Dead," *Hartford Courant*, December 1, 1900, p. 1.

10. Years later, in 1972, Bishop returned to Wilde. "One of my students lent me Oscar Wilde's Letters — a huge book. I just meant to glance at it but found myself still reading it at 4 A M today," she writes. "It gets sadder & sadder — but he was so funny — his U S trip is marvelous — He drank all the miners in Colorado under the table (he was 25 or so) and they respected him very much in spite of his velvet knee-britches" (Ms. letter, Elizabeth Bishop to Loren Frankenberg, January 8, 1972, Elizabeth Bishop Papers).

11. "Manmoth Eggs," *American Farmer* 1 (July 24, 1839): 66.

12. F. M., "Necessities," *Life* 81 (April 5, 1923): 34.

13. Apropos of Spiderman's resemblance to the Man-Moth, the poet Anthony Hecht notes that Bishop "indulge[s] herself in a sort of science-fiction fantasy, not very far removed from such a comic-strip convention as Spider-Man, whose name as well as whose newspaper source seem relevant"; but he does not develop the observation ("Two Poems by Elizabeth Bishop," in Anthony Hecht, *Melodies Unheard: Essays on the Mysteries of Poetry* [Baltimore and London: Johns Hopkins University Press, 2003], p. 164).

14. Bonnie Costello, "Afterword," in Fountain and Brazeau, *Remembering*, 353.

15. Ibid.

16. "Of course I'm amazed at the obvious reflection of Herbert in the 'one tear' stanza [in 'The Man-Moth']," wrote Bishop to U. T. and Joseph Summers. "I'm sure you are quite right,

but it had never occurred to me at all. I'm always delighted when people discover these things" (October 19, 1967, *One Art: Letters*, 477). It would have pleased Bishop, or amused her at least, I think, to learn that Tom Robbins, the author of *Even Cowgirls Get the Blues*, cribbed from "The Man-Moth" his characterization of the poet-songwriter-performer Leonard Cohen as one with "a quill in his teeth, a solitary teardrop a-squirm in his palm" (liner notes to *Tower of Song*, quoted in Tim Footman, *Leonard Cohen: Hallelujah, A New Biography* [Surrey: Chrome Dreams, 2009], p. 143). For Robbins's interview of Bishop when she was teaching at the University of Washington, first published in *Seattle Magazine* in April 1966 (pp. 8–12), see Monteiro, *Conversations*, 33–37.

17. Oswaldino Marques, "O Realismo Alegórico de Elizabeth Bishop," 282.

18. Süssekind, "A Geléia & o Engenho," 344.

19. Britto, *Iceberg Imaginário*, 25–33.

20. Chamberlain and Harmon, *Dictionary of Informal Brazilian Portuguese*, 322.

21. *American Heritage Spanish Dictionary*, 2nd ed. (Boston: Houghton Mifflin, 2001).

22. Chamberlain and Harmon, *Dictionary*, 493.

Chapter 21

1. Elizabeth Bishop to Arthur Gold and Robert Fizdale, December 2, 1958, *One Art: Letters*, 368.

2. *Nuova Corriente di Letteratura* 4 (July-September 1955): insert.

3. "Visite all'Ospedale di Santa Elisabetta," *Nuova Corriente di Letteratura* 5–6 (1956): 28–33. Bishop was also quoted in the same issue (from a letter to Rizzardi, presumably) to the effect that she admired Pound's criticism — "Inchiesta su Ezra Pound e la Poesia Americana," 207–08.

4. It is so dated by Camille Roman in *Elizabeth Bishop's World War II–Cold War View* (New York: Palgrave, 2001), p. 119. But consider the fact that Bishop explained to Howard Moss, her *New Yorker* editor, in 1956 that she acceded to Alfredo Rizzadi's request for a poem about Pound. "I sat down and wrote him a poem, or a kind of a poem — wrote it and sent it off in 24 hours" (June 1, 1956, *Bishop and The New Yorker*, 177–78).

5. Ibid., 178.

6. *Partisan Review* 24 (Spring 1957): 185–87. When Bishop included this poem about Pound's confinement in *Questions of Travel* (1965) she placed it last in the book and dated its composition "November, 1951." Oddly, however, in her copy of the book May Swenson has crossed out the date "November, 1951," as in-

structed to do by the poet, one surmises, since Bishop herself, when she included the poem in *The Complete Poems* (1969), also dropped the "November, 1951" date. Swenson's copy of *Questions of Travel* is in my personal collection.

7. *Words in Air*, 34.

8. The *Hartford Courant* editorialized: "Pound's Pisan Cantos are the latest in a long series of spluttery poetic comments upon life and politics. They include lines in praise of Mussolini for whose fascists he broadcast from Rome during the war" ("Poetry Prize Awarded to Ezra Pound," February 20, 1949, p. 10).

9. Fountain and Brazeau, *Remembering*, 115. In an interview in 1979, Bishop repeated that while she sent Pound books and admired his courage "in some way," she did not like him (www.writing.upenn.edu/pennsound/x/Howe-Pacifica.php).

10. Quoted Millier, *Life and the Memory*, 221. Millier also quotes from Bishop's diary apropos the same visit to Pound taken in the company of Kees. Under the date of February 21, 1950, Bishop writes: "We didn't get there until almost 3:30 because I had completely forgotten (the perfect slip) that visiting hrs. are over at four. He was very talkative — has a new blue back-chair, already broken from his throwing himself back in it, almost full-length. He said he was using my *hair-lotion—* I think it was eau-de-cologne, though!" (221).

11. *One Art: Letters*, 16.

12. Ibid., 31.

13. Ibid., 32.

14. Ibid., 78.

15. *Words in Air*, 93.

16. Ibid., 101–02.

17. Ibid., 105.

18. Ibid., 107.

19. *One Art: Letters*, 276. To Lowell on December 5, 1953, lamenting the early death of Dylan Thomas, Bishop wrote: "*Why*, I wonder ... when people can live to be malicious old men like Frost, or maniacal old men like Pound, or — well — I gather that J. Malcolm Brinnin had the worst of it all, too?" (*Words in Air*, 147).

20. Ibid., 186.

21. *One Art: Letters*, 338.

22. *Words in Air*, 274.

23. *One Art: Letters*, 576.

24. *Words in Air*, 669–70.

25. Brett C. Millier offers an excellent reading of "Visits to St. Elizabeths" (*Life and the Memory*, 280–84).

26. Paulo Henriques Britto, "Functionality of Form in Elizabeth Bishop's Poetry: Implications for Translation," in *The Art of Elizabeth Bishop*, 95. Of course the question of Pound's madness may also be related to the question of Bishop's mother's madness and death in a "house of Bedlam." The connection is fortuitously made (ironically) in Bishop's decision to risk the iden-

tity that readers might make between her given name and the name of the institution housing Pound. Then there is the teasing possibility that there are below-the-surface connections to be made among the terms "Saint," "Pope" (as applied to Pound) and "Bishop."

27. *Words in Air*, 259.

28. "Visits to St. Elizabeths" was first set to music by Ned Rorem; see his *Visits to St. Elizabeths (Bedlam): For Medium Voice and Piano* (New York: Boosey and Hawkes, 1964). On October 17, 1963, Bishop wrote to Lowell: "I was sent a photostat of the cover of the music of 'Visits to St. E's' by Cocteau. It must be one of his very last drawings. The usual Cocteau thing, but a weird wreath of names around it: Ned Rorem, Ezra P, E.B., and Cocteau — (the only one I really like is E.B.)" (*Words in Air*, 512). An image of this cover can be viewed at http://www.betweenthecovers.com/btc/item/278073/.

29. Randall Jarrell to Elizabeth Bishop, February 1957, *Randall Jarrell's Letters*, 419.

Chapter 22

1. *One Art: Letters*, 86.

2. Millier, *Life and the Memory*, 142; *One Art: Letters*, 85–86.

3. Charles A. Pearce to Elizabeth Bishop, October 27, 1939, *Bishop and* The New Yorker, 3.

4. Elizabeth Bishop to Robert Lowell, March 1, 1961, *Words in Air*, 354. Millier comments on Bishop's allusion to Baudelaire and his notion of *correspondances* in her birthday poem: "'The Bight' is a wonderful example of a Bishop speaker viewing a scene, telling 'what really happened,' and at the same time demonstrating her individuality, even personality." She also writes, "The poem avoids all explicit reference to the viewer of the excavation except in its sub-title." In addition, "The 'objective' description of the animals and machines is charged from the outside with Bishop's personal perspective, her own 'correspondences.' Surely these are Baudelaire's *correspondances*, his '*forêts de symboles / qui l'observent*'" (*Life and the Memory*, 196).

5. "Dust of Snow," *New Hampshire* (1923), in *Collected Poems, Prose, & Plays*, 205.

6. "Choose Something Like a Star," in *An Afterword* (1959), *Collected Poems*, 365. Or at least what Frost, on another occasion, called poetry: "The freshness caught of an idea dawning on you," for "poetry has that freshness forever, of having caught the feeling that goes with an idea just as it comes over you" ("'Anxiety for the Liberal Arts,'" in *Robert Frost Speaking on Campus: Excerpts from his Talks 1949–1962*, ed. Edward Connery Latham [New York and London: Norton, 2009], p. 32).

Chapter 23

1. Elizabeth Bishop, "Gerard Manley Hopkins: Notes on Timing in His Poetry," in *Poems, Prose, and Letters*, 665–66.
2. See Elizabeth Bishop to Jerome Mazzaro, April 27, 1978, *One Art: Letters*, 621.
3. Quoted in Millier, *Life and the Memory*, 181. The cross-out is Bishop's.
4. F. S. Bassett, "Nautical Proverbs and Sayings," *United Service; a Quarterly Review of Military and Naval Affairs* 2 (October 1889): 355.
5. Elizabeth Bishop to Ashley Brown, June 11, 1974, *One Art: Letters*, 586.
6. Alex Comfort, "Sixth Elegy," *New Road 1944*, 99.
7. This connection is also made by Ashley Brown in "An Interview with Elizabeth Bishop," *Shenandoah* (Winter 1966), 3–19; reprinted in Monteiro, *Conversations*, 18–29.

Chapter 24

1. Camille Paglia, "Final Cut: The Selection Process for *Break, Blow, Burn*," *Arion* 3rd series (Fall 2008): 3.
2. September 3, 1974, *Words in Air*, 767.
3. Robert Lowell, *Life Studies* (New York: Vintage, 1959), p. 68.
4. Edwin Morgan, "The Poet in the City," *Sonnets from Scotland*, in *Collected Poems* (Manchester: Carcanet, 1990), p. 451. Emphasis added.
5. April 27, 1978, *One Art: Letters*, 621.
6. Quoted in Charles F. G. Masterman, *The Heart of the Empire* (London: T. Fisher Unwin, 1901), p. 47, note.
7. Silviano Santiago, "The Status of Elizabeth Bishop's Descriptive Poem," trans. Julio Pinto, in *The Art of Elizabeth Bishop*, 16.
8. March 22, 1949, *One Art: Letters*, 184.
9. Bishop, *The Complete Poems*, 192.
10. Isabel Burton, *The Life of Captain Sir Richard F. Burton*, 1:426.
11. Whether Bishop intended this as a "coming-out" poem — prompted by what appears to

me an uncharacteristically blunt use of the term "gay" at the end of the poem — is a legitimate bio-critical question. Bishop's friend from their Vassar days, the writer Mary McCarthy, expressed puzzlement at Bishop's use of the word. When Frani Blough Muser, a mutual friend, called her attention to "Sonnet," she found that she was puzzled at Bishop's use of the word "gay." There were possibly three meanings of the word but she doubted that Bishop would have approved of the current meaning (May 19, 1982, Mary McCarthy Papers, Vassar College, Poughkeepsie, New York). Other readers, however, have had less doubt. See, for example, Elizabeth Burns's chiding of Bishop: "So, I was thinking, once you knew that your poems were being sent to, say, Marianne Moore, did you take away anything about sexuality?" she asks. "Would you have shown her 1979's 'Sonnet' had she still been living? Did you worry that poems of love/passion would be relegated to the land of Edna St. Vincent Millay?" She persists, "Was calling a sonnet by its name a gesture towards the language of love (the traditional love form being a sonnet — why didn't I mention that before?) that you would not have allowed yourself earlier in your life?" (*Letters to Elizabeth Bishop* [Buffalo: Leave Books, 1991], p. 20).

Epilogue

1. This card, along with May Swenson's copy of *Questions of Travel*, is in my possession. Swenson also notes that there are errors on pages 16 and 40.
2. Quoted in Kirstin R. Hotelling, "Afterword: Urged by the 'Unknown You': May Swenson and Elizabeth Bishop," in *Four Poems and a Letter to Elizabeth Bishop* (Torrance, CA: Bear River Press, 1997), p. [13].
3. www.writing.upenn.edu/pennsound/x/Howe-Pacifica.php.
4. Frank Bidart, "Elizabeth Bishop" (paper, American Literature Association meetings, Cambridge, Massachusetts, May 2004).

Bibliography

A.,"Casabianca." *The Child's Friend and Family Magazine* 8 (April 1847): 17–19.

Adorno, Theodor et al. *The Authoritarian Personality*. New York: Harper & Row, 1950.

Alighieri, Dante. *The New Life*. Translated by Dante Gabriel Rossetti. London: George G. Harrap / New York: Brentanos, 1916.

Almeida, Sandra Regina Goulart, Gláucia Renate Gonçalves, and Eliana Lourenço de Lima Reis, *The Art of Elizabeth Bishop*. Belo Horizonte: Editora UFMG, 2002.

Almeida; *American Heritage Spanish Dictionary*. 2nd ed. Boston: Houghton Mifflin, 2001.

Anderson, Jon Lee. "Gangland." *New Yorker*, October 5, 2009, pp. 47–55.

Andrade, Mário de. *Macunaíma*. Translated by E. A. Goodland. New York: Random House, 1984.

_____. *Macunaíma: O herói sem nunhum caráter*. Edited by Telê Porto Ancona Lopez. UNESCO Coleção Arquivos 6. Forianópolis, SC, Brasil: Editora da Universidade Federal de Santa Catarina, 1988.

Andrews, E. Benjamin. "A History of the Last Quarter Century in the United States." *Scribner's Magazine*, 18 (September 1895): 269–89.

Andrews, Norwood, Jr. *The Case Against Camões: A Seldom Considered Chapter from Ezra Pound's Campaign to Discredit Rhetorical Poetry*. Utah Studies in Literature and Linguistics 27. New York: Peter Lang, 1988.

Arnold, Matthew. "Dover Beach." In *Masters of British Literature*, vol. B. Edited by David Damrosch and Kevin J. H. Dettmar, 863–64. New York: Pearson Longman, 2008.

Arroyo, Leonardo. *A Carta de Pêro Vaz da Caminha*. São Paulo: Melhoramentos / Rio de Janeiro: Instituto Nacional do Livro, 1971.

Atwood, Margaret. *Survival: A Thematic Guide to Canadian Literature*. Toronto: Anansi, 1972.

de Azevedo Filho, Leodegário A. *História, Metodologia, Corpus*. Vol. 1 of *Lírica de Camões*. Vila da Maia: Imprensa Nacional-Casa da Moeda, 1985.

Bandeira, Manuel. *Estrêla da Vida Inteira*. Rio de Janeiro: José Olympio, 1966.

Bassett, F. S. "Nautical Proverbs and Sayings." *United Service; a Quarterly Review of Military and Naval Affairs* 2 (October 1889): 352–63.

Bell, Pearl K. "Dona Elizabetchy: A Memoir of Elizabeth Bishop." *Partisan Review* 58, no. 1 (1991): 29–52.

Biele, Joelle, ed. *Elizabeth Bishop and* The New Yorker*: The Complete Correspondence*. New York: Farrar, Straus and Giroux, 2011.

Bishop, Elizabeth. *The Ballad of the Burglar of Babylon*. New York: Farrar, Straus and Giroux, 1968.

_____. "The Buck in the Snow." *Gettysburg Review* 5 (Winter 1992): 19.

_____. "Cape Breton." *New Yorker*, June 8, 1949, p. 24.

_____. *The Complete Poems 1927–1979*. New York: Noonday Press / Farrar, Straus and Giroux, 1983.

_____. "A Drunkard." *Georgia Review* 46 (Winter 1992): 608–09.

_____. *Edgar Allan Poe & The Juke-Box: Uncollected Poems, Drafts, and Fragments*. Edited by Alice Quinn. New York: Farrar, Straus and Giroux, 2006.

_____. "A Flight of Fancy." *The Blue Pencil*, December 1929, 22–26.

_____. *Geography III*. New York: Farrar, Straus and Giroux, 1976.

_____. "Gerard Manley Hopkins: Notes on Timing in his Poetry." *Vassar Review* February 1934, pp. 5–7.

_____. "Gregorio Valdes, 1879–1939." *Partisan Review* 6 (Summer 1939): 91–97.

_____. "Jeronymo's House." *Partisan Review* 8 (September/October 1941): 382.

_____. "Love from Emily." *New Republic* 125 (August 27, 1951): 20–21.

_____. "On 'The Man-Moth.'" In *Poet's Choice*, edited by Paul Engle and Joseph Langland, 102–104. New York: Dial, 1962.

_____. "On the Railroad Named Delight." *New York Times*, March 7, 1965.

_____. *One Art: Letters*. Edited by Robert Giroux. New York: Farrar, Straus and Giroux, 1994.

_____. *Elizabeth Bishop: Poemas*. Horácio Costa, translator. São Paulo: Companhia Das Letras, 1990.

_____. *Poems*. New York: Farrar, Straus and Giroux, 2011.

_____. *Poems, Prose, and Letters*. Edited by Robert Giroux and Lloyd Schwartz. New York: Library of America, 2008.

_____. *Prose*. Edited by Lloyd Schwartz. New York: Farrar, Straus and Giroux, 2011.

_____. *Questions of Travel*. New York: Farrar, Straus and Giroux, 1965.

_____. Review of *XAIPE: Seventy-one Poems* by E. E. Cummings. *The United States Quarterly Book Review*, June 1950, pp. 160–61.

_____. "Sandpiper." *New Yorker*, July 21, 1962, p. 30.

_____. "Unseemly Deductions." *New Republic* 127 (August 18, 1952): 21.

_____. "Visite all'Ospedale di Santa Elisabetta." Translated by Alfredo Rizzardi. *Nuova Corriente di Letteratura* 5–6 (1956): 28–33.

_____. "Visits to St. Elizabeths." *Partisan Review* 24 (Spring 1957): 185–87.

_____, and Emanuel Brasil, eds. *An Anthology of Twentieth-Century Brazilian Poetry*. Middletown, CT: Wesleyan University Press, 1972.

_____, and The Editors of *Life*. *Brazil*. New York: Time Incorporated, 1962.

_____, trans. *The Diary of "Helena Morley."* New York: Farrar, Straus and Cudahy, 1957.

_____, trans. "A Hen." *Kenyon Review* 26 (Summer 1964): 507–09.

Blake, William. "London." *Songs of Experience*. In *Blake: The Complete Poems*, 2nd ed., edited by W. H. Stevenson, 213–14. London and New York: Longman, 1989.

Borges, Jorge Luis. "Partial Magic in the Quixote." In *Labyrinths: Selected stories & Other Writings*, translated by Donald A. Yates and James E. Irby, 193–96. New York: New Directions, 1964.

Britto, Paulo Henriques, trans. *O Iceberg Imaginário e outros poemas*. São Paulo: Companhia das Letras, 2001.

Brown, Ashley. "An Interview with Elizabeth Bishop." *Shenandoah* 17 (Winter 1966): 3–19.

Brown, Stephen. "Chopin came from Ipanema." *Times Literary Supplement*, June 30, 2003, pp. 20–21.

Bryson, Bill. *A Short History of Nearly Everything*. New York: Broadway Books, 2003.

Burns, Elizabeth. *Letters to Elizabeth Bishop*. Buffalo: Leave Books, 1991.

Burton, Captain Richard F. *Explorations of the Highlands of Brazil*. 2 vols. London: Tinsley Brothers, 1869.

Burton, Isabel. *The Life of Captain Sir Richard F. Burton, K.C.M.G., F.R.G.S.* 2 vols. New York: D. Appleton, 1893.

Butler, Samuel. *The Way of All Flesh*. New York: Modern Library, 1998.

Cabral de Melo Neto, João. "On Elizabeth Bishop." Translated by Celso de Oliveira. *Verse* 4 (November 1987): 58.

C[ampbell], J[ames]. "X-rated." *Times Literary Supplement* 5623, January 7, 2011, p. 32.

Camões, Luis de. *Lírica Completa*. Vol. 2, *Sonetos*. Preface and notes by Maria de Lurdes Saraiva. Vila da Maia: Imprensa Nacional-Casa da Moeda, 1980.

_____. *Lusiad; or, Portugals Historical Poem* (1655). Translated by Sir Richard Fanshawe. Reprinted in *The Lusiads*. Edited by Geoffrey Bullough. Carbondale: Illinois University Press, 1963.

_____. *Os Lusíadas*. Edited by Frank Pierce. Oxford: Clarendon Press, 1973.

Cesar, Anna Cristina. *A Teus Pés*. 8th ed. São Paulo: Brasiliense, 1992.

Chamberlain, Bobby J., and Ronald M. Harmon. *A Dictionary of Informal Brazilian Portuguese*. Washington, DC: Georgetown University Press, 1983.

"Chronicle." Channel 5. Boston, Massachusetts, February 6, 2001.

Cidade, Hernani, ed. Preface to Luis de Camoens, *Obras Completas*. Vol. 1, *Redondilhas e Sonetos*. 4th ed. Lisbon: Sá da Costa, 1961.

Clifford, James. *The Predicament of Culture: Twentieth-Century Ethnography, Literature, and Art*. Cambridge: Harvard University Press, 1988.

Comfort, Alex, and John Bayliss, eds. *New Road 1944: New Directions in European Art and Letters*. London: Grey Walls Press, 1944.

"Comment on New Books." *Atlantic Monthly* 69 (January 1892): 137.

Conrad, Joseph. *Heart of Darkness* (1902). Harmondsworth: Penguin Books, 1983.

"Contemporary Sayings." *Appletons' Journal of Literature, Science and Art* 12 (September 19, 1874): 383–84.

Cordeiro, José. "Visita de Lampião a Juazeiro." In *Literatura de Cordel: Antologia*, 3rd ed, ed. Edison de Souza Leão Santos, 394–415. Fortaleza, CE: Banco do Nordeste do Brasil, S.A., 1994.

Costello, Bonnie. *Elizabeth Bishop: Questions of Mastery*. Cambridge: Harvard University Press, 1991.

_____, Celeste Goodridge, and Cristanne Miller, eds. *Selected Letters of Marianne Moore*. New York: Knopf, 1997.

Croll, Morris W. "The Baroque Style in Prose." In *Studies in English Philology: A Miscellany in Honor of Frederick Klaeber*, eds. Kemp Malone and Martin B. Rudd, 427–56. Minneapolis: University of Minnesota Press, 1929.

Cummings, E. E. *XAIPE: Seventy-one Poems*. New York: Liveright, 1930.

"Death of Oscar Wilde," *New York Times*, December 1, 1900.

Dickinson, Emily. *The Poems of Emily Dickinson*. Edited by R. W. Franklin. Cambridge, MA and London: Belknap Press of Harvard University Press, 1999.

Diehl, Joanne Feit. *Women Poets and the American Sublime*. Bloomington: Indiana University Press, 1990.

Dodd, Elizabeth. *The Veiled Mirror and the Woman Poet: H.D., Louise Bogan, Elizabeth Bishop, and Louise Glück*. Columbia: University of Missouri Press, 1992.

Doreski, C. K. *Elizabeth Bishop: The Restraints of Language*. New York: Oxford University Press, 1993.

Douglas, Tom. *Scapegoats: Transferring Blame*. London and New York: Routledge, 1995.

"Edwin A. Robinson, Poet, is Dead at 66." *New York Times*, April 6, 1935.

Eliot, T. S. *Collected Poems 1909–1962*. New York: Harcourt, Brace & World, 1963.

_____. *The Waste Land: A Facsimile and Transcript of the Original Drafts*. Edited by Valerie Eliot. New York: Harcourt Brace Jovanovich, 1971.

Elizabeth Bishop Papers, Vassar College Libraries, Vassar College, Poughkeepsie, New York.

Faggen, Robert, ed. *The Notebooks of Robert Frost*. Cambridge: Harvard University Press, 2006.

Feaver, Vicki. "Hemingway's Hat." *New Yorker*, December 23, 1996, p. 108.

Footman, Tim. *Leonard Cohen: Hallelujah, A New Biography*. Surrey: Chrome Dreams, 2009.

Fountain, Gary and Peter Brazeau, eds. *Remembering Elizabeth Bishop: An Oral Biography*. Amherst: University of Massachusetts Press, 1994.

Frank, Waldo. *South American Journey*. New York: Duell, Sloan and Pearce, 1943.

Freyre, Gilberto. *The Masters and the Slaves: A Study in the Development of Brazilian Civilization*. 2nd English-Language Version, Rev. Translated by Samuel Putnam. New York: Knopf, 1956.

_____. *New World in the Tropics*. New York: Vintage Books / Random House, 1963.

Frost, Robert. "'Anxiety for the Liberal Arts.'" In *Robert Frost Speaking on Campus: Excerpts from his Talks 1949–1962*, ed. Edward Connery Latham, 30–41. New York and London: Norton, 2009.

_____. *Collected Poems, Prose, & Plays*. Eds. Mark Richardson and Richard Poirier. New York: Library of America, 1995.

Gilbert, Roger. "Framing Water: Historical Knowledge in Elizabeth Bishop and Adrienne Rich," *Twentieth Century Literature* 43 (Summer 1997): 141–6.

Girard, René. *Violence and the Sacred*. Trans. Patrick Gregory. Baltimore and London: Johns Hopkins University Press, 1977.

Goldensohn, Lorrie. *Elizabeth Bishop: The Biography of a Poetry*. New York: Columbia University Press, 1992.

Gottlieb, Robert. "Nearly Anything Goes." *New York Review of Books* 56 (December 3, 2009): 33.

Gray, Jeffrey. "Bishop's 'Brazil, January 1, 1502.'" *Explicator* 54 (Fall 1995): 36–39.

Greenberg, Michael. "Freelance." *Times Literary Supplement*, July 29, 2005, p. 14.

H. R. "Walt Disney and René Clair." *Life and Letters To-Day* 13, no. 1 (September 1935): 199–201.

Harrison, Victoria. *Elizabeth Bishop's Poetics*

of Intimacy. Cambridge: Cambridge University Press, 1993.

Hecht, Anthony. *Melodies Unheard: Essays on the Mysteries of Poetry.* Baltimore and London: Johns Hopkins University Press, 2003.

Hemans, Felicia. *The Poetical Works of Felicia Hemans.* Boston: Phillips, Sampson, 1858.

———. *Selected Poems, Letters, Reception Materials.* Edited by Susan J. Wolfson. Princeton and Oxford: Princeton University Press, 2000.

Henneberg, Sylvia. "Elizabeth Bishop's 'Brazil, January 1, 1502' and Max Jacob's 'Etablissement d'une Communauté au Brésil': A Study of Transformative Interpretation and Influence." *Texas Studies in Literature and Language* 45 (Winter 2003): 337–51.

L'Homme Armé Masses, http://music.olivet.edu/nwoodruff/1%27homme.htm.

Hotelling, Kirstin R. *Four Poems and a Letter to Elizabeth Bishop.* Torrance, CA: Bear River Press, 1997.

Insert. *Nuova Corriente di Letteratura* 4 (July-September 1955).

Jarrell, Mary, ed. *Randall Jarrell's Letters: An Autobiographical and Literary Selection.* Boston: Houghton Mifflin, 1985.

Jewett, Sarah Orne. *The Country of the Pointed Firs and Other Stories.* London and New York: Penguin Books, 1995.

Joyce, James. *A Portrait of the Artist as a Young Man: Text, Criticism, and Notes.* Edited by Chester G. Anderson. New York: Viking, 1968.

Kalstone, David. *Becoming a Poet: Elizabeth Bishop with Marianne Moore and Robert Lowell,* Edited by Robert Hemenway. Afterword by James Merrill. New York: Farrar, Straus and Giroux, 1989.

———. *Five Temperaments: Elizabeth Bishop, Robert Lowell, James Merrill, Adrienne Rich, John Ashbery.* New York: Oxford University Press, 1977.

Kearful, Frank J. "Elizabeth Bishop's 'The Prodigal' as a Sympathetic Parody." *Connotations* 12, 1 (2002/2003): 14–34.

Kipling, Rudyard. *Brazilian Sketches.* New York: Doubleday, Doran, 1940.

Kitchin, George. *A Survey of Burlesque and Parody in English.* London: Oliver and Boyd, 1931.

Klintowitz, Jacob. *Pedro Luiz Correia de Araújo.* N. p.: André Galeria de Arte, 1981.

Krähenbühl, Olívia (trans.). *Poesias Escolhidas de Emily Dickinson.* São Paulo: Saraiva, 1956.

Lask, Thomas. "Modern Verse." *New York Times,* March 10, 1957.

The Letter of Amerigo Vespucci Describing his Four Voyages to the New World, 1497–1504. Introduction by Oscar Lewis. San Francisco: Book Club of California, 1926.

Liddell, H. G., and R. Scott. *Lexicon.* Oxford: Clarendon Press, 1896.

Lowell, Robert. *Collected Poems.* Edited by Frank Bidart and David Gewanter. New York: Farrar, Straus and Giroux, 2003.

———. *The Letters of Robert Lowell.* Edited by Saskia Hamilton. New York: Farrar, Straus and Giroux, 2005.

———. *Life Studies.* New York: Vintage, 1959.

M., F. "Necessities." *Life* 81 (April 5, 1923: 34.

MacMahon, Candace W. *Elizabeth Bishop: A Bibliography 1927–1979.* Charlottesville: Bibliographical Society of the University of Virginia / University Press of Virginia, 1980.

McCabe, Susan. *Elizabeth Bishop: Her Poetics of Loss.* University Park: Pennsylvania State University Press, 1994.

McClatchy, J. D. "Elizabeth Bishop: Some Notes on 'One Art.'" In *White Paper on Contemporary American Poetry,* 139–45 New York: Columbia University Press, 1989.

McCorkle, James. "'Flowing, and Flown' Reveries of Childhood in Elizabeth Bishop's Poetry." In *Jarrell, Bishop, Lowell, & Co.,* ed. Suzanne Ferguson, 165–85. Knoxville: University of Tennessee Press, 2003.

Manguel, Alberto. *In the Library at Night.* New Haven & London: Yale University Press, 2006.

"Manmoth Eggs." *American Farmer* 1 (July 24, 1839) 1: 66.

Marques, Oswaldino. *O Laboratório Poético de Cassiano Ricardo,* 2d ed. Rio de Janeiro: Civilização Brasileira, 1976.

———. "O Realismo Alegórico de Elizabeth Bishop." In *Ensaios Escolhidos,* 267–82. Rio de Janeiro: Civilização Brasileira, 1968.

———. *Teoria da Metáfora & Renascença da Poesia Americana.* Rio de Janeiro: Livraria São José, 1956.

Masterman, Charles F. G. In *The Heart of the Empire.* London: T. Fisher Unwin, 1901.

Merrill, James. "Elizabeth Bishop (1911–1979)." In *Recitative: Prose,* ed. J. D. McClatchy, 121–23. San Francisco: North Point Press, 1986.

Milford, Nancy. *Savage Beauty: The Life of Edna St. Vincent Millay*. New York: Random House, 2001.

Millay, Edna St. Vincent. *Fatal Interview*. New York and London: Harper & Brothers, 1931.

Millier, Brett C. *Elizabeth Bishop: Life and the Memory of It*. Berkeley and Los Angeles: University of California Press, 1993.

Monteiro, George, ed. *Conversations with Elizabeth Bishop*. Jackson: University Press of Mississippi, 1996.

Moore, Marianne. *Poemas*. Edited by João Moura, Jr. Translated by José Antonio Arantes. São Paulo: Companhia Das Letras, 1991.

de Moraes, Vinicius. "Garota de Ipanema." In *O Operário em Construção e Outros Poemas*, ed. Sérgio Buarque de Holanda, 108. Rio de Janeiro: Nova Fronteira, 1979.

Moreira, Luiza Franco, ed. *Cassiano Ricardo*. São Paulo: Global, 2003.

Morgan, Edwin. "The Poet in the City," *Sonnets from Scotland*. In *Collected Poems*, 451. Manchester: Carcanet, 1990.

Moser, Benjamin. *Why This World: A Biography of Clarice Lispector*. New York: Oxford University Press, 2009.

"Mrs. Hemans: A Gentle Poet." London *Times Weekly Edition*, May 23, 1935, p. 18.

Note. "Squatter's Children." *Anhembi* 6 (April 1956): 288–89.

"Oscar Wilde Dead." *Hartford Courant*, December 1, 1900.

Paglia, Camille. "Final Cut: The Selection Process for *Break, Blow Burn*." *Arion* 3rd series (Fall 2008): 1–23.

"Poetry Prize Awarded to Ezra Pound." *Hartford Courant*, February 20, 1949.

Przybycien, Regina M. "Feijão Preto e Diamantes: O Brasil na Obra de Elizabeth Bishop." Ph.D. dissertation. Faculdade de Letras da Universidade Federal de Minas Gerais, Belo Horizonte, Brasil, 1993.

_____. "Tainted Paradise: Elizabeth Bishop's Vision of Brazil." Paper Presented at the XXIV SENAPULLI meetings, João Pessoa, PB, January 27, 1992.

Reed, Justin. "Manners of Mistranslation: The *Anthrofagismo* of Elizabeth Bishop's Prose and Poetry." *CR: The New Centennial Review* 3 (Spring 2003): 297–327.

Ricardo, Cassiano. *Martim Cererê*, 11th ed. São Paulo: Saraiva, 1962.

Roman, Camille. *Elizabeth Bishop's World War II–Cold War View*. New York: Palgrave, 2001.

Rorem, Ned. *Visits to St. Elizabeths (Bedlam): For Medium Voice and Piano*. New York: Boosey and Hawkes, 1964.

Schwartz, Lloyd. "Annals of Poetry: Elizabeth Bishop and Brazil." *New Yorker* 67 (September 30, 1991): 85–97.

_____, and Sybil P. Estess, eds. *Elizabeth Bishop and Her Art*. Ann Arbor: University of Michigan Press, 1983.

de Sena, Jorge de Sena. *Os Sonetos de Camões e o Soneto Quinhentista Peninsular*, 2nd ed. Lisbon: Edições 70, 1980.

Skidmore, Thomas E. *Brazil: Five Centuries of Change*. New York and Oxford: Oxford University Press, 1999.

Southey, Robert. *Robert Southey's Life of Nelson*. Edited by Edwin L. Miller. New York: Longmans, Green, 1898.

Stevens, Holly, ed. *Letters of Wallace Stevens*. New York: Knopf, 1972.

Stevens, Wallace. *Collected Poems of Wallace Stevens*. New York: Knopf, 1955.

Stevenson, Anne. *Elizabeth Bishop*. Twayne's United States Authors Series. New York: Twayne, 1966.

_____. *Five Looks at Elizabeth Bishop*. London: Bellew, 1998.

_____. "Letters from Elizabeth Bishop." *Times Literary Supplement*, March 7, 1980, pp. 261–62.

Süssekind, Flora. "A Geléia & o Engenho: Em Torno de uma Carta-poema de Elizabeth Bishop a Manuel Bandeira." In *Papéis Colados*, 331–65. Rio de Janeiro: Editora UFRJ, 1993.

Sussman, Warren I. *Culture as History*. New York: Pantheon, 1984.

Symons, Arthur. "Arthur Rimbaud." In *Studies in Two Literatures*. London: Martin Secker, 1924.

Thoreau, Henry David. *Cape Cod*. New York: Penguin, 1987.

Travisano, Thomas J. *Elizabeth Bishop: Her Artistic Development*. Charlottesville: University Press of Virginia, 1988.

_____. "Emerging Genius: Elizabeth Bishop and *The Blue Pencil*, 1927–1839." *Gettysburg Review* 5 (Winter 1992): 32–47.

_____, with Saskia Hamilton, eds. *Words in Air: The Complete Correspondence Between Elizabeth Bishop and Robert Lowell*. New York: Farrar, Straus and Giroux, 2008.

Van Der Post, Laurens. *Venture to the Interior*. New York: Viking, 1961.

Van Ghent, Dorothy. *The English Novel: Form*

and Function. New York: Holt, Rinehart and Winston, 1953.

Vaz de Caminha, Pêro. "Letter of Pedro Vaz de Caminha to King Manuel." In *The Voyages of Pedro Álvares Cabral to Brazil and India,* 3–33. Works Issued by The Hakluyt Society, 2nd Ser., No. 81. Trans. William Brooks Greenlee. London: Hakluyt Society, 1938.

Vendler, Helen. *Last Looks, Last Books: Stevens, Plath, Lowell, Bishop, Merrill.* Princeton and Oxford: Princeton University Press, 2010.

Vianna, Hélio. *História do Brasil.* Vol. I, *Período Colonial.* 3rd ed., rev. São Paulo: Melhoramentos, 1965.

Warnke, Frank J. "The Voyages of Elizabeth Bishop." *New Republic* 154 (April 9, 1966): 19.

Williams, William Carlos. "Comedy Entombed: 1930." In *Make Light of It,* 322–32. New York: Random House, 1950.

Wright, Albert Hazen. *Letters to C. F. Hartt.* Studies in History No. 16, Pre-Cornell and Early Cornell II Series. Ithaca, New York: Privately printed, 1953.

Yeats, William Butler. *The Collected Poems of W. B. Yeats.* 2nd edition. Edited by Richard J. Finneran. New York: Simon & Schuster, 1996.

Index

Aesop 155
Agnew, Spiro T. 165
Alberto, José 22
Alexandra (Princess) 137
Aliança para o Progresso (Alliance for Progress) 47
"Aliança para o Progresso da Esso" 47
All Souls' Day 119
Alves, Antônio de Castro 23, 117; *The Slave Ship* 23, 117
Amazon (forest) 105, 111
Amazon (river) 8, 79, 177
Amazonas (state) 113
American Farmer 158
Anastácio, Sílvia Maria Guerra 7–8; *O Jogo das Imagens no Universo da Criação de Elizabeth Bishop* 7–8
Andrade, Carlos Drummond de 8, 23, 81, 84, 85, 86, 88–89, 94; "Infância" ("Infancy") 88; "No Meio do Camino" ("In the Middle of the Road") 81, 84, 85, 86
Andrade, Mário de 32; *Macunaíma* 32
Anhembi (journal) 58, 93
An Anthology of Twentieth-Century Brazilian Poetry (with Emanuel Brasil) 7, 23–24, 51, 79–80, 81, 84–85, 95, 97
Anthon (Scott), Kate 12
Anti-Semitism 162, 165
Aquinas, Saint Thomas 117
"The Armadillo" 8, 15, 34, 52, 53, 54, 55, 56, 57, 68; "The Armadillo — Brazil" 52; "Owl's Nest" (earlier title) 52, 55, 56
Arnold, Matthew 56; "Dover Beach" 56–57
"Arrival at Santos" 8, 12, 13, 15, 34, 35, 36, 36–37, 38, 70, 123, 128, 179; "To the Interior" (earlier title) 37
The Art of Elizabeth Bishop 7
"The Art of Elizabeth Bishop: An International Conference & *Celebração* in Brazil" 7
"As true as the sea burns" (proverb) 171
Assis, Machado de 117
Associated Press 162
"At the Fishhouses" 170–72
Atwood, Margaret 50, 85, 86, 137; *Survival: A Thematic Guide to Canadian Literature* 50, 137

Auden, W. H. 142, 146; "Musée des Beaux Arts" 142, 146

Bacchus 145
Bacon, Leonard 25–26; *The Lusiads of Luiz de Camões* 25, 26
Bahia (city) 47, 102, 117
The Ballad of the Burglar of Babylon 5, 59, 61
Bandeira, Manuel 7, 23, 91–95; "Acalanto" ('Lullaby") 91; "Parabens, Elizabeth!" ("Congratulations, Elizabeth!") 93, 94
"The Baptism" 155
Barker, Ilse, and Kit 7; letters from Bishop 124, 126, 131
Bathsheba (scripture) 78
"Batman" 159
Battle of the Nile 151
Baudelaire, Charles 83, 117, 167, 168; "Le Cygne" 168; "Spleen" 167
Baumann, Annie: letters from Bishop 2, 6, 34, 42, 177
The Beats 149
Bedlam, House of 165, 166
Bellow, Saul 82; *Henderson the Rain King* 82
Belo Horizonte (city) 7, 37
Berlin, Irving 77; "Blue Skies" 77; "Easter Parade" 77
Berryman, John 2
Besner, Neil K. 5; *Rare and Commonplace Flowers* 5
Bidart, Frank 138, 139; letters from Bishop 138
"The Big Bear of Arkansas" 82
"The Bight" 3, 60, 66, 174, 175, 177
Bilac, Olavo 23, 24, 32; "O Brasil" ("Brazilian Land") 24; *As viagens* (*The Voyages*) 24
"Black Beans and Diamonds" 8, 37, 98–99
Blackmur, R. P. 163
"The Bishop" 127, 166
Blake, William 27, 64, 65, 66, 70, 72–73, 83, 96; *Auguries of Innocence* 65; "London" 72, 83; *Songs of Experience* 72; "The Tyger" 27
Blessed Virgin 14, 145
Blough (Muser), Frani 163, 167; letters from Bishop 163, 167
Bollingen Prize 161–62

Bonaparte, Napoleon 105
Bonifácio, José 109
Boston 5, 86, 138, 147, 181
SS *Bowplate* 4, 36
Brant, Alice Dayrell Caldeira 35, 92, 176; *Minha Vida de Menina* 13, 92, 124, 176
Brasil, Emanuel 7, 24, 51, 80, 81, 84–85, 95, 97, 132; *Pedra Fantasma* 132
Brasília 8, 89, 99, 101, 109, 110, 111, 119, 120
Brazil 8, 26, 67, 78, 82, 98–122
"Brazil, January 1, 1502" 12, 15, 23–32, 35, 123
Brazilian Academy of Letters 117
"Brazilian Tragedy" (by Manuel Bandeira) 95
Brinnin, John Malcolm 127
Britto, Paulo Henriques 7, 160; *Esforços do Afeto e outras histórias* 7; *O Iceberg Imaginário e outros poemas* 7; *Poemas do Brasil* 7; *Uma Arte: as Cartas de Elizabeth Bishop* 7
Brooks, Paul: letters from Bishop 92
Brown, Ashley 35, 74, 75, 78; letters from Bishop 74, 75
Browning, Elizabeth Barrett 11; "Catarina to Camoens" 11
Browning, Robert 47; "Pippa Passes" 47
Brush, Marjorie 162; letters from Bishop 162
Bryant, William Cullen 54; "To a Waterfowl" 54
Bryson, Bill 129
Bulmer, Grace: letters from Bishop 39, 84
Bumba-meu-boi 67–69
"The Burglar of Babylon" 5, 15, 59, 60, 61–63, 97; "O Ladrão da Babilônia" 97
"Burro que vai a Santarém burro vem" ("An ass that goes to Santarém comes back an ass"); (proverb) 176
Burton, Isabel 125–26, 178; Friday (Mrs. Burton's servant) 126
Burton, Richard F. 123–24, 125; *Explorations of the Highlands of Brazil* 124
Butler, Samuel 152–53; Ernest Pontifax 152–53; *The Way of All Flesh* 152–53

Cabo Frio 8, 64, 65, 67, 68, 113
Cabral, Pedro Alvares 26, 30, 103
Cabral de Melo Neto, João 51, 62, 94; "On Elizabeth Bishop" 51, 62
Cadernos brasileiros (journal) 97
Cagney, James 156
Camargo, Iberê 116
Caminha, Pedro Vaz de 26, 27, 28–29, 31, 32, 88
Camões, Luis de 12–13, 14, 15, 19, 20, 25, 26, 32, 63, 166; "Island of Love (Canto IX)" 25, 26, 32; *Líricas* 12; *Os Lusíadas* 25; "Quem vê, Senhora, claro e manifesto" 12–14
Cambridge (Massachusetts) 90, 147
Campbell, Roy 20; "Luis de Camões" 20
Canudos (Bahia) 117
"Cape Breton" 33, 46
Cape Breton (island) 46
Cape of Good Hope 104

Caracas (city) 116
Carnaval (Carnival) 41, 52, 58, 67, 74–80, 115
Carvalho, Ronald de 23, 38; "Interior" 38
Casa Mariana 6, 15–16, 32
"Casabianca" 153–54
Casabianca, Giacomo Jocante 151
Casabianca-ism 152
Ceará (state) 114
César, Anna Cristina 5
Chaplin, Charles ("Charlito") 160
Chesterton, G. K. 117
Child's Friend and Family Magazine 151
Christ the Redeemer (Corcovado) 108
"Cirque d'Hiver" 68, 167–69; "Spleen" (earlier title) 167, 168–69
Cirque d'Hiver (Paris) 167–168, 169
Clark, Sir Kenneth 25; *Landscape into Art* 24–25
Clifford, James 83
"Come, my mulatta" (samba) 90
Comfort, Alex 171, 172; "Sixth Elegy" 171–72
The Complete Poems 5, 127, 155, 164, 180, 181
The Complete Poems 1927–1979 181
Congonhas (city) 105
Conkling, Roscoe 151
Conrad, Joseph 37, 38; *Heart of Darkness* 37
Consultant in Poetry to the Library of Congress 4, 161, 162, 163
Cooper, James Fenimore 85; *The Pioneers* 85
Copacabana 27, 71, 77, 108, 140
Cornell, Joseph 83, 176, 180
Correia de Araújo, Lilli 16, 17, 31
Correia de Araújo, Pedro Luiz 17, 31, 32; *Conquistadores e Conquista* (*Conquistadors and Conquest*) 31, 32
Costa, Horácio 7, 38; "Chegada a Santos" 38
Crane, Hart 94
Croll, Morris W. 57, 170; "The Baroque Style in Prose" 57, 170
"Crusoe in England" 88–90, 180; "Crusoe at Home" (earlier title) 89
Cruz e Souza 23
cummings, e. e. 38, 79, 81, 91, 94, 95; "it may not always be so; and I say" 91; letters from Bishop 91; *95 Poems* 94; *Tulips and Chimneys* 91; *XAIPE: Seventy-one Poems* 38, 79, 81
Cunha, Euclides de 117; *Os Sertões* (*Rebellion in the Backlands*) 117

Dante 75, 80; *La Vita Nuova* 80; "My lady looks so gentle and so pure" 80
Darwin, Charles 38, 123; *Voyage of the Beagle* 123
David (scripture) 78
"Dear my compass" 16, 17, 18–19
Defoe, Daniel 88–89, 90; "A Dream Realised" (chapter 14) 90; Friday (character) 89, 90; *The Life and Adventures of Robinson Crusoe* 88, 89, 90; Robinson Crusoe (character) 88, 89, 90;
De Mille, Cecil B. 42; *The Ten Commandments* 42
Dennehy, Brian 144

Diamantina (city) 124
The Diary of "Helena Morley" 3, 13, 35, 124, 176
Dickinson, Emily 1, 11, 12, 14, 18, 83, 87, 141, 177, 178; "After great pain, a formal feeling comes" 87; "The Brain is wider than the sky" 141; "Done with the Compass" 178; "Hope is the thing with feathers" 178; "Pain has an element of blank" 141, 178; "A route of evanescence" 178; "Success is counted sweetest" 141; "Wild Nights" 178
Dictionary of Literary Biography 76
Disney, Walt 157
Dolmetsch, Arnold 163
Dom Pedro I (Emperor) 106
Dom Pedro II (Emperor) 105, 106, 107
Doreski, C. K. 3
Dostoyevsky, Fyodor 159
"A Drunkard" 73, 148, 149
Duarte, Paulo 58
Dublin 132, 144

Ecclesiastes (scripture) 131
Edgar Allan Poe & The Juke-Box 55
Edward (Prince of Wales) 137
Edwards, John 163
"Efforts of Affection: A Memoir of Marianne Moore" 7
Ehrenpreis, Irwin 157
"18 Smart 'n Cheerful Cards" 173
"Electrical Storm" 125–26
"Elegy" 5, 21
Eliot, T. S. 32, 66, 70, 72, 88, 96, 123, 147; "East Coker" 70; *Four Quartets* 70; "The Love Song of J. Alfred Prufrock" 147; "Portrait of a Lady" 123; "Preludes" 147; "Sweeny Among the Nightingales" 147; *The Waste Land* 32
Elizabeth Bishop: An Oral Biography 81
Elizabeth Bishop Collection (Harvard University) 100–21 *et passim*
"Elizabeth Bishop: Intervista con Ezra Pound" 161
Elizabeth Bishop Papers (Vassar College) 8
Emerson, Ralph Waldo 54, 177; "Rhodora" 54
Emily Dickinson's Letters to Doctor and Mrs. Josiah Gilbert Holland 11
"The End of March" 180
Engle, Paul 157; *Poet's Choice* 157–58
Esquadrão da morte (death squad) 75, 79
Evans, Luther 163
"Exchanging Hats" 127–28
"Ezra Pound Song" 161, 166

Faber & Faber 124
Faulkner, William 82, 85, 117; "The Old People" 85
"Faustina, or Rock Roses" 3, 42–45
Feaver, Vicki 128; "Elizabeth Bishop: The Reclamation of Female Space" 128; "Hemingway's Hat" 128
"Filling Station" 35, 46–47, 48, 49; "Station #2" (earlier title) 47

"First Death in Nova Scotia" 130, 136
"The Fish" 48, 49, 50, 128, 173
"Five Flights Up" 180
Fizdale, Robert: letters from Bishop 95
"A Flight of Fancy" 55
Frank, Waldo 30
Frankenberg, Loren, and Lloyd: letters from Bishop 13, 14, 130
"Free City" (Brasília) 110
Freud, Sigmund 1
Freyre, Gilberto 23, 24, 29, 32, 36, 57, 67, 69, 76; *Casa Grande & Senzala* (*The Masters and the Slaves*) 23, 24, 29, 36, 57, 67, 76
"From 'First lessons in Geography,' Monteith's Geographical Series, A. S. Barnes & Co., 1884" 9, 180, 181
"From Trollope's Journal" 88
Frost, Lesley 93
Frost, Robert 1, 49, 66, 67, 85, 91, 93, 145, 164, 169; "Choose Something Like a Star" 169; "The Death of the Hired Man" 145; "Design" 67; "Directive" 49; "Dust of Snow" 169; "For Once, Then, Something" 66, 69; "Two Look at Two" 85

Galentine, Wheaton 81–82; letters from Bishop 82
Galvão, Paulo Costa 74
Gama, Vasco da 25
Gardner, Isabella: letters from Bishop 164; "The Gentleman of Shalott" 179; "The Gentlemen of Shalott (alternate title) 179
Geography III 9, 180–81
George V 137
Georgia Review (journal) 148
"Gerard Manley Hopkins: Notes on Timing in His Poetry" 44, 170
"Giant Snail" 155
"Giant Toad" 155
Giroux, Robert 7, 55, 136, 180–81; *The Complete Poems 1927–1979* 181; *One Art: Letters* 55
Gloucester, Massachusetts 55, 172
Góes, Maria 8; *Um Porto para Elizabeth Bishop* (*A Safe Harbor for Elizabeth Bishop*) 8
"Going to the Bakery" 34, 70–73; "Good-bye to Rio" (earlier title) 70, 72
Gold, Arthur: letters from Bishop 95
Goldensohn, Lorrie 14–15, 19, 20, 21
Golding, William 1
Gorton's Gloucester fisherman 172
Grand Rapids (city) 158
Great Depression 157
"Gregorio Valdes, 1879–1939" 45
Guimaraens, Alfonsus de 23
"Gwendolyn" 135

"The Hanging of the Mouse" 155–57, 159, 180
Hardwick, Elizabeth 14, 68, 139
Harvard University 1, 6–7, 84, 99, 100, 122, 148

Havelock Ellis 1
Hays Office 156
Hellman, Lillian 165
Hemans, Felicia 150–54; "Casabianca" (poem) 150–51
Hemingway, Ernest 49–50, 60, 66, 123, 128, 132; "Big, Two-Hearted River" 49; *A Farewell to Arms* 123; *Green Hills of Africa* 50, 60; "In Another Country" 123; Nick Adams (character) 49; *The Old Man and the Sea* 49, 82, 128; Santiago (character) 49, 82
Herbert, George 69
Hitchcock, Alfred 61; *Rear Window* 61–62
L'Homme Armé 29, 30
Hopkins, Gerard Manley 44, 170
Hound & Horn (journal) 163
"The House That Jack Built" 163, 165, 166
Housman, A. E. 87
Howe, Susan 181
Hughes, Langston 96
Humphrey, Hubert 165
Huxley, Aldous 8

Ilha da Vera Cruz (Island of the True Cross) 74, 88, 90
Imagists 54
"In the Village" 15, 92, 130, 131–35, 136, 180
"In the Waiting Room" 41, 180
Inconfidência Mineira 104, 117
Integralistas 120
Italy 159, 162, 165, 166

Jack Frost 137
Jarrell, Randall 2, 38, 60, 94, 140, 166; letters from Bishop 60
Jeca Tatu 38–39, 55
"Jeronymo's House, Key West" 23, 38, 45, 88, 171
Jewett, Sarah Orne 135
João VI 105, 106
Jobim, Antonio Carlos 80; "Garota de Ipanema" ("The Girl from Ipanema") 80
Johnson, Lyndon Baines 165
Johnson, (Dr.) Samuel 77–78, 128; *A Dictionary of the English Language* 128
Johnson, Thomas 11
Jornal do Brasil 5, 93, 94
Joyce, James 21, 132–34; Dante (character) 133, 134; *Giacomo Joyce* 21; *Portrait of the Artist as a Young Man* 132–34; Stephen Daedalus, Stephen (character) 133, 134

Kafka, Franz 36, 155–56, 157, 159; "The Burrow" 155; "Metamorphosis" 155, 157; "The Trapeze Artist" 155–56, 157, 159; *The Trial* 156
Kalstone, David 136
Karp, Walter 100
Kazin, Alfred 34; letters from Bishop 34
Kazin, Pearl: letters from Bishop 39, 93, 94, 128, 163–64
Kearful, Frank J. 144–45

Keats, John 3, 25, 26, 30, 32, 137; "The Eve of St. Agnes" 137; "Ode on a Grecian Urn" 25, 26, 30, 32
Kees, Weldon 162
Key West 15, 23, 38, 42, 49, 55, 65, 83, 84, 88, 125, 163, 171
Kipling, Rudyard 125; *Brazilian Sketches* 125
Kirkland House (Harvard University) 148
Kitchin, George 145
Kittredge, George Lyman 1
Kraft-Ebing 1
Kubitschek, Juscelino 109, 110

Lacerda, Carlos 5, 6, 42
La Fontaine 155
Lampião 63
Landowski, Paul 108
Langland, Joseph 157; *Poet's Choice* 157–58
Lapa, Rodrigues 12
Latin America 103, 114
Latin Quarter (Paris) 158
Laughlin, James 153
Lawrence, D. H. 139; "The Mystic Blue" 139
Leadville, Colorado 158
Le Corbusier 115
Leeds, Harold: letters from Bishop 82
Leme 5, 27, 62, 71, 77
Leoni, Raul de 23
Leviticus (scripture) 143
Library of Congress 162
Life (journal) 158, 159
Life and Letters To-Day (journal) 155, 157, 158, 159, 160
Lima, Everaldo Dayrell de 24; "Brazilian Poetry" 24
Lima, Jorge de 23
"Lis Bish" 162
Lispector, Clarice 82, 84; "Uma Galinha" ("A Hen") 82, 84
Literatura de cordel (Literature on a string) 62, 63
Livingston, David 38
Lobato, Monteiro 39, 55
Lockeport Beach 171
London (city) 73, 132, 159, 180
London, Jack 85; "The Law of Life" 85
Long, Huey 165
Longfellow, Henry Wadsworth 54; "The Cross of Snow" 54
Los Angeles Times 162
Louis XV 115
Lowell, Amy 54
Lowell, Robert 1, 2, 3, 7, 12, 39, 44, 49, 52–54, 55, 57, 63, 65, 68, 69, 91, 93, 94, 95, 98, 121, 131, 133, 134–35, 136, 138–39, 141, 142, 148, 149, 157, 161, 163, 164, 165, 166, 168, 173, 174; "The Drinker" 148; *For the Union Dead* 135; letters from Bishop 33, 39, 44, 49, 50, 63, 65, 91, 92, 93, 94, 95, 98, 99, 121–22, 135, 142, 163, 164, 173; *Life Studies* 52, 134, 174; "Memories of West Street and Lepke"

38; "The Mills of the Kavanaughs" 57; "The Scream" 134–36; "Skunk Hour" 52–54, 141; "Terminal Days at Beverly Farms" 174

M., F. 158; "Necessities" 158, 159
Mabe, Manabu 118
Maciel, Antônio (*Conselheiro*) 117
MacIver, Lorin 55, 82; letters from Bishop 41, 55
MacKenzie, Rachel: letters from Bishop 83
MacMahon, Candace 97
Magalhães, Aloisio 116
Mallarmé, Stéphane 60
"The Man-Moth" 49, 96, 97, 131, 140, 155, 157–60; "O Homem 'Bruxa'" 97; "Homem-Mariposa" 160
Manaus (city) 37, 105, 111
Manchette (journal) 91
Manguel, Alberto 9; *The Library at Night* 9
"Manuelzinho" 15, 38–41, 42, 55, 88, 140
"The Map" 9, 10, 123
"The Maple Leaf Forever" (Canadian national hymn) 137
Maranhão (state) 114
Marlowe, Christopher 53; "Come live with me and be my love" 53; *The Jew of Malta* 123
Marques, Oswaldino Ribeiro 96–97, 160; *Ensaios Escolhidos* 96; *O Laboratório Poético de Cassiano Ricardo* 96; *Teoria da; Metáfora & Renascença da Poesia Americana* 96
Martins, Lúcia Milléo 8; *Duas Artes: Carlos Drummond de Andrade e Elizabeth Bishop* 8
Marvell, Andrew 129; "To His Coy Mistress" 129
Marx, Roberto Burle 115
Matarazzo, Francisco ('Cicillo') 114
Mato Grosso (state) 8, 113, 121
Mazzaro, Jerome 176; letters from Bishop 176
McClatchy, J. D. 21
McKenna, Rollie 42; letters from Bishop 42
Meireles, Vitor 30, 31, 32; *A Primeira Missa* 30, 31, 32
Melville, Herman 43, 48, 82; "Benito Cereno" 43; *Moby-Dick* 48–49
"Memories of Uncle Neddy" 132, 136; "Uncle Artie" 135, 136
Mendes, Murilo 23
Merrill, James 21–22, 60, 61, 62–63, 78, 81, 164, 174, 175; letters from Bishop 60, 164; "Overdue Pilgrimage to Nova Scotia" 174; "The Summer People" 60–61, 62–63
Metaphysical poets 69, 170, 177
Methfessel, Alice 19
Mickey Mouse 157
Micuçu 59, 61, 62, 140
Millay, Edna St. Vincent 154; *The Buck in the Snow* 154; *Fatal Interview* 154; "First Fig" ('My candle burns at both ends') 154; "Sonnet XXX" 154
Millier, Brett C. 5, 11, 16–17, 21, 37, 39, 68, 129, 130, 142–143
Milton, John 53

Minas Gerais (state) 7, 16, 104, 105, 112
Minas Triangle (Minas Gerais) 112
Minnow (cat) 157
Mirabeau 163; *Memoirs* 163
"A Miracle for Breakfast" 96–97; "Um Milagre Como Café da Manhã" 97
Mongan, Agnes 93
Moore, Marianne 7, 16, 20, 21, 32, 34, 36, 49, 53, 55, 60, 70, 84, 92, 93, 94, 96, 125, 138, 155, 157, 163, 167, 168; letters from Bishop 36, 49, 55, 84, 92, 93, 125, 157, 163, 167; "Marriage" 138
"The Moose" 84–86, 140, 180
Moraes, Vinícius de 58, 79–80, 125; *Black Orpheus Orfeu Negro*) 58, 80, 115; "A Garota de Ipanema" ("The Girl from ; Ipanema") 80; *Orfeu daConceição* 58; "Soneto de Intimidade" 125
Morgan, Edwin 174–75; "The Poet in the City" 175; *Sonnets from Scotland* 175
Morse, Mary Stearns 4, 82
Moss, Howard: letters from Bishop 47, 51, 59, 63, 74–75, 94–95, 97
"Mother Goose" 163
Museu Nacional de Belas-Artes 31
"My Last Poem" (by Manuel Bandeira) 95

Nabokov, Vladimir 164; *Ada* 164
Natal (city) 37
Nemer, Linda 7
Nery, Ismael 23
Nation (journal) 42
New Democracy (journal) 153
New Republic (journal) 11, 49, 128, 160, 180
New Road 1944: New Directions in European Art and Letters 23–24, 38, 171
New Testament 143, 146
New World Writing 127
New York (city, state) 2, 4, 6, 8, 50, 68, 77, 81, 82, 83, 139, 140, 151, 158, 159
New York Review of Books (journal) 68
New York Times 51, 90, 142, 158, 159, 162
New Yorker (journal) 4, 12, 16, 17, 24, 35, 37, 39, 40, 45, 47, 52, 58, 59, 64, 65, 70, 74, 82, 83, 92, 94, 97, 98, 123, 126, 127, 128, 130, 136, 140, 149, 167, 170, 174, 176, 177, 179
Niagara Falls 106
Niemeyer, Oscar 109
"Night City" 180
Nims, John Frederick 47; letters from Bishop 47
North & South 4, 5, 9, 10, 91, 153, 179
"North Haven" 138–39
North Haven, Maine 138
North Shore (Massachusetts) 56
North Shore Country Day School (Saugus, Massachusetts) 56
Nova Scotia 2, 15, 18, 55, 84, 93, 130, 131, 133, 134, 135, 136, 137, 142, 143, 174, 180
Nuova Corriente di Letteratura (journal) 161

Objective correlative 53, 66, 70, 147
Office for the Dead 145
Oliveira, Alberto de 23
Oliveira, Carmen L. 5, 6, 7; *Flores Raras e Ba-nalíssimas (Rare and Commonplace Flowers)* 5, 7
"On the Railroad Named Delight" 90
"One Art" 19, 20–21, 86–87, 88, 90, 180, 181
O'Neill, Eugene 144; *The Iceman Cometh* 144; Jimmie Tomorrow (character) 144
Orient (ship) 151, 152
Ouro Prêto (city) 6, 7, 16, 17, 21, 31, 48, 80, 124, 178
The Owl (journal) 56
"The Owl's Journey" 55, 57
Oxford English Dictionary (OED) 42, 127, 128

Paglia, Camille 173; *Break, Blow, Burn: Camille Paglia Reads Forty-three of the World's Best Poems* 173
Pará (state) 113
Paraná (state) 114
Paris 115, 126, 132, 158, 167, 168
Partisan Review (journal) 23, 45, 49, 161
Paternoster 145
Patterson, Rebecca 11–12; *The Riddle of Emily Dickinson* 11–12
Paz, Octavio 180, 181; "Objects & Apparitions" 180–81
Pegasus 168
Penteado, Darcy 14
Pernambuco (state) 8, 76
Petrobras 114
Petrópolis (town) 4, 5, 7, 27, 33, 34, 42, 54, 56, 124, 125, 137
Pharmakos 144
Phi Beta Kappa (Harvard University) 84
Philoctetus 160
Philomela 32
Piauí (state) 114
Picchia, Menotti del 23
"Pink Dog" 74–80, 140; "Farewell to Rio" (earlier title) 74
Plath, Sylvia 2, 147
Plaza of the Three Powers (Brasília) 111
Poe, Edgar Allan 20, 55, 66, 82, 136; *The Narrative of Arthur Gordon Pym* 82; "The Raven" 20
"Poem" 83, 180
Poems: North & South — A Cold Spring 4–5, 12, 14, 35, 128, 179
Porter, Katherine Anne 135
Portinari, Cándido 116
Portugal 10, 28, 94, 105, 159
Post, Laurens van der 37; *Venture to the Interior* 37
Pound, Ezra 54, 96, 126, 161–66; *Drafts & Fragments of Cantos CX-XXVII* 164; "In a Station of the Metro" 126; *Pisan; Cantos* 161–62
Pound, Mrs. (Dorothy Shakespear Pound) 162, 163, 166
Pouso do Chico Rey (Ouro Prêo) 16, 31

"The Prodigal" 3, 55, 73, 140–49
Prodigal Son, Parable of the (scripture) 142, 144, 145, 146
Prose 2, 99–100, 122
Proust, Marcel 134
Provençal poetry 163
Przybycien, Regina M. 7, 41, 74; "Feijão Preto e Diamantes: O Brasil na Obra de Elizabeth Bishop" (dissertation) 7
The Public Enemy (movie) 156
Putnam, Samuel 76

Queen Mary 137
Queen Victoria 137
Questions of Travel 5, 12, 13, 14, 15, 16, 19, 35, 47, 59, 64, 68, 123, 126, 128, 131, 136, 179, 180
"Questions of Travel" 15, 89, 124, 125
Quinn, Alice 55, 148

"Rainy Season; Sub-Tropics" 155, 180
Ransom, John Crowe 94
Rattigan, Terrence 1
Recife (city) 119
Rexroth, Kenneth 165
Ricardo, Cassiano 69, 96–97; "Anoitecer" (Nightfall") 97; "O Canto da Juriti" ("The Song of the Wild Dove") 97; *Martim Cereê (o Brasil dos meninos, dos poetas e dos heróis)* 69, 96–97
Rich, Adrienne 2
The Riddle of Emily Dickinson 11–12
Rilke, Erich Remarque 34, 132
Rio de Janeiro 4, 5, 6, 8, 12, 16, 24, 26, 27, 29, 30, 31, 33, 34, 36, 37, 47, 54, 55, 56, 59, 61, 62, 64, 68, 70, 72, 73, 74, 75, 76, 79, 80, 82, 90, 93, 96, 101, 103, 108, 110, 111, 113, 115, 116, 118, 119, 120, 125, 137, 166
"Rio de Janeiro" (samba) 72
Rio Negro (river) 105, 111
"The Riverman" 3, 15
Rizzardi, Alfred 161, 164; "Visite all'Ospedale di Santa Elisabetta" 161
Robinson, Edwin Arlington 50–51
Rockefeller Foundation 37
Roethke, Theodore 2, 6, 94
Rondon, Cândido Mariano da Silva 119
"Roosters" 49, 82
Rossetti, Dante Gabriel 80; *La Vita Nuova (The New Life)* 80
Roth, Philip 164; *Portnoy's Complaint* 164
Roy, Gabrielle 50, 85; *The Hidden Mountain* 50, 85
Royce, Josiash 9; *The World and the Individual* 9
Ruas, Charles 181
Ruskin, John 176; *Flors Clavigera* 176

"St. Elizabeth of Petrópolis" 54
St. Elizabeth's Hospital 161, 162, 163, 166
St. Ignatius Loyola 103
St. John's Night 52, 56, 57
St. Luke (scripture) 144, 146

St. Patrick's Day 140
Salvador (city) 37
Samambaia (Fazenda Samambaia) 5, 6, 7, 27, 94, 124, 126, 137, 166, 168, 178
San Francisco (city) 59, 162
"Sandpiper" 64–66, 67
"Santarém" 79, 83, 175–76, 177
Santiago, Silviano 176
Santos (city) 12, 33, 35, 36, 37, 39, 125, 126
São Francisco (river) 8
São Paulo (city, state) 36, 37, 58, 69, 93, 104, 110, 113, 114, 125, 126, 166
Saturday Review (London journal) 152
Saugus, Massachusetts 56
Saugus High School (Massachusetts) 56
Schiller, Beatriz 94
Schwartz, Lloyd 16, 17, 18, 21, 99–100
"The Sea and Its Shore" 155
Selected Poems 180
Selzer, Richard 141
Sena, Jorge de 167
"Sestina" 130–31
Sexton, Anne 2, 147
Shakespeare, William 1, 3, 27, 48, 126, 128, 138; *As You Like It* 48; Jacques 48; *Love's Labour's Lost* 138; *The Tempest* 126
"The Shampoo" 27, 61, 90, 128–29, 179–80
Shelley, Percy Bysshe 96
"Sleeping on the Ceiling" 155
"Sleeping Standing Up" 155
Smart, Christopher "Kit" 123; Jeoffrey (cat) 123; *Jubilate Agno* 123
Snodgrass, W. D. 147
Soares, Lota de Macedo 2, 3, 4, 5, 6, 7, 8, 12, 13, 14, 15, 16, 17, 19, 21, 22, 33, 34, 36, 38, 39, 40, 41, 42, 54, 64, 68, 70, 82, 89, 90, 92, 97, 98–121, 124, 125, 178, 179
"Song for the Rainy Season" 8, 57
"Songs for a Colored Singer" 91
"Sonnet" 177–78
Sousa, Ireneo Evangelista de 106
Sousa, Octavio Tarquinio de 105
Southey, Robert 151; *Life of Horatio, Lord Nelson* 151
"Spiderman" 159
"Squatter's Children" 58–59, 93–94; "Filhos de favelado" 58
Stafford, Jean 57, 67–68; *In the Zoo* 68; letters from Bishop 67–68; Lottie Jump (character) 68; *A Reading Problem* 68
Stanford, Donald: letters from Bishop 57, 163
Stanley, H. M. 38
Starbuck, George 2
Stein, Gertrude 85; "Rose is a rose is a rose is a rose" 85
Stevens, Wallace 2, 44, 57; "On Modern Poetry" 44; "An Ordinary Evening in New Haven" 57
Stevenson, Anne 3, 37; letters from Bishop 37
Stonington, Connecticut 60, 61
"Strayed Crab" 90, 155
Summers, Mary Eliot: letters from Bishop 56

Summers, U.T., and Joseph: letters from Bishop 34, 35, 36, 38
"Superman" 159
Süsskind, Flora 7, 160
Swampscott, Massachusetts 56
Swenson, May 1, 7, 11, 34, 39, 58, 59, 179–80; letters from Bishop 33, 34, 39, 59

Tapajos (river) 79, 177
Tate, Allen 94
Thoreau, Henry David 64; *Cape Cod* 64; *The Maine Woods* 64
TLS (*Times Literary Supplement*) 1
Tobias (Bishop's cat) 123, 124, 126
Travisano, Thomas 148
"Trouvée" 67, 81–84, 176
Tuileries (Paris) 115
"Twelfth Morning; or What You Will" 8, 14, 15, 34, 67–69; "Dia de Reis" 14
"12 O'Clock News" 180
Tyndale, William 143; New Testament 143, 146

Übermensch 159
Uialapiti (tribe) 89
"Under the Window: Ouro Prêto" 8, 16, 35, 47–49, 97; "Debaixo da Janela: Ouro Prêto" 97
United States Quarterly Review (journal) 79
University of Washington 6, 13

Valéry, Paul 117
Van Ghent, Dorothy 133
Vassar Review (journal) 170
Vendler, Helen 21
Venezuela 116
Venus 25, 145
Vespucci, Amerigo 24, 26, 27
Vidal, Piere 163
Villa-Lobos, Heitor 118
Villegaignon, Nicolas Durand de 107
Virgil 105; *Aeneid* 105
Visão (journal) 97
"Visits to St. Elizabeth" 161–66

Wagley, Charles 3; *Amazon Town: A Study of Man in the Tropics* 3
Walnut Hill School (Natick, Massachusetts) 55, 56
Warnke, Frank 13, 14
Washington, D.C. 161, 162
Wegenen, Theodora Van 11; *Emily Dickinson's Letters to Doctor and Mrs. Josiah Gilbert Holland* 11
Wharf Harbor (Boston) 181
White, Katherine 64, 128, 130; letters from Bishop 47, 64, 130
Whitman, Walt 96
Whittier, John Greenleaf 106, 137; "The Cry of a Lost Soul" 106; "Snow-Bound" 137
Wilde, Oscar 158, 160; "Sebastian Melmoth" (pseudonym) 158
Williams, Tennessee 1

Williams, William Carlos 2, 45, 83; "Comedy Entombed: 1930" 45
Wilson, Edmund 160, 163; "Philoctetus: The Wound and the Bow" 160; *The Wound and the Bow* 160
Wilson, Robert 121
Wolfson, Susan J. 153
Woolf, Virginia 89

Worcester, Massachusetts 173
Wordsworth, William 172; "Resolution and Independence" 172
World War II 162

XAIPE: Seventy-one Poems 79, 80

Yeats, William Butler 49, 164; "The Fish" 49